Domestic Workers in Indonesia

Domestic Workers in Indonesia

Feminist Activism and a Politics of Presence

Mary Austin

LIVERPOOL UNIVERSITY PRESS

First published 2024 by
Liverpool University Press
4 Cambridge Street
Liverpool
L69 7ZU

British Library Cataloguing-in-Publication data
A British Library CIP record is available

ISBN 978-1-80207-457-4 (cased)

Typeset by Carnegie Book Production, Lancaster
Printed and bound by CPI Group (UK) Ltd, Croydon CR0 4YY

Contents

Figures

Acronyms and Abbreviations

AJI	Alliance of Independent Journalists
Baleg	Legislative Council in Indonesian parliament
DPR	People's Representative Council/House of Representatives, or Parliament
FDPY	Yogyakarta Women's Discussion Forum
IAIN	State Institute for Islamic Studies
IDWF	International Domestic Workers Federation
IDWN	International Domestic Workers Network
ILO	International Labour Organization
JAKERLA PRT	Network for Decent Work for Domestic Workers
JALA PRT	National Advocacy Network for Domestic Workers
JP	*Jurnal Perempuan*, the Indonesian feminist journal
KAPAL Perempuan	Institute for Women's Alternative Education
KAPPRT-BM	Action Committee for the Protection of Domestic and Migrant Workers
KOMPERATA/OPERATA	Domestic worker-led organization
KOWANI	Indonesian Women's Congress
KOY	Yogyakarta Domestic Workers' Congress
KP	Komnas Perempuan, National Commission on Violence against Women
KPI	Indonesian Women's Coalition for Justice and Democracy

KSBSI	Indonesian Confederation of Prosperous Trade Unions
KSPI	Confederation of Indonesian Trade Unions
LBH	Legal Aid Institute
LBH APIK	Indonesian Women's Association for Justice
MI	Mitra Imadei, Jakarta-based domestic worker organization
PKI	Partai Komunist Indonesia, Communist Party of Indonesia
PRT	Domestic helper(s) or domestic worker(s), the latter preferred by JALA PRT
PSW/PSG	Centre for Women's/Gender Studies
RTND	Rumpun Tjoet Nyak Dien, domestic worker NGO in Yogyakarta
RUU PPRT	Draft Bill for the Protection of Domestic Workers
RGP	Rumpun Gema Perempuan, domestic worker NGO in Jakarta
SP	Solidaritas Perempuan, Women's Solidarity for Human Rights
SPRT	Domestic workers' union
UI	University of Indonesia
UGM	Gadjah Mada University, Yogyakarta
UPC	Urban Poor Consortium
Yogyakarta DIY	Yogyakarta Special Province

Glossary

Bupati	The directly elected head of a regency or second-tier local administrative unit immediately below a Province.
Gotong Royong	Traditional mechanism of mutual self-help, understood as a feature of Indonesian identity
Jaringan	Net or network: term commonly used in the names of groups of civil society organizations working together on a cause
Kampung	Village or traditional residential area in a town or city
Kodrat Wanita	Women's destiny, nature, role
Korban	Victim
Masyarakat	Society, community
Mudik	The annual exodus from cities as millions of people return to their hometowns or villages to celebrate Idul Fitri.
New Order	The period of the Suharto Presidency, 1966–1998
Ngenger	To live with someone (especially a relative) and do housework in return for room and board
Pekerja	Worker
Pembantu	Helper
Pemuda	Youth
Perempuan	Woman
Priyayi	Term used to describe traditional Javanese aristocratic and bureaucratic elites

Rakyat	The people
Reformasi	The name for the political era leading up to and following the fall of President Suharto

Acknowledgements

This book would not have been possible without the generosity of the activists, trade unionists, journalists, researchers, domestic workers, ILO staff, and others in Indonesia who gave time to meet me and allowed me to join their activities. Many are named in the book; others have informed my understanding. I hope I have captured something of their collective commitment, perseverance, creativity, and achievement in what follows. Behind the scenes, in Indonesia, staff at the SMERU research institute in Jakarta offered me an internship and supported the first stages of my project. Hariyanti Sadaly, SMERU's NGO Partnership Officer, set up many of my first hesitant interviews, went with me on visits, and offered warmth and friendship. Teachers at the Wisma Bahasa language schools in Yogyakarta and Jakarta pushed me to improve my language skills, facilitated meetings, and helped translate many of my interviews. In Jakarta, the staff at the apartment hotel I stayed in cared for me "like family". They kept an eye on my comings and goings, printed out my papers, and ensured I was well fed. The energy and efficiency of my research assistants, Tyas Pusposari and Zahra Sakinaruzzahara, made the latter stages of my fieldwork far more productive and enjoyable than would otherwise have been the case. Ade Indriani Zuchri, Puji Maharani, and Valentina Utari became both friends and collaborators, aiding my research and encouraging me to take social time while in Jakarta. Maria Pakpahan, whose involvement in the movement is charted in Chapter 2 and who now lives in Edinburgh, offered her friendship and advice about completing my project. Nona Evita and her family welcomed me to their home on my first field trip, spoiling me with their generosity, and Tjie Ferry Nugroho translated several interview recordings.

My project grew from my MA studies at SOAS. Ben Murtagh and Sallehuddin Abdullah Sani patiently helped me acquire some language skills. Mandy Sadan and the fellow students in her class reminded me of the pleasures of taking an historical approach to current issues. Nadje Al-Ali, Katherine Natanel, and Ruba Salih guided my encounters with gender theory, and Carol Tan pushed me to get an essay published, an endeavour that would not otherwise have crossed my mind. My decision to embark on a doctorate was kindled by Ati Nurbaiti who steered me towards my topic and continued to support me throughout. It was further fuelled by the enthusiasm of Henk Schulte Northolt, Ward Berenschot, and Laurens Bakker at a conference in Lisbon in 2013.

I owe much to members of my PhD supervisory team. They assuaged my doubts and encouraged me in my writing. Carol Tan helped sharpen my arguments, pointed to places where I could look beyond northern scholarship, and taught me the intricacies of formatting. My "second supervisor", Gina Heathcote, offered care beyond the call of duty, always tactful and thoughtful in suggesting readings in gender theory that might enrich my work. She kindly took over as lead supervisor during my final year and supported me through my (online) viva. Ben Murtagh was my team's Indonesian specialist; his interventions helped produce a study that hopefully resonates among readers concerned with developments in Southeast Asia and Indonesia as much as with those interested in domestic work. SOAS helped fund my fieldwork with grants for language acquisition and an Ousley Memorial Scholarship. The Annette Lawson Charitable Trust gave me a generous award for my final visit to Indonesia. I want to thank George Lawson, from the Trust, for helping me set my project in a broader context.

Vanja Hamzic from SOAS University of London and Mina Roces from the University of New South Wales in Sydney examined my thesis. Coming from different backgrounds, their generous and perceptive comments and suggestions were invaluable in helping me extend my thinking, consider the needs of a range of readers, and have confidence in the power of the stories that informants had shared with me. Mina lured me into writing about domestic worker activism from the perspective of fashion and dress studies (as well as embarking on this book), an intriguing diversion I immensely enjoyed.

Some scholars and individuals outside SOAS also deserve my thanks. Rebecca Elmhirst advised me sagely as I scoped my project. Petra Mahy and Wayne Palmer offered friendship and professional input, suggesting new venues to explore. Early on, long before her name came up as a possible examiner, Mina Roces' enthusiasm for studying women's movements in Southeast Asia was infectious; after talking with her, I began to imagine a PhD as not only possible but something to be wished for. David Jordhus-Lier generously shared his findings and encouraged me in my research. Sri Eddyono, Muryanti, and Debbie Prabawati challenged my thinking diplomatically from their more expert, insider perspectives. Carol Chan, whom I first met at the Wisma Bahasa language school in Yogyakarta, generously shared her experiences of turning a thesis into a monograph.

An earlier version of parts of Chapter 4 appeared in *Jurnal Perempuan* 22 (3) (2017) with the title "Challenging Disregard: Advocacy journalism and the campaign for domestic worker legislation in Indonesia". I have reused some quotations from informants already published in Chapter 11 of *Citizenship and Democratization in Southeast Asia*, edited by Ward Berenschot, Henk Schulte Northolt, and Laurens Bakker (2017). Some of the material in Chapter 3 relating to protest movements is included in a special edition of *International Quarterly for Asian Studies* 53 (1) (2022) on "Dress as Symbolic Resistance in Asia", edited by Mina Roces. It also features in *Local Responses to Global Challenges: A Transregional Studies Reader*, edited by Lina Knorr, Andrea Fleschenberg, Sumrin Kali, and Claudia Derichs (World Scientific Publishing Company, 2023). Incisive comments from reviewers and editors proved extremely helpful in clarifying my arguments. I am also grateful to participants and co-panellists in conference workshops in Indonesia and Europe, where I tested my ideas.

I owe an enormous debt to Anthony Grahame and Mona Roces at Sussex Academic Press for their belief in the value of my project and patient encouragement to persevere through the trials of lockdown and COVID-19. Catherine Pope guided me through sticky patches, Beth Dufour was a model of efficiency and determination in helping get permissions for the pictures that enliven this book, and Maartje Scheltens not only did the copy editing meticulously but kept me calm as deadlines approached. Alison Welsby and her colleagues at Liverpool University Press took over responsibility for my manuscript at a crucial moment and steered the book to publication with great sensitivity. I am grateful, too, to the anonymous reviewers who offered new perspectives, helpful advice, and encouragement.

There is no way I could have completed this project without the love and support of friends and family. Some I have neglected, others I have overburdened. I am sure all have heard more about Indonesian domestic workers than anyone could reasonably wish for. Most of all, I thank Mark Austin. He took me to Indonesia in the first place and has looked after me with love throughout this return journey.

Finally, I dedicate this book to my daughter, without whom it would never have come about.

A Note about Names

In this book I refer to many individuals by name. The use of names varies across Indonesia; some people go by one name. Hence, when introducing people, I give their first and last given names, indicating in brackets if they use, or are generally referred to by, a short form or variant – where this is known to me. In discussing interview material or recounting stories about people, I use the short form where appropriate. Yuli Maiheni, for example, a founder member of Indonesia's first domestic worker union, is frequently referred to as "Heni". In citing works by Indonesian authors, I use the author's final name, or the name adopted for publications.

Deciding when to use names and when to withhold them was complicated. In many instances I rely on published and archival sources such as autobiographies, journal articles, media reports, or NGO or organizational websites. In these cases, with due regard to the source, I use people's names. Many of the protagonists – including many of my informants – are well-known in Indonesia (and in some cases, beyond) for their political activism. I see naming these individuals and describing their involvement in the domestic worker movement as an act of recognition of their courage and resilience, often in challenging times. Several domestic workers who feature fall into this category.

My approach was shaped by the principles of informed consent, the need for fairness, respect, trust, and integrity in research and writing, and the paramount importance of the rights, welfare, safety, dignity, and interests of my informants. I discussed my ideas with key stakeholders during an initial scoping visit and adjusted my research questions and proposed participants in the light of these discussions. On subsequent visits, these stakeholders/gatekeepers introduced me to informants who, most often, were members or employees of NGOS or other organizations deeply involved in or supportive of the domestic worker campaign.

Key stakeholders included Lita Anggraini (coordinator of JALA PRT, the lead organization fighting for domestic worker rights in

Indonesia); a senior staff member of ILO Jakarta; and the then chair the Alliance of Independent Journalists. Lita Anggraini brokered my introductions to many interviewees: indeed, agreement to meet me was often predicated on the knowledge that she was supportive of my research and my goal of producing a book that celebrates activist efforts to improve the position of domestic workers in Indonesia. Lita provided me with a list and contact details of some fifty people; I met with as many of those based in Jakarta or Yogyakarta as I could. The head of the ILO Project PROMOTE, which focuses on domestic workers in Indonesia, introduced me to others involved in the project.

Some other meetings, including some with academics, were brokered by two organizations that hosted me during my research. These were the SMERU independent research institute in Jakarta and the Wisma Bahasa language school in Yogyakarta. Both organizations freed up staff to negotiate interviews, accompany me on interviews, and help review my findings. Such invaluable assistance helped build trust. As mentors, they translated and elaborated my explanations where needed and helped me handle any questions that arose around the use of data.

Having gained consent, I began interviews by outlining my research project briefly, explaining that I planned to publish articles and a book alongside and following my PhD. I discussed the use of names and affiliation, asking informants if they wanted to choose a pseudonym. At the close of interviews, I asked whether people were still comfortable with my using their responses. Out of sixty-five informants, two added caveats. One did not want her name to be used. Another did not want me to name the news outlet he worked for. Everyone else urged or preferred for me to name them in my work. However, on a few occasions, when discussing or quoting from people who were not part of the movement and whose views are not a matter of public record, for example, I have not included identifying details.

Some data is drawn from observations made at meetings of JALA PRT or domestic worker organizations. I made five visits to the field between 2012 and 2016, becoming known to leading members of such groups. If it was not a public meeting like a press conference, I might be asked to introduce myself and explain my purpose in researching the movement. Alternatively, if a special meeting had been set up for me, the host would explain that I was researching the movement for my PhD and a book.

Despite establishing, I hope, a level of trust, I had not set out, or negotiated permission, to write a critique. Consequently, I was careful, and I hope sensitive in my writing. Of course, the story I tell reflects my own history, experience, and predilections, as well as mistakes and misremembering. I hope, nevertheless, that my ever-generous informants will see how their words add to the patchwork of voices and experiences that give the book its power.

Introduction

"Let Me Speak!"

One evening in May 1980, two Javanese women whom I came to know as Ibu Jum and Ibu Mortinah entered the room where my husband and I were sitting.[1] It was our first ever day in Indonesia, and we had just arrived at the house in central Jakarta provided for us by the British Council for our three-year stay. What I remember most vividly about that first meeting with the women who were to be our *pembantu* (helpers), as domestic workers were then called, was that they came into the room crouching low, addressed my husband with the Indonesian honorific *Tuan*, and left the room backwards, almost on their knees. *Tuan*, our dictionary told us, translated as "lord, master, owner", associated in the past with the "higher classes" or "ruling caste". As a young woman who had spent the 1970s reading her way through the modern women's classics published by the ardently feminist British publisher Virago Press, the discovery that our home came with live-in servants was shocking indeed.

A few weeks in Jakarta made it obvious that if I were to continue my professional life as a teacher and enjoy the opportunities Indonesia offered, we could not do without *pembantu*. Who else, we realized, would boil and filter our drinking water, do the washing without hot water or a machine, iron everything, mop the floors, shop at the market, cook for us and our many visitors (my husband's job was looking after the British volunteer programme [VSO] in Indonesia), cut the grass, and tend the flowers, so that we could relax when we came home after what, even then, were traffic-nightmare commutes? How quickly I came to accept, I see on reflection, that having live-in domestic workers was essential to the task of managing life as a

1 *Ibu*, the Indonesian word for mother, was used as a term of address for older/married women in New Order Indonesia.

middle-class wife in my newly adopted city. In any event, we told ourselves, with their extended families dependent on their wages, we could hardly send Ibu Jum and Ibu Mortinah away. Instead, as a photograph taken in 1981 (Figure 0.1) reminds me, we began to see our *pembantu* as members of our substitute "family", a means, no doubt, of dealing with (post-) colonial ambivalence. Seeing domestic workers as family was not something we had encountered in our upbringings. Our suburban houses were peopled by "charwomen"[2] and the rather more genteel "daily helps"; familial relationships were neither expected nor inferred.[3]

Yet, even though the crouching walk[4] was never repeated, and however generous employers we might have been, our "helpers" lived apart, in cramped quarters, spoke to us in tones of deference, and never shared meals at our table except on ceremonial occasions like Christmas, when they and their families were invited guests. Just like other housewives and expatriates at the time, I pushed aside uncomfortable feelings in the interest of my own "modernity".

This book traces the development of a social and political movement in Indonesia that originated in the work of a few feminist activists and organized workers not content to leave the tropes of domestic worker as "helper" and "one of the family" alone. Their stories span three periods in Indonesia's postcolonial history: the period of President Suharto's "New Order" that ran from 1966 to 1998; the period of "reformasi" that precipitated and followed Suharto's downfall; and, at the book's close, a time some observers are beginning to describe as "Neo-New Order Indonesia" or Indonesia's period of "Democratic Decline" (Lindsey 2017; Warburton 2022). Over the same time frame, member nations of the UN (and its specialist agency, the International Labour Organization ILO), have agreed on a series of Conventions designed to ensure complete and equal enjoyment of human rights.

2 In 1950s Birmingham, where I grew up, charwomen did the dirtiest work, coming in for a few hours each morning. For a discussion of the term's origins, see Steedman's *Master and Servant* (2007: 77–81).

3 On ambivalence about servants in late colonial Indonesia, see Locher-Scholten (2000) and Stoler (with Strassler) (2002).

4 We discovered later that the crouching walk was a traditional Javanese form of deference known as *jongkok*. For a vivid account of Dutch colonial appropriation of the practice and calls for its abolition in the rise of Indonesian nationalism, see van der Meer (2020).

Fig. 0.1 The VSO family in Jakarta, 1981 (Photo: author's collection)

Activists in Indonesia have contributed to setting such international norms and used them as ammunition in local campaigns.[5]

Many people whose stories figure in this book are, or have been, associated with JALA PRT, Indonesia's "National Network for Domestic Worker Advocacy", sometimes referred to more simply as "JALA". JALA PRT is an acronym, one of many that abound in Indonesia's socio-political landscape, derived from "*Jaringan Nasional Advokasi Pekerja Rumah Tangga*". *Jaringan* is the word used to describe the loosely networked alliances that were common in the crowded landscape of women's and human rights organizations following President Suharto's momentous downfall in 1998. The "PRT" part of JALA's name was even more familiar; it stood for *pembantu rumah tangga*: the paid

5 Appendix 1 provides a timeline that sets these periods in Indonesia's political history alongside relevant developments at the UN and ILO.

"helpers" inside Indonesian homes. From the outset, the movement challenged the *pembantu* nomenclature. Its oft-repeated mantra was "PRT=*Pekerja*" – *pekerja* being the Indonesian word for worker or labourer. Short and to the point, "PRT=*Pekerja*" encapsulates JALA's key demand that domestic workers are entitled to the better regarded – and legally defined – status of an employee.

However, in 1980, when I encountered *pembantu*, some of the movement's founders and longest-serving leaders were still at school. Lita Anggraini, who has served as JALA's national coordinator since 2004 and whose commitment and determination have, by all accounts, held the movement together, was eleven. In the eyes of her upper-middle-class family in the port city of Semarang, she was en route to a career as a diplomat. Lek Jumiyem, one of the founders of Tunas Mulia, the first domestic workers' union in Indonesia, was only five. Daughter of a small farmer and furniture-maker and the seventh of nine children living in a village in the Special Region of Yogyakarta, her destiny was to start work at the age of fifteen, unable to fulfil her dream of going to college (although, through her own efforts, she did so eventually). When activists like Anggraini and domestic workers like Jumiyem began to organize together across class boundaries at the end of the Suharto era, they created a movement that has pursued cases of abuse through the courts, lobbied for legislation, and provided havens in which workers could meet and learn. It has mounted media campaigns, staged demonstrations, and even resorted to hunger strikes. The experiences of those involved provide the grounds for this book's thesis: that a feminist politics of presence has wrought changes in the discursive and political landscape surrounding domestic work in Indonesia and enabled the emergence of a new kind of domestic worker class. Together, the creative responses and tenacity shown by people whose endeavours make up the substance of this book offer a compelling case study of how feminists have managed alliances across differences, called gender injustices into question, and built new social imaginaries and solidarities.

While there is a plethora of scholarship analyzing the agency and resistance of Indonesia's overseas domestic workers, the existence of a domestic worker movement inside Indonesia is much less widely known. Scholarship published in Indonesia can be elusive: the development of the "Indonesia OneSearch" portal, for example, dates from 2015, and much of what is listed there features migrant domestic labour. A handful of studies have analyzed the reasons for the movement's failure to achieve a domestic workers bill or establish more powerful unions. These studies cite the depth of political and cultural resistance to change; class and gender divisions between potential supporters; issues of funding, leadership and strategic direction; and the spatial and logistical challenges involved in organizing across the archipelago (Irawaty 2011; Eddyono, Fanani, and Maurice 2015; Eddyono et al. 2016; Gastaldi et al. 2017; Jordhus-Lier 2017; Jordhus-Lier and Prabawati 2018). They have revealed aspects of Indonesian society that cemented the institution of unregulated domestic work in place. Depending on the research paradigms employed, researchers have proffered different solutions to the movement's problems: a focus on cultural change, a return to gender-based advocacy, or a pursuit of industrial citizenship, for example. This book exploits the advantages of a full-length study. It puts aside "if onlys" to highlight what has been achieved, against the odds. As a study of a social movement and an exercise in women's and gender history, it adopts an interdisciplinary approach. Looking over a longer timescale and larger canvas, it sets the interventions of social actors in the context of Indonesia's broader pro-democracy, labour, and women's rights activism.

Social Actors and Feminist Alliances

This account of Indonesia's domestic worker movement concentrates on the contributions made by members of three interconnected and overlapping groups: activists, journalists, and knowledge producers working as researchers or academics. Others, such as ILO officers, sympathetic politicians or political advisers, and committed individuals signed up to JALA's agenda also feature. Assigning individuals to groups is not to suggest rigid boundaries but to allow a focus on interventions operating in different parts of the uncertain terrain of *reformasi* Indonesia. Many of the most prominent characters in this book belong to a larger group of activists with pro-democracy and populist concerns for the people (Lee 2009). However, they are also unusual in championing local rather than migrant domestic workers. More extraordinary still are the domestic worker activists who co-star. Like the NGO activists in JALA PRT, domestic workers who became activists are among the main protagonists. They have taken leadership roles in worker-led unions and other local domestic worker groups, their influence counting for more than mere numbers. Their presence has supplied grit; it raised the question of who speaks for whom in cross-class and domestic worker alliances.

Having studied media coverage of the moratorium Indonesia imposed on sending domestic workers to Malaysia between 2009 and 2012, I had more than an inkling that journalists could be crucial to JALA's campaigns. By giving extensive coverage to victim stories and framing these in popular anti-government and anti-corruption rhetoric, sympathetic and headline-seeking reporters and editors helped push Indonesian governments into negotiating better bilateral agreements with countries where they exported labour (Austin 2017: 283). Yet, as Carol Chan convincingly established, victim stories can be double-edged. Media reporting tends to categorize victims as deserving or undeserving, which places responsibility or blame onto individuals and diverts readers' attention from the everyday injustices and indignities of paid domestic work (Chan 2018: 52–9). This book uncovers the work of feminist and advocacy journalists who challenged members of their profession to do better, just as one senior journalist challenged me when I discussed my ideas for further research with her. She urged me to move away from the familiar topic of migrant domestic work and document the campaign for a national domestic worker law, a little-known campaign her newspaper, the *Jakarta Post*, had long backed.[6]

Investigating the contribution of academics and researchers was more speculative. A book called *The Future of Asian Feminisms* (Katjasungkana and Wieringa 2012) introduced me to "triangles of women's empowerment". Initially associated with political settings in Europe where activists, feminist politicians, and feminist civil servants had collaborated to advance women's interests (Vargas and Wieringa 1998; Holli 2008;) the construct was taken up by the "Kartini Asian Network" (KAN), co-founded in 2003 by prominent Indonesian feminist activist, lawyer, and politician Nursyahbani Katjasungkana. The Kartini network believed that women and gender studies academics and activists could work together with policymakers to forge a "transversal politics of recognition and redistribution" that would work with and across differences in class, age, gender, religion, or education (Katjasungkana and Wieringa 2012: 33). Most relevant to this book's shaping was the idea that personal relationships and shared histories could bind feminist triangles strongly enough to act as counterweights to male-dominated networks of power. Women needed counterweights in Indonesia; patronage democracy had long sustained "collusive networks connecting bureaucrats, politicians, businessmen and armed forces" (Schulte Nordholt 2014: 239).

6 Interview with Ati Nurbaiti, Jakarta, 27 June 2012.

Structurally, the potential for such feminist triangles existed in Indonesia. Governments have promoted gender mainstreaming, including women's and gender studies centres in universities, since the late 1970s. Independent feminist-inspired research institutes, such as the Women's Research Institute founded in Jakarta in 2002, were also pioneering Participatory Action Research (Hadiwinata 2003). However, my speculative enquiries revealed complexities. Academics encountered challenges within their institutions and in the field. Homing in on examples of how some Indonesian scholars tackled these challenges, this book delves into questions about the boundaries and relationships between activists and academics, researcher and researched (Grossman 2011; Azzarello et al. 2014).

As well as charting contributions, this book investigates, to the extent that people were prepared to share with me, the dynamics between the actors involved. Alliances between feminist/women's rights and domestic worker movements are not axiomatic. Research on domestic worker movements in nine nations (not including Indonesia) found examples of ambivalence and evasion at the organizational level, even where individual feminists had played pivotal roles (Marchetti et al. 2021). In Indonesia, observers noted that many activists, scholars, and policymakers have focused on overseas migrant labour rather than domestic work at home (Blackburn 2004: 188; Robinson 2009: 117; Irawaty 2011: 80–85; Elmhirst 2012). Middle-class activists and professionals, including those signed up to pro-women legislative reform, were caught in a familiar bind; as one informant put it, "Our husbands would nag about our working if we did not employ a whole range of domestic workers, the alternative is never the men doing more".[7]

Talk of feminist alliances draws attention to the use of the term "feminist", a critical issue across Asia, where feminists have been stigmatized as extremist, anti-men, and pro-lesbianism (Roces 2010: 4). Furthermore, as pointed out by three Indonesian feminists who described their experiences of studying gender studies in the UK, talk of "Asian feminisms" amongst those in the global north can homogenize difference and marginalize – if not wholly overlook – the diversity of Indonesian feminisms and feminist activism (Adriany et al. 2017). Mindful of such matters, in this book, I follow others in using "feminism" as a label for discourse and praxis premised on ideas of gender justice and equity. I use "feminist" to describe organizations and groups sharing a commitment to reducing gender inequalities and

7 Interview, Jakarta, 27 June 2012.

discrimination and name particular individuals as "feminists" when they self-identify as such (Wichelen 2010: 18; Rinaldo 2013: 8).[8] Rather than eliding difference, this book seeks to elucidate how one transnational and transversal movement in Indonesia has dealt with differences in its turn.

Domestic Workers and the Law

In the period this book spans – the 1980s to the early 2020s – organized domestic workers across the globe have engineered a step-change in their legal rights and social recognition.[9] Sustained campaigning by workers and their supporters pushed delegates at the 100th International Labour Conference (ILC) in Geneva to adopt the pathbreaking "Domestic Workers Convention, 2011 (No. 189)" on 16 June 2011. To the "joy" of domestic workers and "the astonishment" of others, the Convention, referred to as "C189" in this book, established the principle that domestic workers should enjoy decent work – like all other workers – and be legally protected from the unique vulnerabilities of their sector (Blackett 2019:10–11; Seiffarth et al. 2023: 2). In Indonesia as elsewhere, C189 has sustained calls for respect and rights, offered a set of standards as the basis for national legislation, and served as a chastening rod with which to chide governments for failing to implement internationally agreed norms.

The call for "respect" and "rights" stemmed from the first international conference of domestic worker organizations hosted by the Dutch Trade Union Federation FNV in Amsterdam in November 2006. Lita Anggraini and Susi Apriyanti (the then chairperson of the Tunas Mulia domestic worker union in Yogyakarta) attended. Both played active roles. Apriyanti described her union's pioneering work in negotiating contracts between employers and domestic workers. She also explained how, in her home city, domestic workers and supporters had drafted and advocated for local regulations as a precursor to a national law.[10] Anggraini became secretary of the

8 For a discussion of self-identification as "feminist" amongst members of women's and gender studies centres in public and Islamic universities in Yogyakarta, see Qibtiyah (2010).

9 Appendix 1 (a timeline) lists some of these global developments and sets them alongside political changes in Indonesia.

10 Tragically, Susi Apriyanti died in a traffic accident the following year. When the IDWN steering committee published a report on the Amsterdam

International Domestic Workers Network (IDWN), a transnational group established after the conference ended. In 2008, the IDWN published a conference report. Entitled *Respect and Rights: Protection of Domestic/ Household Workers!*, the report spoke forthrightly of outrage, rights, demands, servitude, exploitation, failure, and urgency. Workers, the authors reminded readers repeatedly, were tired of others speaking for them. They wanted their voices heard and their representatives officially recognized in negotiations about labour laws (IRENE and IUF 2008).

By 2010, the IDWN had formulated a *Platform of Demands* for discussion at the 2010 International Labour Conference. Workers said they wanted an International Convention (and national labour laws) to secure for domestic workers the same rights to decent work as any other worker. The *Platform* set out what legislation needed to cover. First, a statement that "anyone who works in the private home of another, doing household and care work" full- or part-time, live-in or live-out, migrant or not, counts as a domestic worker. Second, a set of terms and conditions that place domestic workers on a par with other workers. Third, clauses addressing the unique vulnerabilities and needs of domestic workers. These should include the regulation of employment agencies, the right to choose one's place of abode and keep personal documents, the right to tailored education and training, access to specific dispute resolution mechanisms, and effective monitoring procedures (Mather 2010). These proposals incorporated what Indonesia's domestic worker movement – and movements worldwide – knew from experience were needed. However, in many jurisdictions, agreeing the definition of a domestic worker or the age at which a child can start work has proved contentious. So too has reaching consensus on what constitutes equal treatment, especially regarding wages, hours of work, and payments in kind (ILO 2021). In the case of Indonesia, such matters were still holding up the passage of a domestic worker law in the spring of 2024, twenty years after Indonesia's parliament had first put a draft law on its list of priority legislation.

Despite opposition and prevarication, domestic workers and their allies continue to campaign for "respect and rights", twin themes that thread through this book. They have good reason to do so. As Adelle Blackett has argued convincingly, where labour laws do not cover them

Conference in 2008, they dedicated it to her memory. For an account of the complex campaign for regulation in Yogyakarta, written by activist participants, see Sargini et al. (2017).

or employers or agencies ignore legislation in practice, domestic workers are subject to deeply embedded norms that oblige them to show duty and deference to their employers but assign them few or no rights in return. Whether described as the "asymmetrical, unequal and largely invisible law of the household workplace" (Blackett 2019: 11) or the expression of "cultures of servitude" (Ray and Qayum 2009), taken-for-granted and unwritten laws have left domestic workers without enforceable limits on their working time, without entitlement to days off, paid holiday, or maternity leave, and unable to appeal against unjust wages, unfair dismissal, or insalubrious or unsafe conditions. In Indonesia, hard-won protections other workers enjoy, enshrined in a Manpower Act passed in 2003 (and still in place after the deregulatory changes made in a much-contested "Job Creation" or "Omnibus" law passed in 2020) do not apply to PRT. The 2003 Act classifies those who employ domestic workers as *pemberi kerja* or "work-givers". Unlike "entrepreneurs", who must apply specific provisions in the act on matters such as the minimum wage, working hours, or paid leave, "work-givers" have only a "general obligation" towards employees (Sheppard 2009: 18–20). In January 2015, after a succession of public protests analyzed later in this study, the movement secured a partial victory when a new minister of manpower and transmigration announced a Ministerial Regulation, *Permenaker* No. 2/201, on the protection of domestic workers. Activists welcomed the Regulation as a sign of goodwill, even though it did not meet all their demands and was not legally binding (*Jakarta Post* 2015). It did, however, mark a significant step from silenced political invisibility and symbolic confinement in the *belakang*, the private backyard areas of Indonesian homes, to public recognition of PRT as independent workers and worthy citizens.

Lobbying for legal reform has only been one part of the movement's activities, but – this book argues – a crucial part. The commodification of reproductive labour and the continuing exploitation of domestic workers underpin global economic development while humanity's shared precarity, mutual interdependencies, and ethical responsibilities are disavowed (Gutiérrez-Rodríguez 2009; Fish 2017). The differential impact of COVID-19 on domestic and care workers cruelly exposed this reality (see, for example, Ismail and Ogando 2023). Pre-pandemic, an estimated four to five million PRT were employed in Indonesian homes (Suhaimi and Farid 2017; Liem et al. 2023). A 2022 survey of employers and migrant domestic workers in Thailand, Singapore and Malaysia found evidence of continuing bad practice including low wages, long hours, restricted access to social security, limited rights to organize, and cases of forced labour, alongside a rhetoric that cleaning and caring in the home is not "real" or skilled work (Holliday 2023). As the world's fourth most populous nation, third-largest democracy, and the leading democracy in ASEAN – where in 2023, the Philippines remained the only nation to have ratified ILO C189 – Indonesia could transform the landscape of domestic worker rights beyond as well as inside its borders if it acceded to the demands of JALA PRT.

Ten years after the adoption of C189, most commentators judge that legislation that secures equal standing with other workers is an essential first step towards "decent work" for the world's estimated 75.6 million domestic workers (ILO 2021). Furthermore, as the testimony in this book confirms, organized domestic workers express a desire for dignity, respect, and recognition of the moral, social, and economic value of their labour – and of themselves as human beings – as often as they give vent to outrage. In such a context, shared feelings can be directed towards campaigning for a national law or the ratification of C189 (Schwenken et al. 2011).

However, some caveats remain. Ally (2008, 2011b) has argued (as she says, "provocatively") that despite material and symbolic benefits, regulation of domestic work in South Africa has depoliticized workers, reduced the scope for personalized relationships, and left the institution of domestic work intact to do its work of reproducing inequalities. Similarly, Gutiérrez-Rodríguez, studying migrant domestic work in Europe, questions whether rights-based remedies alone will address the unease engendered by the inequalities of paid domestic labour. Contrasting the happiness domestic workers create for employers with the feelings of disgust and disregard that workers she interviewed spoke of, she argues for a new, decolonizing, and "cosmological" language of interdependence that would go beyond professionalization or the class-based politics of labour (Gutiérrez-Rodríguez 2009: 160–69). Indeed, "going beyond" the scope of national legislation and C189 is crucial for migrant domestic workers. Immigration laws and bilateral agreements can make aspirations of equal treatment meaningless, as a tied visa system introduced in the UK in 2012 amply illustrates (Mullally and Murphy 2014).

In the context of such debate, this book concerns itself with the micro-politics of the quest by Indonesian domestic workers for both "happiness" and a revaluing of their labour. If it is in the nitty-gritty of "the bathroom where a domestic worker scrubs" that racism and patriarchy are sustained, as internationally renowned feminist theorist and writer Cynthia Enloe has suggested (in Prasad and Zulfiqar

2021: 730), this book journeys into the many and varied spaces where Indonesia's domestic workers and their supporters have strategized and sustained their campaign to get PRT voices heard, and laws changed.

Sources and Spaces: Archive and Field

This book has been long in the making. That has given me the advantage of reflecting on changes over time, compensating to some degree for the fact that no "archive" of Indonesia's domestic worker movement is ready for researchers to mine. Three types of material proved indispensable: postings on NGO websites, media accounts of events and personalities, and the published work of researchers and scholars whose work touched on relevant themes. As time progressed, materials foregrounding PRT voices came into play, such as the blog *Tungku Menyala*, its title conveying the sense of a flame that, once lit, will never be put out.

NGO websites were invaluable but unstable. JALA used to manage a substantial website. Well-populated sections covered its history, mission, advocacy, media campaigns, casework, news, consultations, and domestic workers schools, material I used to build a narrative and understand activist strategies. A gallery of photographs chronicled street protests, goings-on at the JALA house-cum-office, and meetings with officials and politicians, illuminating shifts between public, political, and semi-private spaces, and supplying visual evidence of the growing participation of PRT. The websites of NGOs and unions within the JALA network revealed shared histories, values, and personal connections between protagonists. In the middle of my research, however, JALA stopped maintaining its website, prioritizing a presence on social media. Evidence disappeared. Similarly, the ILO Jakarta website contains press releases, features, newsletters, and video and audio stories about the movement, but it, too, is subject to change. Consequently, some material used in making this book is no longer easily accessible.[11]

Media accounts and images feature large in this book's story. Journalists, I argue, were no mere observers. Some engaged in advocacy, others interviewed the movement's opponents. While news reports are not infallible – I found one, based on a press release, about an event

11 I have included URLs and the date I last accessed material in the reference list. In a few cases, the sources may no longer be available to follow up.

that activists called off at the last minute – Indonesian journalists quote government officials and activist speeches extensively and publish profiles of leading figures. Such sources illustrate how the movement managed its public face. However, the *Jakarta Post* and *Kompas*, two national newspapers I had used extensively, imposed paywalls part-way through my research; this last barrier but one of the challenges of "toiling in the archives of cyberspace", not least the matter of deciding when to call a halt (Sentilles 2005: 140–47). Indeed, ever hopeful, I found myself scanning the internet repeatedly, eager to see whether this book could close with the news that Indonesia's parliament had finally passed the long-awaited National Domestic Worker Law.

Along with documentary evidence, this book relies on interviews and observations conducted during five visits to Indonesia between 2012 and 2016, seven months of fieldwork in all. Appendix 2 lists my interviewees. People's memories of and reflections on their involvement with the movement highlighted continuities – in personnel, principles, loyalties, and leadership – along with the tensions inherent in contentious politics and intersectional alliances. I interviewed sixty-six informants, using an outline interview map focused on feminist affiliations, contributions to the movement, and recollections of events. Since many were figures already in the public eye, I tailored my questions accordingly once I had researched their careers. As outlined in the introductory 'Note on Names', this book uses names, not pseudonyms, for domestic workers, naming those already operating in the public sphere as movement advocates or citizen journalists. In a few cases, interviewees spoke of their practices as employers of domestic workers as an aside or junior journalists commented on editorial cultures. In such cases, I have not used their names. The aim has been to give voice to individuals and groups and convey something of the emotions and experiences they shared.

Place and space proved significant, affecting movement dynamics and the emergence of political identities. I divided my time between Yogyakarta and Jakarta, with a short side trip to Palembang (Sumatra) to observe developments outside Java. Yogyakarta was the birthplace of domestic worker unionism, and many of the activists in the movement met there. Seen by its residents as "a center of Javanese 'traditional culture'" and as representative of "the best that the modern community of Indonesia has to offer" (Strassler 2010: 10), evidence collected there illustrates the dexterity with which movement leaders developed a rights-based discourse that reflected and utilized Javanese values. Jakarta, on the other hand, was crucial as the capital city. JALA, leading feminist and women's rights NGOs, trade union confederations, national newspapers, and the ILO have their headquarters there. The University of Indonesia hosts the nation's longest-established gender studies centre. Population growth, a burgeoning middle class, outward movement to the suburbs, expansion of industry in the periphery, and widening income inequalities have resulted in increased social segregation and growing anxieties about security and what it means to be "modern" amongst Indonesia's wealthier classes (Hudalah and Firman 2012: 42–45; van Leeuwen 2008: 65, 262–8). In Jakarta, I could see the JALA network in operation and explore how social actors challenged and tuned in to public concerns. Using press reports, the findings of other researchers, and, for the later years of the movement, the published writings of organized domestic workers, this book also provides glimpses of developments in other regions and cities, where diverse cultural traditions and activist trajectories come into play.

Gender History and Feminist Storytelling

After forty years as a history teacher, school inspector, and senior local education officer, finding an appropriately academic storytelling voice for writing my PhD thesis and this book presented a challenge. How was I to conceptualize my new role? Historians sometimes describe themselves as "promiscuous" (Olcott 2017: 258) or as "critical gadflies" (Scott 2011: 42). Ephraim Chambers, compiling his 1728 *Cyclopaedia*, preferred the metaphor of the bee to that of the jackdaw – his sources "a thousand Flowers", his industry spent not for "Pride" but the common good (quoted in Kennedy 2013: 41). My preferred metaphor for the work of producing this book is that of the feminist needlewoman constructing a quilt, journeying to collect scraps, devising and discerning patterns, stitching individual pieces and layers together, binding all with threads of feeling. Like quilting, feminist research troubles Cartesian binaries; research is as much "an emotional and embodied set of practices" (Elmhirst 2012: 274) as an exercise of the mind. Quilts, like intersectionality, can uncover marginalized lives. Multi-layered, constructed of fabrics representing events in, and aspects of, individual or collective lives, quilts conjoin past and present, signal agency as well as tradition, and have been used, most famously by British artist Tracy Emin, to subvert gender hierarchies (Prichard 2010).[12]

12 For discussions of quilting bees and the quilting metaphor in academic

At the heart of this book's construction, providing, as it were, the backing layer, are some fellow travellers: feminist scholars whose work does not necessarily feature prominently in the text but whose thinking influenced my epistemology, shaped my investigations, and helped me craft the whole. First is Kimberlé Crenshaw's classic account of intersectionality, of how legal accountability and responsibility could be side-stepped when Black women found themselves "on the subordinate side of both the race and the gender divide" (2011: 230). JALA PRT has built its campaign on an intersectional analysis: as Lita Anggraini argued in an interview in 2015, Indonesian domestic workers have been on the subordinate and subservient side in terms of "gender bias, class bias, feudalism [and] issues of trust"; indeed, she went on, "everything blends here" (Madewanti 2015: 1).

Raewyn Connell's formulation of gender regimes offered a path between structure and agency. Her argument that relatively stable gender hierarchies become open to change during periods of transition (such as those precipitated by colonialism or globalization) and that social practice can be "ontoformative", bringing "new social realities into existence" sat well with my own feminist critical realist standpoint and with recent Indonesian history (Connell 2009: 85–7, 2018: 342). New constructs of masculinity that valued men "as hard-as-nails soldiers and hard-nosed politicians", for example, arose out of Indonesia's struggle for independence (Gouda 1999: 171), while in 1965, a contest between the Indonesian army and the Communist party was "played out over women's bodies", leading to the institutionalization of hegemonic militarized masculinity and a counterpart, conservative, femininity (Wieringa 2011: 556). The period this book encompasses, bifurcated by the rupture of 1998, exemplifies another time when "ontologies of exploitation" (Gutiérrez-Rodríguez 2009: 126) could be open to change. Similarly, Joan Scott sees the potential for change during political upheaval or shifts in employment patterns. She warns, however, of the possible re-inscription of fixed polarities of masculine and feminine when conservatives mobilize "implicit" understandings of gender to secure the status quo (Scott 1986: 1072–4). Hence, this book explores the political, social, and cultural construction of gender differences and gender identities as it chronicles activist experiences, agency, and subjectivities.

research, teaching, and feminist activism, see Brown (1989), Flannery (2001), Wilson (2001), Koelsch (2012) and Robertson (2014). For a recent discussion of Indonesian batik quilting and its associated cultural values, see Ekawati Dukut (2018).

Nancy Fraser's framing of gender justice as three-dimensional and Ruth Lister's analysis of feminist citizenship also inform this book's conclusions. In the mid-1990s, alarmed that feminists were sidelining structural issues, Fraser argued in a much-debated series of lectures that "only an approach that redresses the cultural devaluation of the 'feminine' precisely *within* the economy (and elsewhere) can deliver serious redistribution and genuine recognition" (1998: 10; italics in original). Furthermore, on the principle that all should have a voice in decision-making and a fair opportunity to contest their claims, societies should foster "parity of participation in a multiplicity of interaction arenas", which might include the workplace, the family home, and a community or civil society (Fraser 2013: 166). Lister similarly suggested that a synthesis of liberal and participatory citizenship would reduce the political exclusion women experience. Such a change would require a shift in the boundaries between public and private, redefining what counts as the common good, and efforts to build women's confidence as political operators (Lister 1997: 33–42). With such ideas in mind, this book asks questions about how, how far, by what means, and in what sorts of spaces Indonesia's domestic worker movement has fostered PRT participation in its efforts to change the political playing field in favour of those currently kept out.

Second, three studies of gender and class in eighteenth- and early nineteenth-century England alerted me to relevant themes. Leonore Davidoff and Catherine Hall's celebrated study, *Family Fortunes*, first published in 1987, showed how gender and class shaped the "ideologies, institutions and practices" of a growing middle class (2002: 13).[13] Their research established that domestic service underpinned modern capitalism and new constructions of middle-class femininities and masculinities. By the mid-nineteenth century, three-quarters of middle-class families had at least one live-in servant, enabling male heads of household to concentrate on business. At the same time, their wives supported family enterprises, built social capital, and nurtured the next generation. Servants helped create smooth-running homes-as-havens that helped restore a sense of order at a time of "exceptional turmoil" following a period marked by economic crises, war with France, political unrest, rapid population expansion, industrialization, and urbanization. New anxieties and

13 Citations refer to a second edition of *Family Fortunes* published in 2002. The publishers brought out a third edition in 2018. For an account of the book's reception, see Laura Lee Downs (2019: 103–6).

tensions, however, arose as an increasingly cash and market-driven economy encroached on familial forms of master-servant relationships (Davidoff and Hall 2002: 30, 357, 383–96). Perhaps similar processes were operating at the end of President Suharto's thirty-two-year rule of Indonesia when, as one US policy adviser described it, "financial chaos, inflation, unemployment, hunger, and civil commotion" beset the nation (Friend 1998: 387).

Like *Family Fortunes*, Carolyn Steedman's *Labours Lost* (2009) argues that domestic servants were significant in constructing a modern labour force in late eighteenth-century England. Castigating E. P. Thompson, noted author of *The Making of the English Working Class* (1963), for sidelining servants as not engaged in productive labour, Steedman considers the social imaginary (a notion I take up in the next chapter) and concludes that in social imaginaries and their own minds, servants "*were* the people, or if you will have it this way, the working class" (2009: 356; italics in original). Three aspects of Steedman's work informed my thinking. First, the commentators used the position of servants as a synecdoche for the social order. Second, hidden histories revealed that eighteenth-century servants spoke and wrote about themselves – represented themselves – in "astonishing" ways. Third, spaces and objects – kitchens, laundries, nurseries, and the tools of the trade therein – were sites of and the means whereby relationships between servants and their employers were negotiated and redefined (2009: 346–54).

Amanda Vickery was deeply critical of *Family Fortunes*. Nevertheless, in *Behind Closed Doors* (2009), she too seams richly detailed stories together and conveys the gendered materiality of domestic worlds. Her interest in the thresholds and boundaries of Georgian homes, the role of the mistress in policing the borders, and her interest in rooms and objects inflected my observations of the activist spaces the Indonesian domestic workers' movement created to provide workers with "homes-from-home". Vickery's insights into employers' perspectives enriched my understanding of middle-class housewives' fears. And, in the confines of my own workspace, her vivid prose and ability to pen succinct sentences helped me write to the point on many occasions.

These "fellow travellers" reflect my age, cultural roots, and education. Returning to formal study at SOAS in 2012, I began researching Indonesian feminism, which had passed me by when I lived in Jakarta in the 1980s. As I read, I was impressed by the figure of Siti Musdah Mulia, the first Indonesian woman to receive a doctorate in Islamic political thought from Syarif Hidayatullah State Islamic University in Jakarta. An outspoken and progressive feminist theorist and activist, she provoked controversy when, as a senior adviser in the ministry for religious affairs, she headed a ministerial team tasked to revise the "Compilation of Islamic Law" that stipulated legal marriage arrangements for Muslims in Indonesia. The task group published a "Counter Legal Draft" (CLD) in 2004. It proved highly controversial. It argued that the social subordination of women arose from misguided interpretations of religious texts. It proposed changes to marriage, divorce, and inheritance. It looked forward to the prohibition of polygamy. The ministry quickly withdrew the draft as too incendiary. Reflecting on it later, Mulia reiterated her belief that the Islamic principle of "making one" should apply to social relationships between men and women. Women, she averred, should not "acquiesce" in being dominated by men, but take part in public life and politics as Muslim women have done in the past (Mulia 2015: 7–9). A strong advocate of religious pluralism and lesbian and gay rights (and a supporter of the domestic worker movement from the outset), Mulia continues to argue that religious conservatism and extremism threaten Indonesia's democracy. She calls out governments, the most affluent, and the middle classes for not seeking justice and prosperity for ordinary Indonesians (Diani 2014; Soparianti and Narulita 2022). Her words and her work helped me grasp something of the fervour and optimism of the *reformasi* period and be better prepared for meeting feminists for whom religious belief was a crucial source of strength and political commitment.

Finally, Clare Hemmings's warnings against nostalgia, unwarranted optimism about feminist progress, or a focus on loss in feminist storytelling are especially pertinent to feminists of my generation (2005). As a scholar whose earliest encounters with feminism were mediated through the material lens of the second-wave feminist classic *Our Bodies, Ourselves* (Boston Women's Health Book Collective 1973) with its gospel of global sisterhood and who now looks back through the dismal lens of post-Brexit Britain, a narrative of loss is hard to resist. Even so, looking for progress rather than failure, this book errs on the side of hope, cherishing the expectation that PRT and activist persistence will succeed in winning concessions from employers and the state.

Threads of Feeling: A Chapter Outline

This account of Indonesia's domestic worker movement combines chronology and theme. In chronological terms, the first three chapters move from New Order Indonesia in the 1970s and 1980s to the close of 2016 (when my fieldwork concluded). The next two look more thematically at journalism and knowledge production over a similar period. The book ends with an update and overview, its final layer of topstitching, but not the end of the story as far as the movement is concerned. Such an approach allows me to trace the emergence and development of the movement as it came into being and investigate aspects of the temporal and the spatial in depth. Each chapter functions, perhaps, as the "block" of a quilt, made up of its scraps of evidence and selection of literature and theory, linked to the whole with threads of connectivity and recurrent motifs. In this quilt, the stories of individuals who move between different, but connected, networks and spaces of activism are explored.

Chapter 1 introduces the cultures of servitude prevalent in New Order Indonesia, revealing reasons for stasis and the potential for change. It uncovers tensions between employer imaginations of kinship, generosity, and fondly remembered, more harmonious, domestic pasts, and the materiality of economic necessity found in the voices of domestic workers that spoke of the monetary value of gifts, access to loans, and the avoidance of precarity. Chapters 2 and 3 constitute the book's chronological core. Focusing on the contribution of activists, both interweave the temporal and spatial in exploring questions of representation and political participation. Chapter 2 situates the early history of Indonesia's domestic worker movement in the context of the radical anti-Suharto student activism and feminist organizing that developed in the late 1980s and '90s. It reveals how workers and middle-class NGO activists negotiated tensions between each other and shows how activists drew on feminist and liberatory theory to promote participation amongst women whose voices society had long ignored.

Chapter 3 follows the movement from Yogyakarta to Jakarta. It examines the JALA network as a model of cross-class organizing founded on feminist principles. Detailing how women's and children's rights NGOs, and, later, trade union confederations were drawn in, it illustrates the evolution of a domestic worker activist street style, charts a shift towards adversarial street politics, and uses the story of one domestic worker to illustrate activist support for domestic worker unions. Chapters 4 and 5 work in parallel. They shift attention to the symbolic power of words and ideas in changing the landscape of what people take for granted. Chapter 4 charts changes achieved by a small group of journalists who became JALA advocates and contested prevailing patterns of media coverage of domestic worker issues. Chapter 5 problematizes boundaries between activism and academia, excavating evidence of contributions made by feminist scholars in the academy, by Indonesia's first feminist journal, *Jurnal Perempuan*, and by a group of overseas and Indonesian scholars who entered the field in the wake of C189.

Despite the disastrous impact of COVID-19 on the lives of Indonesian domestic workers – many of whom lost their jobs without compensation or found their workloads doubled as families stayed at home – they have supported each other and the movement throughout, keeping up their demands on the political agenda through social media. The concluding chapter provides a brief update on recent developments and draws the threads of the chapters together to reflect on the politics of presence and what it might mean in a post-pandemic world.

CHAPTER

1

On Not Sitting on Chairs: Social Imaginaries of Servitude in New Order Indonesia

The coursebook I used to study Bahasa Indonesia soon after my arrival in Jakarta contains a revealing story about “a capable housewife”, Nyonya (Mrs) Harun, a graduate with a degree in medicine. The textbook aimed to introduce foreigners to the culture as well as the language of Indonesia. Indeed, Mrs Harun exemplifies a culture described memorably as “state ibuism” (state motherism), a means whereby the Suharto regime “depoliticized and mobilized” women “to support the New Order’s developmental goals” (Suryakusuma 2012: para. 1). Like all wives of civil servants, Mrs Harun was required to participate in an organization named Dharma Wanita (Women’s Service), attend official functions, and do charitable work alongside tending to the needs of her husband and three children. Her career is secondary; despite her qualifications, Mrs Harun is described as “helping” at the hospital. Servants were a *sine qua non*, as the text explains:

> Mrs Harun has two very good servants, Mbok Kromo and Bibik Ikem. Although she doesn’t have to cook, wash the clothes, and clean the house, her days are always full. Apart from helping at the hospital, Mrs Harun is very active in several organizations. On Fridays, she stays at home and reads medical books and journals. When she is at home, the telephone never stops ringing. Her friends ring up to discuss this and that about the organizations. Once a week, on Saturdays, if there are no meetings, she plays tennis with

> her friends. On Sundays, if the weather is fine, Mrs Harun and her family often go to the swimming pool. They are all fond of and good at swimming. (Johns and Stokes 1977: 169–70)

This passage gives no hint of any tension arising from the contrast between the modern lifestyle achieved by Nyonya Harun and the circumscribed lives of the women who work for her. Mrs Harun's middle-class modernity is signalled by her possession of a car (she takes her youngest child to school by car), her collegial relationship with her husband who "helps his wife if necessary", her always-ringing telephone, her love of tennis and swimming at weekends, and her two servants. She maintains a harmonious household, looking after the emotional side of her family's lives while servants, in the background, keep everything spotless. The textbook's authors explain in a gloss that the terms *Mbok* (mother) and *Bibik* (aunt) are "used in Java to address an older female household help" and that "it would be very impolite to use the [person's] name alone (1977: 171). Javanese culture and familial nomenclature thus provide the frame for a colonially inflected mistress–servant relationship bolstered by the state's prescribed gender norms.

This story encapsulates the theme of this chapter, the intertwining of vestiges of feudal and colonial premises and practices within prevalent social imaginaries of domestic work and modernity in New Order Indonesia. Similarly concerned with the interplay between past and present, Raka Ray and Seemin Qayum use the term "cultures of servitude" to characterize the situation of domestic workers in contemporary Kolkata. Interested in the "interstices of the social imaginaries of feudalism and capitalist modernity", they analyze domestic service as a site where India's influential middle classes shape and reproduce class boundaries. Three long-held beliefs, they argue, underpin servility. Having servants is seen as a necessity. Servants are regarded as part of the family, encased in a "rhetoric of love". Nevertheless, boundaries between employers and servants must be maintained through the quotidian "politics and practices of eating, sitting, sleeping, bathing, and clothing". Such mechanisms confer distinction on the middle classes and categorize servants as a class apart (Ray and Qayum 2009: 3, 19, 25–6).

These same tropes of necessity, family membership, and distinction often recur in histories and ethnographies of domestic life and work in Indonesia. However, one could argue that in the Indonesian context servitude is not peculiar to waged domestic work. A study of relationships between restaurant workers and employers in Yogyakarta, for example, identified similar patterns of dependency, subordination, and inequality, but characterized them as customary patron–client relationships that exemplified an Indonesian notion of *kekeluargaan* (family-ness) (Mahy et al. 2017). Nevertheless, locating the figure of the domestic worker in the interstices between feudal and modernist imaginaries is instructive. An interstice, after all, is not only a space to be caught in, like a crevasse in a glacier, but a crack, a fissure, or an opening from which movement may be possible. Exploring such spaces emphasizes adaptation, adjustment, and upheaval – the tensions between movement and stasis in paid domestic work.

Moreover, as Sheila Jasanoff points out in *Dreamscapes of Modernity*, the notion of social imaginaries can encompass the large scale – as in Benedict Anderson's imagined national communities (2006) or Charles Taylor's broadly defined "ways people imagine their social existence, how they fit together with others, how things go on between them" (Taylor 2004: 23) – but also accommodate the smaller-scale, the material, and the performative. For Jasanoff, "coproduction" in contemporary societies is a collective "reformation" of conceptual and social orders in response to rapid technological and socio-political change. Investigating the "time and space" dimensions of the imaginaries surrounding domestic work in New Order Indonesia, in that case, should illuminate not only the institution's stickiness but its susceptibilities to change (Jasanoff 2015: 5–14).

Following this line of reasoning, this chapter looks, Janus-like, both to the *longue durée* and to possible harbingers of a new future. "On Distinction" contrasts two contemporary readings of New Order imaginaries, arguing that a preoccupation with order held together apparently opposing constructs: servants as cogs in a metaphorical modernist machine and servants as elements in complex hierarchies and codes of behaviour grounded in belief and ritual. "On (Happy) Families" investigates and historicizes different manifestations of the notion of servants as kin or family members and considers the function of such rhetoric. Finally, "On Openings" explores the potential for change in domestic worker–employer relationships becoming apparent by the beginning of *reformasi*.

On Distinction

A social imaginary of servant as hidden cog in a modernist machine, exemplified in the middle-class lifestyle of Nyonya Harun and her family, was not new. Advertisements and posters displayed in schools attended by indigenous elites in the 1930s foregrounded almost identical bourgeois values: not wasting time, cleanliness, the nuclear family, and the role of women as upholders of stability. Servants, if shown, were in the background, performing subservience (Schulte Nordholt 2011: 441–6). Nyonya Harun's telephones, cars, and sports equipment – then coveted markers of modernity and distinction – were amongst numerous consumer items displayed at the spectacular fairs and exhibitions which mushroomed in late colonial Indonesia (van der Meer 2017). Two photograph albums belonging to Javanese elites dating from the 1920s and '30s show a younger generation swimming, playing tennis, and going on excursions, even as older relatives adopt formal poses inside the house. Movement signified modernity. Photographs depicted "respectability", "conjugal civility", and "familial contentment and unity", yet servants did not feature. They provided the essential underpinning of the new social imaginary but were excluded from it (Protschky 2012: 28–34).

It seems taken for granted in the rendering of the Nyonya Harun story that even "good servants" could only enjoy the fruits of modernity by association. Unsurprisingly, in a textbook aimed at northern audiences, with many readers coming to Indonesia as experts to bolster Suharto's developmentalism, no mention is made of Mrs Harun's servants not being permitted to sit on the family's chairs. However, as Japanese anthropologist Saya Shiraishi's reflections on her visits to Javanese middle-class homes in the 1980s demonstrate, the politics of sitting mattered much. In an essay entitled "Silakan masuk, silakan duduk" (Please come in, please sit down), Shiraishi suggests that sitting on chairs in New Order Java served as a metaphor for knowing one's place, for being included or excluded, and for feeling secure. Servants featured strongly in her account. Once, when staying in a guest house in Solo, she recalled, she and the other guests were "offered seats on the red-cloth covered, carved wood-framed sofas or chairs". The house manager perched on a bench, housemaids sat on the "floor steps", and a "gentle floor sweeper" sat on the floor, entertaining the small children present. When Shiraishi broke protocol and knelt down to play with the children, placing herself on the same level as the lowliest servant, the sweeper leapt to his feet and retired from the room backwards. The mistress of the house restored order, inviting Shiraishi to come immediately and sit with her on the sofa, smoothing ruffled relationships (Shiraishi 1986: 110). Her role, like Mrs Harun's, was to maintain harmony.

Not everyone in the household had the right to invite visitors into New Order Javanese homes. In Shiraishi's account, "a young housemaid" was sent back to her village after inviting a friend to sit with her in her room without permission. Fear of losing one's place and becoming a victim or *korban*, a person without a sitting room or a chair to sit on and thus no entitlement to inhabit the neighbourhood or city, seemed to be pervasive. Householders contained their anxieties by strengthening and extending the walls and fences around their houses to provide a "thick security blanket". At the same time, popular performances by a theatre group called *Sri Murat*[1] enacted a state of disturbing "deregulation" precipitated by the arrival on the stage (set as a sitting room) of an unbidden stranger in the form of a Dracula figure. The actors jump to their feet in alarm; at that moment, the "distinction between the chair-sitters and the floor-sitters is nullified". Shiraishi concludes that "tranquillity" depends on respecting symbolic and material boundaries of who might legitimately sit on the chairs (1986: 108, 112).

John Pemberton's *On the Subject of Java* puts New Order seating practices into historical perspective. Ensuring people sat according to their rank was one expression of *tata*, a Javanese term that encapsulates both the physical arrangement of kings, court officials, and guests in choreographed positions and the "theoretical arrangement of the realm" (1994: 56). Drawing on court manuscripts describing grand ceremonial occasions held at the royal palace (known as the *Kraton*) in Surakarta (Solo) in Central Java from the eighteenth century onwards, Pemberton concluded that:

> In two centuries of Kraton Surakarta texts, nothing was *tata-ed* more frequently than *kursi*: European style, straight back chairs. For the potential power of chairs in matters of ceremonial [...] was that they were always set out beforehand in a predesignated and precisely measured formation so that provocative issues of status might be taken care of before the ritual fact [...] thus the origins of an orderly tranquil kingdom became peculiarly embodied in chairs. (1994: 56)

---

1 Shiraishi speaks of *Sri Murat*. James Siegel, who writes about the theatre company at length, suggests the group was named *Sri Mulat* after its founder (1986: Chapter 4).

For "provocative issues of status", Pemberton argues, read the unwelcome presence of victorious Dutch colonial officials at Javanese court rituals following the disorderly rout of the Surakarta king, Pakubuwana II, in 1743. Pakubuwana had had to cede full sovereignty of the wealthiest part of his kingdom, agree to enormous rice duties, and accept having a Dutch East India Company garrison at his court before being reinstated in a new palace in Solo (Ricklefs 2008: 121–5). Only once seated in his new throne room with the Dutch *Commandant* and his soldiers standing alongside and two banyan trees from the ransacked former residence ritually planted was everything judged, once again, to be "in good order" (Pemberton 1994: 34–6).

Good order was what united modernist and traditional/hierarchical modes of distinction. The promise that all Indonesian citizens, even servants, might eventually share in the benefits of modernity justified the privileged existence of an educated middle class acting as the avant-garde. Alongside future visions, feudal imaginaries originating in Javanese principalities and adopted by Dutch colonialists in their homes and within the civil service continued to enshrine rituals of subservience. Knowing one's place was cemented as a cornerstone of stability.

On (Happy) Families

During my childhood, in the aftermath of the Blitz, the card game "Happy Families" was a popular pastime. As Sara Ahmed points out (though it did not trouble me at the time), the game, in which players compete to collect as many "happy" families as possible, creates "a shared orientation towards the family as being good, as being what promises happiness in return for loyalty" (2008: 12). There were no war widows in the UK version, no "only" children who had never seen their fathers, no divorcees, and no maiden aunts. The model family comprised Father, Mother, Son, and Daughter. "Miss Bun the Baker's Daughter" or "Master Dose, the Doctor's Son" had only to accept their allotted roles and follow the rules, reproducing the "happiness object" that is the family in their turn. In the game, you lose your turn if you fail to say "please" and "thank you". In life, Ahmed reflects, those who reject norms risk being cast as "killjoys" around the family table or losing their space altogether (2017: 36–9).

The connection between happiness, loyalty, and proper behaviour Ahmed pinpoints is a leitmotif linking the narratives that follow.

Drawing on ethnographies and histories of the New Order period (or those written shortly afterwards), and on the recollections of some of my informants who grew up in President Suharto's Indonesia, I outline four embodiments of the "one of the family" or " like kin" imaginary, labelling these as "Retainer", "Nursemaid", "Adoptee", and "Follower". This is not to suggest these were fixed and discrete categories. "Retainers", for example, often joined families as nursemaids. Indeed, part of the power of the kinship idiom in relation to domestic work in New Order Indonesia was its pervasiveness. Imprecise and elastic, the notion could shapeshift. Distinctions between "family" and "not family" were blurred, varied from region to region, and changed over time – the nuances of belonging slippery and ambivalent but well-buttressed by elements of traditional moralities and an appeal to affect. Familial models of domestic service represented harmony and happiness to many employers. Even those committed to change could, willy-nilly, express ambivalence and nostalgia when comparing new social imaginaries of domestic work with those of earlier times.

Retainer

The first and most cherished embodiment of servants as family members I encountered was that of the faithful, generally female, long-serving domestic worker, characterized by Ray and Qayum in their study of domestic work in India as the "family retainer" (2009: 98). Some of my informants still had such persons in their households, referring to them as friends or companions. In my second week of fieldwork, I was invited to visit the home of an academic following a meeting at a university in Yogyakarta. My host explained that her domestic worker had been with her for twenty-two years and was "very close" with the family. Amongst this PRT's duties, I discovered, was taking the daughter of the house, whom she had looked after in childhood, to and from university each day; caring companionship carried from one generation to the next. Later, in Jakarta, a senior women's rights activist said of one of her PRT (who had served her family for forty years) that "now she stays with me, she's not working anymore […] having grown up together, we are very close". She remembered servants in her childhood as "dedicated […] very proud […] part of the family […] we trusted each other more in those days. I looked on them as my friends". Closeness, loyalty, trust, and friendship – such were the attributes of the ideal domestic worker–employer relationship these informants underlined.

This same social imaginary came to light part-way through another interview in Yogyakarta when an older woman came in to serve tea.

She was not introduced and left the room at once. Later, unbidden, my informant explained:

> The older woman who brought in tea for us earlier, she is my friend. My relationship with her is not about money. She will stay with me until she dies. We feel secure in our relationship and that feeling cannot be guaranteed by the law.

Knowing my interest in the Domestic Workers Bill, she elaborated:

> Too much expression of money culture, this culture hindered the progress of the Bill in parliament. For example, the people in the Kraton [palace] who *abdi dalem* there receive very little money, but they feel protected and at peace. They don't value money. But PRT nowadays demand high wages and are not always loyal in their work.

A passionate advocate of women's rights and domestic worker empowerment, this informant wanted legal recognition and protection for domestic workers. Nonetheless, her reference to *abdi dalem* speaks to a different register. *Abdi dalem* were (and remain) the quintessential Javanese family retainers who served the Sultan of Yogyakarta. Traditionally living in enclaves surrounding royal palaces and mosques or within the palace, they were paid little, but gained respect through their contribution to "the culture of the *kraton*" (Schlehe 2017: 7). Comparing PRT with *abdi dalem* elevated the intangible – security, protection, and a feeling of peace – over financial gain.

Historian Rudolf Mrazek supplies further evidence of this link between servants, loyalty, and happiness. In the 1990s, he held conversations with eighty-two "elderly" members of Indonesia's pre-and post-Independence intellectual elite. Recounting memories of growing up in colonial Indonesia, his informants talked about servants who had lived with them. Professor Selo Soemardjan, an eminent Indonesian social scientist and former high-ranking civil servant born into an aristocratic Javanese family in 1915, for example, explained that in his childhood:

> Our servants were family servants. There was no contract or anything. They were just there, and if the family liked them, they were ours, accepted as servants. Some stayed for many years. I recall one servant who grew old in our house. She actually became like a member of the family. We treated her as if she were of our family. [...] Yes, as I said, we were happy. (Mrazek 2010: 37)

Pointing to the "inner living quarters" on a plan of his childhood home, Soemardjan spoke of happiness, a happiness which rested in part in the knowledge that family servants were in the house. In poetic mode, Mrazek concluded that servants were recalled "as being a tightness of the house, the bricks, the plaster, the bamboo", their presence making home life "wholesome", their absence, in the case of former family retainers, "missed" (2010: 36–8). Employers, such comments imply, assumed that servants would share the happiness and harmony. Similar assumptions, I discovered, persisted into and beyond the New Order. "We have a common saying", a senior journalist told me in 2012, "that if the employer is happy, then the domestic worker will be happy too" – a platitude she believed militated against any domestic worker law.

Happiness, however, depended on both parties embracing distinction. Amongst Javanese families, using "respectful" language of the proper linguistic level and observing seating protocols marked the boundaries of family (Mrazek 2010: 37; Supardo 2007: 11–13). As one informant told me, the servants she grew up with addressed her mother, a member of an aristocratic Javanese family closely related to the Sultan of Yogyakarta, as "Your Highness". Another explained that when she was small, "maybe because we were still feudal", she "wasn't allowed to talk to the domestic workers in Bahasa [Indonesian]", because Javanese enabled employers and servants to "show the class". Even now, she continued, her long-serving live-in domestic worker, "the old one", does not address her in Indonesian, only breaking the rule occasionally if, for example, "she is mad at me or doesn't want to serve the meal or wash the dishes". While this discomforted my informant, she savoured such moments of greater equality. "Am I still feudal?" she mused, "because my PRT still sit on the floor and don't want to sit on the chair unless I ask them."

Such reflections suggest that maintaining harmonious retainer relationships depended on employers and domestic workers using – and sometimes circumscribing – inherited codes of speech and behaviour that had the status of rules. More than a show of manners, *tata krama*, the term used to describe expectations around ordered social relations, was a complex system constructed to mark and maintain harmony and distinction. It encompassed matters such as bodily comportment, deference, and humility: Javanese children, for example, were taught to ask permission and bend their heads low before passing in front of their grandparents. Keeping low (*andhap*) and humbling oneself (*asor*) while exalting the other were valued qualities in Javanese culture. At the same time, the practice had colonial connotations. In the early part of the twentieth century, young, educated Indonesians in the colonial civil service had resisted practices such as crouching or sitting on the floor in the presence of European officials as part of a demand for greater recognition and respect (Luttikhuis and van der Meer 2020).

Conversations between domestic workers and employers conducted in Javanese, as my informant explained, are grounded in complex speech levels that demonstrate different degrees of "formality" and "respect" based on social status (Kraube 2018: 72). Hence, while speakers defer to age, as a rule, an older domestic worker talking with an employer much younger than herself would nonetheless use a higher speech level. The employer would use a lower level in return (Sukarno 2010: 65). *Tata krama* could allow for resistance – witness my informant's observations about her domestic worker's switch to Bahasa Indonesia. Indeed, I have a memory of Ibu Mortinah, our cook in Jakarta, serving a warmed-up chicken carcass to a volunteer for breakfast to let her know that she had outstayed her welcome and was creating too much work. Ibu Mortinah and my informant's domestic worker were well-established in their positions and able to transgress – and negotiate – within boundaries.

Ibu Mortinah, however, had chosen to work for expatriates, exchanging higher pay and clear working arrangements for the security and closer relationship staying with one family might provide.

Nursemaid

A second role in the cast of "servants as family" in affluent households was that of childminder/nursemaid or *mbok mban/emban*. Koentjaraningrat, who belonged to the same generation of Indonesian intellectuals as Soemardjan and was regarded as the founding father of Indonesian anthropology, discussed childrearing in his tour de force, *Javanese Culture*, published in 1985. Delineating the lifestyle of his class, the *priyayi* or civil servant class, in colonial and New Order times, he spoke about nursemaids in this way:

> It is customary among priyayi families to have female servants, mbok mban, if possible one for each child until it reaches school age. A pre-war or high-ranking priyayi family may therefore have three to four such female servants, whose exclusive duties are taking care of the family's small children. Since servants in Javanese priyayi families usually serve for a lifetime and reside in the house, they often become very much part of the family. The mbok mban

> especially may become very close to the children they have taken care of. (Koentjaraningrat 1985: 237)

In this account, acceptance into the family was, in part, a consequence of long service and closeness to children. Such status remained conditional. It might happen "often", a servant "may" become close. The practice of having a servant for each child emanated from the *Kraton*; in the 1920s and '30s, after ten months with a wet nurse, royal children were reportedly delivered into the care of a *mbok emban* who accompanied them everywhere, including staying with them at school while they were still young (Amini 2016: 168–72). *Mbok emban* were trusted to train children of the elite in the "behavioural style of speaking, pointing, sitting, and so on" prescribed in Javanese etiquette for their elevated position in the web of asymmetrical and hierarchical social relationships surrounding them (Errington 1984: 278, 282).

A nursemaid, Koentjaraningrat explained, was not a maid-of-all-trades. Indeed, one of my informants was at pains to tell me that, as a young married woman in the 1970s, she employed three when her (three) children were small. What made relationships in the household "fair" was that once home from work, she looked after the children herself, enabling the PRTs to "go out and play with their friends". Her mother and husband "also helped out". She explained that "we made a dialogue between us so that they got a good annual bonus if they worked well. We gave them two grams of gold, which was a pretty good bonus in those days". In the past, she concluded, employers attended to the needs of their PRT and, in return, received loyal service, a form of equality she feared was in danger of being displaced.[2] Another told me that "every child had a caretaker [...] I saw mine more than I saw my mother [...] one stayed with my mother for 60 years into her eighties [...] we felt very attached to them".[3] The point was reiterated to me later when a senior academic at a university where I had given a talk argued that the issue was not wages but whether domestic workers were being made to work "too hard".[4]

According to Koentjaraningrat, employing several *mbok mban* became too expensive for all but a few during the Japanese occupation, the fight for independence, and the two decades of economic hardship that followed. Noting a re-emergence of the practice in the 1980s,

2 Interview, Yogyakarta, 1 March 2016.
3 Interview, Jakarta, 22 August 2015.
4 Discussion, Yogyakarta, 6 December 2016.

Koentjaraningrat feared that families were hiring nursemaids to "enhance status and prestige", not out of concern for young women's moral development (1985: 238–40). In similar vein, another of Mrazek's informants, Pram Sukitno (whose civil servant father had a degree from Leiden University), expressed disapproval of servants indulging the nation's children. When he was young, he reflected, his parents had forbidden him to ask servants to do "frivolous things"; children needed to understand that servants were "paid labour [...] not slaves" (Mrazek 2010: 36).

Towards the end of the New Order, there were fears that aristocratic traditions were being co-opted in the service of consumerism, threatening Javanese values. In the memories of elite Javanese employers, the nursemaid, like the retainer, personified an ideal balance between loyalty, trust, and reciprocity. Hence, for some, a social imaginary of ethical, harmonious relationships between employers and "family helpers", albeit carrying markers of feudalism, was preferable to one predicated on legal contracts or the merely monetary.

Adoptee

A third embodiment of the domestic worker as family member was the *anak angkat* or "lifted child". Using the term "adoptee" is not to suggest a uniformity of practice across the archipelago. Different kinds of child circulation were common. They included *ngenger*, the acceptance into a better-off family of a child past infancy or a young teenager who would help around the house in return for board, lodging, and (sometimes) school fees. This was not the same as the permanent transfer of care of, for example, a baby or infant born out of wedlock to a childless couple within an extended kin network (Bennett 2018), but did create expectations of parental and filial obligations. the same practice but with more emphasis on "following" or "joining" a family as a means of advancement (Kutanegara 2017: 152).

Adoption and *ngenger* had long histories. Dutch East India Company records of the workforce in the Cirebon-Priangan region of Central Java at the close of the seventeenth century, for example, mention *ngenger* (palace servants) alongside *parekan* (concubines). Both groups, as "royal retainers", were amongst the "most bound" but respected for their closeness to nobility (Hoadley 1983: 97, 112). The rulers of the Mataram dynasty, which held sway across much of Java from the sixteenth to the eighteenth century, maintained large numbers of concubines and female attendants; some the daughters of noblemen, some sent as tribute from other kingdoms, and many from poorer families looking to gain status and connections, for example if their daughters produced sons (Kumar 1980: 18–19). The story of Sumantri Ngenger or "Sumantri enters the King's Service" continues to feature in Javanese wayang performance (a tradition dating back to the tenth century) and in contemporary educational discourse as exemplifying Javanese tenets of loyalty, duty, altruism, and the virtues of sacrifice (Nurgiyantoro 2019: 428–9). In Blora (Central Java), *ngenger* tradition required would-be sons or daughters-in-law to work for, and live with, their intended's family for shorter or longer periods (without pay) to demonstrate loyalty and "manners" (Kurnianingsih and Brata 2015). Binding children into servitude to pay off parents' debts was an established means of securing labour across the archipelago, which continued after the abolition of slavery (Boomgaard 2003a: 207–10). In the central highlands of Sulawesi, adoption and fosterage were commonplace, emerging in part as a continuation of slavery after abolition, the practice dependent on a "kinship" culture where calculation of costs and benefits was "supposed to be moot" (Schrauwers 1999: 311, 320).

If kinship rhetoric framed *ngenger* and adoption, class interests were close to the surface. Koentjaraningrat concedes that, in the past, ambitious *priyayi* sometimes took on "too many children" as status symbols and "treated them as servants", suggesting, however, that those joining households through *ngenger* were allowed "to sit on chairs and eat at the same table with the family, which servants never did". By the mid-1980s, *ngenger* had become "a convenient arrangement" for urban middle-class families to obtain domestic help (Koentjaraningrat 1985: 259–61).

Working from a bottom-up rather than *priyayi* perspective, Jan Newberry and Pande Made Kutanegara drew on fieldwork in poor neighbourhoods to demonstrate the class basis of *ngenger*-type practices during the latter part of New Order (and beyond). Newberry investigated child-sharing in an urban *kampung* in Yogyakarta, defining *kampung* as "urban enclaves understood to be home to lower-class Javanese". Kutanegara researched the rural hamlets of Sriharjo, a village some twenty-five kilometres further south. Both describe the circulation of children as a survival strategy for poorer households (Newberry 2014: 83–4; Kutanegara 2017: 152–3). Newberry noted how frequently children were returned to families of origin if the circumstances of an adoptive family changed. On the other hand, Kutanegara found examples of lasting family-like relationships established through *ngenger* being re-activated after the devastating earthquake that hit Yogyakarta in 2006 (2017: 224). Both authors concluded that Indonesian governments capitalized on the tendency of residents in villages and in urban *kampungs* to valorize practices such as *ngenger* (Nooteboom and Kutanegara 2002: 26; Newberry 2014: 76). Ignoring structural inequalities, the government could leave the poor to look after themselves in hard times. At the same time, a reserve army of cheap, flexible labour underpinned the economy. Nevertheless, the dream of achieving the "happiness object" of social mobility through the circulation of children remained a powerful one.

Follower

G. G. Weix's analysis of servitude in the household of an employer she names "Bu Haji", the wealthy owner of a cigarette factory in a north-coast Javanese town in the 1980s, introduces a fourth category of New Order "one of the family" constructs, the "family follower". Bu Haji's followers were constantly on call – "subjects whose interests are deferred to familial authority rather than contractual relationships" (Weix 2000a: 151).

What stands out in Weix's analysis is her discussion of gift-giving. The homes of elite employers became "icons of largesse" (2000b: 311). Gifts generated feelings of moral obligation and served as a management tool. Or, to use Ahmed's critique of the family as a "happiness object", a "powerful legislative device" (2008: 12). Each year Bu Haji distributed bounty to staff and servants at Lebaran (Eid-al-Fitri), signalling satisfaction or dissatisfaction with services rendered: those considered "close" might receive cash, jewellery, fabric, furniture, coveted white goods, televisions, sports equipment, and suchlike, in addition to salaries and bonuses. A servant deemed lazy or disliked would receive only the minimum expected payment and not be invited to return. The gift-giving ceremony, followed by the departure of servants for the holidays, marked "the boundary between stranger and family" (2000a: 146).

Bu Haji's maternalistic generosity was the ambivalent obverse of her servants' filial gratitude. Servants Weix spoke to focused on "the materiality of the gift". Goods made life more pleasant. Servants could invest cash as insurance against the vagaries of the economy, ill health, or disaster. Gifts offered the possibility of social mobility and a taste of luxury. Unhappiness – in Weix's terms, "disruption of the logic of the gift" – resulted if the loyalty of staff and servants was strained (1990: 152). Disharmony could ensue if employers asked a servant to complete a task below their station or cancel plans for a day off. Even willing servitude entailed estrangement, continuous performance of low status, and unquestioning acceptance of gifts given or withheld (Weix 2000a: 149–53).

The elite families Weix researched were exceptional. Bu Haji employed around forty men, women, and children in her household. Weix's generalizations about "Javanese servitude" need to be set against other studies to be taken as typical. Here I consider two. Feminist geographer Rebecca Elmhirst studied the "spatial stories" of sixteen domestic workers and a sample of employers in Jakarta in the mid-1980s. In collaboration with cinematographer Sandeep Ray, anthropologist Laurie Rothstein directed a film about a domestic worker named Miyah. It was released in 1999. Both sources illustrate what "following" a family was like in smaller households where two parents worked outside the home.

The families Elmhirst researched employed perhaps five domestic staff: a cook (often an older woman), laundry maid, childminder, driver, and gardener. There were six in the household Miyah worked for as cook-housekeeper in Rothstein's film: two other live-in servants, two drivers and an indeterminate general "help". Rothstein had known her protagonist for nine years and had researched women's work in Java and Bali. Elmhirst drew on fieldwork conducted in Jakarta in 1986 and 1994 and South Sumatra in 1994–5.

Elmhirst provides a space–time map of what being a loyal follower entailed. Comparing the movements of domestic workers and family members in expatriate and Indonesian servant-keeping households, she illustrated the physical toll and personal sacrifice involved in being always available. A servant's day revolved around the needs of the family. It would likely include rising at 4 AM to boil water and go to the market before making breakfast for the family and readying children for school. It might not end until after 10 PM, with scant time for rest, prayer, personal, social, or community life. Meanwhile, the PRT's own children were left with grandparents in villages and towns across Java for the duration (Elmhirst 2003: 257–8). As in Bu Haji's household, familial rhetoric brought "genealogies of obligation" into play. Domestic workers might receive gifts, borrow money, or have their families' medical or school bills paid. They might also be pressurized into making life decisions, even their choice of marriage partner, in line with their employer's wishes. Furthermore, just as Weix had found, domestic servants were "reluctant" to challenge the parent-like authority of employers; they too embraced a social imaginary of "mutual assistance" in which servitude played an "organic" part (Elmhirst 2003: 254–5).

Rothstein and Ray's film (*Miyah: The Life of a Javanese Woman*, 1999) underscores structural inequalities. Intended as a film about food cultures, it became one about a woman "entrapped" in the institution of domestic work (Close 2000; Heider 2000: 6). Miyah, the film's eponymous heroine, had worked for the same family for nineteen years, beginning when she was thirteen. Her words (spoken in English by a translator) provide the film's narrative.[5] Miyah eschews kinship rhetoric. She refers to her employer as the "Missus", calling her a woman of "real blue blood from Yogyakarta", whom she always addresses in "high Javanese". Her employer's cast-offs become her "better clothes". Her employer shops in the supermarket while she has had to bargain at the market – on her employer's behalf – "every day for nineteen years". Miyah dreams of opening a food stall in her village but, deeply in debt to her employer, recognizes that she is as likely as her hardworking aged parents to face penury when she can no longer work in the city. As a domestic worker, she "follows" out of dire necessity and a strong sense of obligation to meet the needs of her parents, children, and grandchildren. Debts tie her to the job: her long service evidence not so much of loyalty but of little choice.

Miyah testifies that the only place she feels at home in her employer's house is the bijou servants' room she shares with another "maid". Similarly, in the Indonesian homes Elmhirst studied, domestic workers had a place in the family, albeit a subservient one, sharing "intimate family space" at the back of the house. By contrast, in expatriate households PRT arrived for work each morning with no "place" in the family home. They were, nonetheless, expected to make sacrifices, such as not taking leave at Lebaran. In both cases, female employers counted on servants' loyalty as they juggled competing, socially sacrosanct demands on their time. Live-in domestic service was a safety net for poor women from rural areas and "an important backstop" for women entering the paid workforce without subsidized public services such as day or elder care (Elmhirst 2003: 242, 249, 254). From an employer and government perspective, maintaining a female labour force of family followers was a matter of "win-win".

5 Reviewing the film in 2000, however, Heider pointed out that in the absence of film notes it is difficult to judge the extent to which Miyah's words had been scripted for her.

Outside Java

Outside Java, different pre-colonial and colonial pasts inflected social imaginaries. In Java, slavery had been unusual outside Dutch-owned enclaves, ports, and urban areas (where it was ubiquitous) and it was abolished in the Netherlands Indies on 1 January 1860. Slavery was only proscribed across the archipelago around 1910, when the Dutch secured control of all the territory now constituting Indonesia. It continued in some places well into the twentieth century (Boomgaard 2003b: 83–7).

Anthropologists Janet Hoskins and Kathleen Adams were nevertheless shocked to discover that slavery still figured in the imaginaries of servanthood when they embarked on fieldwork in Sumba and South Sulawesi, respectively. In Sumba, employers described servants in public as "poor relatives" but did not recognize those they saw as the descendants of "slaves" as equal citizens or worthy marriage partners (Hoskins 2004: 92, 97). Indeed, in the 1970s, Hoskins found herself living in a household with two young slave girls who had joined the family when their father defaulted on a marriage debt. As one police chief explained:

> Slavery may not exist anymore, but people without homes and without family could become thieves or troublemakers. These people have to understand that it is better for them to watch the livestock of these noble families or serve them in their homes than to be cast by the wayside with no one to protect them. (Hoskins 2004: 98)

Similarly, Adams discovered in the 1980s that her "Torajan aristocrat" informants spoke of servants as descendants of slaves or "the people from behind", calling them "child" or "grandchild" to differentiate them from family members and describing them as "good children, obedient and quiet [...] good at helping around the house". In such a mindset, Indonesian independence "only means freedom from the Dutch, they [the servant class] are not free because they were bought by our ancestors [...] that's our tradition" (Adams 2000: 161, 163, 169–70). Uncomfortable in a "feudally structured" setting, Adams learned that such hierarchies rested on still-repeated origin myths, feeding a more static social imaginary than Javanese *ngenger*, one which a servant might "obliquely challenge" but rarely escape.

If Torajan elites saw descendants of slaves as inferior, Bugis and Makassarese communities in the south tended to marginalize people coming from the northern, upland, and largely agricultural part of South Sulawesi designated by the Dutch as "Tana Toraja" (Toraja Land), considering them inferior. Torajans, many of whom were Christian, in their turn, regarded Islamic lowlanders as the "other" or even the "enemy people" (Volkman 1984: 155). Despite entrenched prejudices, however, Torajan elites had long traded with Bugis and Makassarese elites, exchanging coffee and slaves for firearms. After the ending of slavery, land hunger in the north was matched by a demand for labour in the south and this, together with the social imperative for Torajans to accrue honour by staging expensive funeral rituals, cemented a pattern of outmigration (Volkman 1984: 158–62).

In this context, more affluent urban-dwelling Torajan families brought young relatives from the highlands into their households as family helpers, offering access to education in return. Middle-class Bugis and Makassarese families in South Sulawesi's capital also employed Torajans; they expressed "abhorrence" of servitude and generally refused to allow their daughters to work as servants to avoid violating "highly developed notions of honour and dignity" (Robinson 1991: 42, 47). Indeed, to avoid shame and loss of status, some Bugis women undertook domestic work in Malaysia – although the work itself was "not respected" – while their families employed Javanese or Torajan women to do the domestic work in their own homes (Idrus 2008: 166). In such situations, Torajans could find themselves derided as "not Bugis, not Muslim, and not urban" (Adams 2000: 172). Chinese families, on the other hand, favoured Torajan domestic workers; as Christians they would cook and eat pork, and their families were reputed to be unlikely to get involved with disputes between domestic workers and employers (Adams 2000: 171–2). Social imaginaries of servitude predicated on longstanding patterns of ethnic dominance in such situations made for more formal relationships between employers and employees.

Rebecca Elmhirst's experience suggests that ethnicity and religion affected degrees of distinction elsewhere in the archipelago. She found that in Lampung, South Sumatra, the Lampungese considered Javanese children "more culturally equipped" than their own children to work as domestic servants. In their eyes, servanthood entailed "serious loss of status". Javanese migrants settling in the region who could afford domestic help, on the other hand, always preferred to employ Javanese (Elmhirst 2003: 246–7).

For female domestic workers in eastern Indonesia, loyalty was a daughterly duty owed to families of origin. In a small community in

Maluku, elder daughters were encouraged to work as domestic servants in Ambon to send essentials – "money, clothes, plates, pots, an iron" – back to the village and enable their brothers to continue schooling. Parents instructed them not to make demands, to be grateful for a low wage, and always appear "hardworking, respectful and compliant" (Florey and Healey 2002: 366–9).

Though couched differently, the familial rhetoric surrounding the different roles and relationships discussed so far functioned in each case as a means of bringing servants inside the walls of the master's house. Other terms of address used in different times and places – *babu*, *batur*, *beinde*, *rewang*, *jongo*, *pramuwisma* – similarly signalled degrees of possession and proximity and, as argued in a study of the term "babu", can carry connotations of "the good old days" even while being rejected as remnants of colonial or feudal thinking and practice (Dragojlovic and McGregor 2022).[6] Domestic workers, then, formed part of a defence mechanism against social and political upheaval, threats to the sanctity of inscribed gender norms, and the possible devastation of war or natural disaster. As one of Mrazek's informants recalled, when he first heard about Indonesia's Declaration of Independence, "I had an image that we would live in our servants' quarters and that servants would move to the front" (2010: 67). Just as Ahmed points out, narratives change if we start from the perspective of those without chairs; family walls can be brick walls, a job description, and, like those ascribed to servants in Suharto's Indonesia, tough to break through (2017: 6–7).

On Openings

With family rhetoric firmly entrenched in social imaginaries of domestic work during the New Order, where then were the cracks? Three texts, Carla Jones's "Whose Stress?" (2004), Lizzie van Leeuwen's *Lost in Mall* (2008), and Anne-Marie Fechter's *Transnational Lives*

6 The terms *babu* (Indonesian female nursemaids working for "European" families in the Netherlands East Indies), *jongo* ("houseboys" or male servants in colonial households), and *beinde* (paid household workers) are associated with colonialism and considered derogatory terms. Words like *batur* (servant), *rewang* (helper), and *pramuwisma* (housekeeper, a euphemism for "maid") have Javanese or Indonesian connotations. For a discussion of the term *rewang* in relation to provision of childcare for women who work in factories see Fauzi et al. 2021.

(2007), led me to conjecture that towards the end of the 1990s, some employers were grappling with change. They could no longer assume domestic workers would show unwavering loyalty, embrace distinction, or forego consumerism.

Anxieties

The middle-class women Jones got to know while researching her doctoral thesis in Yogyakarta and Jakarta between 1996 and 1998 told her they suffered from stress. Their lists of anxieties were long: husbands; children's education; the rapidly changing urban environment; New Order expectations of female domesticity; and keeping their homes spotless, shining, hygienic, and harmonious, in line with images shown on billboards and in TV soaps and women's magazines. Wives felt pressured to serve their husbands and children constantly, resorting to subterfuge to maintain the appearance of the household as a smooth-running yet deeply caring machine (Jones 2004: 514–17).

Some wives defined themselves as the manager or "CEO of the house", responsible for the "productivity" of their "teams". Others, though still describing servants as one of the family, increased surveillance and suspected PRT who asked for loans of duplicity. A few looked for better-educated and more experienced women to act as "personal assistants". Most demanded shows of gratitude in return for working in "an urban, higher-class home" and worried that servants might malinger or find work elsewhere if they felt disrespected (Jones 2004: 513, 521–3). Despite concluding that New Order gender politics and globalizing consumerism were entrenching women in the roles of unpaid or lowly paid carers, cleaners or household managers, Jones ends with a "perhaps". "Perhaps", she muses, "the simple act" of employers and servants gathering to watch TV serials that validated the domestic efforts of women might encourage recognition of the work that goes into creating and maintaining wellbeing (2004: 524).

Read in this vein, the anxieties Jones uncovered can be seen as a fault line, opening a way for domestic workers to capitalize on their indispensable place in pressured households. If employers were managers, PRT could be workers. If employers wanted educated assistants to carry out complex tasks or provide scientific childcare, cooking or cleaning, domestic workers could upskill and command better wages as professionals. "Perhaps" a space was opening for workers to exert some bargaining power.

Jabotabek, or, Pastures New

Lizzie van Leeuwen sets her ethnography chronicling the lives of some of Jakarta's new rich in the late 1990s in a location known as Bintaro Jaya. The new development is in Jabotabek (the acronym coined to describe the ever-expanding conurbation consisting of Jakarta, Bogor, Tangerang, and Bekasi) and calls itself "The Professionals' City".[7] Estate agents offered buyers access to an exclusive, prestigious, and transformative lifestyle away from the pressures of central Jakarta. Van Leeuwen's study, based on "intermittent and long-term" participant observation and close relationships with families living in Bintaro, is a perfect place to look for evidence of change in relationships between "new middle-class suburbanites" and their domestic worker employees (2008: 2–3, 15).

Jabotabek represented a massive market growth area for domestic workers. Brand-new housing, electrical appliances, and generally smaller households did not remove the perceived necessity for servants. As van Leeuwen points out:

> More than a third of Bintarese women had college degrees and career ambitions. For these women, middle-class life without servants was inconceivable, in the same way as married life without children was not an option. (2008: 33)

All but the cheapest houses included a tiny space for a live-in servant, without the air-conditioning otherwise deemed *de rigueur*. Bintaro is some thirty-four kilometres from central Jakarta, and a one-way trip can take up to two hours. With parents commuting for several hours each day, even small families needed nannies, caretakers, cooks, and handypersons to care for their homes and children while their drivers took them to and fro. In some ways, this looked like business as usual. Citing studies of late colonial Indonesia, van Leeuwen points out that class aspirations and behaviours in Jabotabek were analogous to notions of middle-classness circulating in the 1920s and '30s. Then, as in the new Bintaro, social imaginaries included clear demarcations between those "within" the embrace of modernity and those not yet ready.

In hypermodern Bintaro, on the other hand, the logic of capitalist modernity was that as many people as possible should join the

---

7 In 1999, the acronym was changed to Jabodetabek to accommodate the expanding city of Depok.

consuming class. Hence tensions arose between "feudal" practices in dealing with servants and the consumerist culture defining life in its Elysian fields. Difficulties included recruiting and training the right people and establishing "comfortable controlling mechanisms". Chairs, long symbols of security, were becoming a source of contention. Indeed, van Leeuwen begins her account with a story she had heard with some bewilderment. In 1999, "an elderly lady" living in her street had "enquired, weeping, whether *demokratisasi* (democratization) meant she had to allow servants to sit on her chairs from now on". Reportedly this lady had "almost suffered a stroke (*strok*) that morning after catching a servant sitting in an armchair while watching television" (2008: 2–3). Later, van Leeuwen writes of joining an affluent family for Christmas in Puncak, Jakarta's nearest hill resort. There she observed "a bit of an event". An unknown domestic worker was spied occupying one of the two "easy master's chairs" on a porch, leading to anxious enquiries about to whom she belonged (2008: 85). Finally, at the close of her book, van Leeuwen revisits the servant/chair theme. She notes that employers now feel obliged to supply their live-in PRT with "servant necessaries", including small plastic chairs and a TV. Asked to check on a house while a family was away, van Leeuwen encountered servants busy taking over "untransgressable middle-class roles", sitting in easy chairs, switching between channels on the wide-screen TV, smoking expensive cigarettes, or off on a visit to the mall for fun (2008: 267). The repeated expression of such concerns mirrored what Shiraishi had seen as a fear of unbridled bodies out of place.

Anxiety about servants was one aspect of what van Leeuwen identified in Bintaro as a widespread "suppressed fear" of Indonesia's underclass. For domestic workers, however, the garden cities of Jabotabek and the anxieties of employers offered possibilities. Domestic services were in high demand, and workers could live at home in neighbouring villages or cheaper housing areas on the periphery. Compared with mansions in Menteng – the iconic residential area in central Jakarta laid out by the Dutch along garden city lines as an enclave for European residents at the beginning of the twentieth century and taken over by Indonesian elites and foreign ambassadors after Independence – most Bintaro properties had smaller footprints. However, families moving there had high incomes. The situation opened avenues to professionalization; there might be more jobs for nannies and assistants. For "new" middle-class employers insecure about managing servants, formal contracts could spell out expectations and obligations on both sides.

Expatriates

Developments like Bintaro targeted expatriate as well as Indonesian markets. Sales brochures emphasized the proximity of housing to international schools and leisure facilities. Fechter's study of corporate expatriates in Jakarta reveals both convergence and divergence between expatriate experiences of employing domestic workers and those of Indonesia's new rich. Both groups experienced anxieties around boundaries, held fears of the city, and felt the need to supervise domestic workers in matters of hygiene. In place of the myth that servants were one of the family, expatriates tended to internalize the colonial "myth of the lazy native". Rather than experiencing servants who know their place as bringing order and tranquillity into households, some expatriates found the constant presence of servants unsettling. Rather than looking for lifelong loyalty, expatriates – always on the move – sought efficient employees to assist them in navigating the complexities of Indonesian life. A new breed of expatriate, the young professional, living in an apartment, eating out, and socializing, nevertheless required a *pembantu* to wash, clean, and iron. Such employers, however, did not need to invoke notions of familial obligation (Fechter 2007: 65, 90–95, 154).

The evidence discussed here is perhaps insufficient to allow me to do more than hypothesize about possible openings. However, it appears that by the end of the New Order and the beginning of *reformasi*, some employers were beginning to sense that inherited conventions of domestic work were no longer fit for purpose. Boundaries were proving difficult to police. Domestic workers had access to television, transportation, and could be seen frequenting the basements of malls where cheaper goods were sold. The rapid growth of a new middle class not schooled in the ways of the *priyayi* left some bewildered. In the new cities of Jabotabek or in expatriate households, domestic workers could work part-time for several families and live out. Even so, none of the texts examined mentioned domestic worker organizing; the possibility of PRT forming themselves into a collective was still far from the common imaginary.

Conclusion

This chapter has portrayed imaginaries of paid domestic work circulating in New Order Indonesia. The level of detail provided by dint of drawing on the fieldwork of others and my own has allowed me to identify some of the intersecting structures that shaped the patterns of employment practices. First, a state-endorsed gender order reinforced the use of powerful familial constructs to maintain social stability and mould compliant workers. Second, rural poverty played out in the circulation of children, justifying child labour and often leaving girls disadvantaged. Third, patron–client relationships were paramount, dependent on generosity on the one hand and subservience on the other. Finally, mechanisms to maintain distinction within households inherited from a feudal past and continued through the colonial appropriation of Javanese practices shaped the everyday politics of sitting, eating, and speaking.

Much of the stasis surrounding domestic work stemmed from the role domestic workers played in "mopping up modernity" (Austin 2014). Their low-paid labours enabled colonial and Indonesian elites to enjoy modern, consumerist lifestyles. At the same time, rapid social, political, and technological change began to stretch the seams of the cherished garment of harmony that clothed the institution of paid domestic work. Corset as well as cloak, the culture of servitude was not simply a colonial evil or insignificant aristocratic anomaly. It was adopted by many of the class who were to become Indonesia's nationalist leaders and intelligentsia.

Chairs have played a central role in this chapter. In 2013, feminist journalist Julia Suryakusuma published a compendium of articles written for the *Jakarta Post* entitled *Julia's Jihad*. The front cover featured a painting by Indonesian artist Sri Astari named *The Flying Chair*. It depicts a young woman holding a chair aloft, ready to hurl it into the space ahead. White-faced, Pinocchio-nosed and with a wide, red-lipped mouth, she was an unmistakable incarnation in female form of one of the court jesters of Indonesian wayang who represent Indonesia's "little people" and critique the status quo (Suryakusuma 2013: xxxv–xxxvi). The book's contents reflect that Suryakusuma has been, by turn, and in tandem, an academic sociologist, feminist activist, and well-known journalist, unflinching in voicing her views.

The following chapters chronicle the contributions of women and men who, in the same mode, as activists, journalists, academics, and often some combination of these, sought to challenge established imaginaries and practices of paid domestic work. Chairs – along with tables, brooms, pots and pans, and dishcloths – will become familiar companions, as will the voices of campaigners and domestic workers themselves.

CHAPTER

2

Yogyakarta Beginnings: 1988–2009

On a hot, humid Sunday in Yogyakarta in August 2014, a dozen or so women were arriving at a suburban house in ones and twos. Leaving their shoes at the door, they greeted friends and drifted into the main room to find a seat on the floor, which had been spread with a deep blue woven bamboo mat in readiness for the morning's activities. Flipcharts and a whiteboard marked the space as a classroom, and the single, somewhat magisterial chair in the room was occupied by the teacher, a well-dressed professional woman perhaps in her late sixties, who explained to me quietly that she suffered from arthritis, hence her need for a chair. After introductions, the next hour and a half was taken up by a lecture and question time on gender theory; only after this were drinks and snacks served.[1]

I was impressed and intrigued by the attentiveness of this group of learners – brought together by Tunas Mulia, Indonesia's first trade union for domestic workers – especially as for many of the women Sunday was their one day off in the week. Some took notes throughout, and most appeared to maintain concentration despite the heat and distraction of small children running in and out. How come, I found myself wondering, the discourse was of patriarchy (the most frequently repeated term in the lecture as far as I could understand), cultural constructions of gender difference, and varieties of feminism rather than wages or working hours? How was feminist vocabulary and ideology supposed to help domestic workers navigate relationships with employers and manage their family lives? If, as indicated in Chapter 1, domestic workers were expected, above all, to accept and embody the social and gender distinctions congruent with their position as the

1 Field notes, Yogyakarta, 10 August 2014.

lowliest members of their employers' households in return for possible acts of generosity, how might they react to being invited to embrace feminism with its emphases on gender equality and women's rights?

Acceptance of new ideas depends, of course, not only on the nature of any proposals made but on how they are presented. Underlying the pedagogic practice in the classroom that day, I discovered when I visited the teacher in her home two years later, was a staunch belief in a certain kind of feminist universalism.[2] As was the case with many of her generation of Indonesian feminists, Agustine (Nunuk) Prasetyo Murniati had encountered feminist theory overseas, in her case while studying theology in New York, where she was strongly influenced by the (self-ascribed) radical lesbian feminist theologian Mary Daly (Fox 2010). Indeed, during our interview, Nunuk disappeared out of the room, returning with a treasured 1973 edition of Daly's *Beyond God the Father*, the first feminist text she had owned; like Daly, she believed that "Words are freed once spoken, and once spoken they act as liberators in their turn"; hence it is vital to intervene in the processes of naming (Suchocki 1994: 64). For women across the globe, using words like patriarchy, which describe "the realities of life" as they experience it, helps loosen "the shackles of social construction" (Daly 1973, quoted in Sendjaja 2009). Spaces like a domestic workers school matter in such a formulation, since, as Nunuk put it to me, "only once PRT are made aware of the special experiences of women can they fight for their rights".

Such a singular feminist framing of reality has long been contested. For feminist activists in Indonesia in the 1990s, discussions of "difference" in global feminist theory ran in parallel with national debates about the role of the middle-class intellectual in speaking on behalf of workers. On the one hand, most Indonesian activists subscribed to the proposition that trade unions should be "from, by and for workers" (Ford 2003: 300–303). On the other hand, feminists had been supporting female workers, including women in the informal sector ignored by unions, since the 1980s and, like Nunuk Murniati, saw consciousness-raising and the acquisition of skills as prerequisites for action (Ford 2004: 110–11). Post-1998, some female workers demanded the right to speak for themselves and rejected what they

---

2 Interview with Agustine (Nunuk) Prasetyo Murniati, Yogyakarta, 1 March 2016. Murniati is generally spoken of as Nunuk and uses that name in her publications. Hence, in writing about her interview, I use the name Nunuk rather than Agustine.

saw as western feminism in favour of class-based analysis, affiliations, and rhetoric (Ford 2008: 514–15).

The picture of the PRT classroom just provided, then, encapsulates the themes this chapter explores. Tracing the evolution of NGO and domestic worker organizations in Yogyakarta from their beginnings in the late 1980s through to 2009, by which time Tunas Mulia was internationally recognized as one of several legitimate domestic worker organizations in Indonesia, it pays attention to political representation – the question of who speaks for whom – and the pedagogies of empowerment. As referenced in the Introduction, both Fraser's account of participation across multiple "arenas" and Lister's emphasis on building confidence among the disenfranchised point to the spatialities of political participation. Andrea Cornwall, in similar vein, suggests that researchers look at spaces where those previously excluded develop "critical consciousness", learn to mobilize and assert rights, and acquire the "weapons of the powerful". Such spaces may include, as is the case with the PRT spaces depicted in this chapter, "invited" spaces created and controlled for political subjects by "external, resource-bearing agents", and "invented" spaces that subjects – now agents – conjure for themselves, each demonstrating different relational dynamics (Cornwall 2002: 17, 28). Following Cornwall, this chapter explores the dynamics of domestic worker spaces as they changed over time.

The place, in this chapter, is the city and region of Yogyakarta. This is not to suggest that the experiences of domestic workers and activists there typify those of workers and activists in cities such as Jakarta or Medan with larger populations of PRT, but because in relation to the domestic worker movement, Yogyakarta was a city of firsts. The birthplace of JALA PRT, it was home to the first neighbourhood-based OPERATA (domestic worker organization), the first feminist-inspired domestic workers school, and the first independent domestic workers' trade union.[3] Furthermore, politics and culture are closely enmeshed in the city; its special political status permits the Sultan to serve as governor, the dual role linking a pre-colonial past to Indonesia's post-authoritarian present. For women, this exacerbates the sorts of tensions between desires for modern, egalitarian gender relationships and idealized notions of an aristocratic, patriarchal, hierarchical but harmonious past grounded in the sorts of distinctions conjured by

---

3 The acronym OPERATA is a contraction of the Indonesian words *Organisasi Pekerja Rumah Tangga*, thus, domestic workers' organization.

"Not sitting on chairs". Yogyakarta is noted for its close links with its rural hinterland (Hudalah et al. 2013: 66, 72–75). Not only have many domestic workers migrated to the city from the region (van Bergeijk 1986), but students in the 1980s and '90s were required to spend a term living in a poor community as part of their degree programmes.[4] At the same time, Yogyakarta was also a hub of the student activism that spread across Indonesia in the closing years of the New Order. Radical students got involved with communities outside the campus and served apprenticeships in mobilizing the rural *rakyat*, or "ordinary people" (Aspinall 2005: 123).[5] From this crucible of youthful idealism and "strange meetings"[6] between rural poor and urbanized, middle-class students, the characteristic discourses of the Indonesian domestic workers' movement emerged.

Opening windows into spaces in the city where students, activists, and domestic workers studied, socialized, and strategized, this chapter investigates the relational dimensions of the intermediary and often home-like spaces created and occupied by domestic workers and activist campaigners as they built a movement, rather than on formal spaces of power. As feminist geographer Doreen Massey pointed out, "that place called home" is not only a gendered space noted for its containment – and too often, abuse – of women, but also a "site of linked and interplaying dichotomies" with the potential to engender a positive re-shaping of social relations, politics, and identities (Massey 1994: 9, 163–7; see also Massey et al. 2009: 401–2, 414–7). Indeed, scholarship on Indonesian transnational migration has demonstrated how spaces inhabited by domestic workers can both liberate and constrain. Killias, amongst others, has shown how the prison-like training camps and other spaces used to house domestic workers en route to overseas placements can inculcate compliancy and a fear of speaking out (Killias 2009: 158–61; see also Rudnyckyj 2004; Lindquist 2010). Silvey, on the other hand, talking with workers in or recently returned from Saudi Arabia and Dubai, acknowledged the "deeply problematic" nature of the camps but found workers describing them as places of sociality, even in one case, as "like home". Researchers, she suggests,

4 Interview with Maria Pakpahan, Edinburgh, 9 August 2017.

5 According to Lee (2016: 231) the word *rakyat* in the 1980s and '90s encompassed "workers, farmers, peasants, artists and the urban poor".

6 I take the phrase from Wilfred Owen's poem because it seems to speak to the unsettling of expected and familiar dyadic relationships and the generation of hope for the future, both of which seem to be features of the post-1988 Yogyakarta scene.

would do well to examine the "micro-spaces" occupied and created by domestic workers in terms of "desire, power, and possibility" and not just as places of confinement, empowerment, or resistance, to better understand the cartographies of "coping" (Silvey 2018: 197–205). Williams demonstrated how migrant domestic workers from eastern Indonesia managed to forge new identities and escape the "circumscribed boundaries" and "grip of male kin's control" as they journeyed and entered the unfamiliar spaces of employers' homes (2005: 406). Similarly, discussing domestic workers in Taiwan, Lan detailed the strategies Filipina domestic workers utilized to shift and maintain the boundaries operating inside employers' homes to protect their privacy, maximize benefits, and assert status (2006: 221–36). Extending the logic of these arguments to explore means of changing the habitus of domestic work within Indonesia, this chapter illuminates the role of activists in promoting agency and participation.

Interweaving the temporal and the spatial, I look first at the earliest phase of the movement when middle-class feminists established the principles, strategies, and practices they believed could challenge existing paradigms. "Student Spaces" explores the key location of the study room; "Activist Spaces", the domestic workers school. Both locations, I argue, served as spaces of enlightenment and reform. "Domestic Worker Spaces" moves to the OPERATA, where workers began to organize themselves, establishing their own understandings of sisterhood. The chapter concludes with "*Mau ke Mana Gerakan PRT?* (Where Does the PRT Movement Go from Here?)", visiting a small hotel in Yogyakarta, the Matahari. At this point the movement's leaders were focused on the opportunities created by ILO plans to table a Domestic Workers Convention for discussion in the summer of 2010. Flexible, fluid, and borrowed spaces, rather than fixed locations, were now needed. Using data collected from interviews with protagonists, personal observations, and a range of texts produced in organizing and mounting campaigns, I explore some of the shifts in subjectivity (to use Williams's phrase) and new collective identities and institutions associated with women in Yogyakarta who spoke and acted outside the ideological, cultural, and concrete boundaries of domesticity and home. Paradoxically, perhaps, the creation of versions of "home" in the form of safe, secluded, and in some ways feminized spaces for domestic workers produced new hierarchies, tensions, and rivalries, which resulted in a reworking of some of the language, strategies, and structures of the movement by the end of its first decade.

Student Spaces: 1988–1995

The women who founded the first domestic workers' organizations in the city describe their lives as having been profoundly changed by going to university in Yogyakarta in 1988 or thereabouts. In discussions with me and in profiles published online, they recounted similar stories of being drawn into student activism soon after starting university, of assuming new identities as feminist activists, of redefining themselves in terms of home, family, and community, and of forming long-lasting friendships that would later sustain the movement in terms of political influence and emotional and practical support. They also spoke of fear and youthful bravado.

Aida Milasari, who now lives in Jakarta and plays a leading role in the national campaign, began her degree in the Faculty of Biology at the University of Gadjah Mada (UGM) in 1989. When I interviewed her in 2015, she reflected on her traumatic initiation into student activism in the following way:

> I think my activism began in my first year at university. My brother was already involved in student activism, and one day, visiting him in his boarding house, I met some of his activist friends. They invited me to join them on an anti-Suharto demonstration, and although I didn't go that time, I remember vividly that my brother did, and that he and the other students came face to face with soldiers with fixed bayonets, even though they were unarmed.
>
> That protest, I think it was in July 1989, was against the burning of the books of Pramoedya Ananta Toer and the imprisonment of him and several sellers of his work. Why, the protestors thought, should the government be afraid of a book?[7]

My own visceral memories of the shock of being confronted by a line of hostile police as a young student protestor in Grosvenor Square on an anti-Vietnam war demonstration in London in 1968 made Aida's revelations about the bayonets facing her brother even more chilling. While students arrested in London had been held overnight and then released, albeit with an undeserved police record, in 1988 in Yogyakarta, three members of a student study group had been arrested and held on charges of subversion for possessing, circulating, and discussing Pramoedya Ananta Toer's novels and later sentenced to

7 Interview with Aida Milasari, Jakarta, 2 July 2015.

prison terms ranging from seven to eight and a half years (Beerkens 2008; Lane 2008).[8] Since it was well-known that Pramoedya had been denied access to paper or pencils for the majority of his time in prison, for students, banning his books constituted a particularly outrageous example of their government's betrayal of nationalist ideals (Augenbraum and Schwalbe 2000).

Righteous anger did not negate the risk of participation in protests, as Aida went on to explain:

> My brother and I hadn't told our parents we were getting into activism for fear of alarming them because it was so dangerous. Indeed, my brother was beaten up and cut by a bayonet and rushed to hospital. As soon as I heard I rushed there and was deeply shocked to see what had happened to him and some of his friends.
>
> The experience didn't deter me, however, from becoming more politically involved through the Women's Discussion Forum. But it wasn't until later that we told our parents about our activism; after all, we thought, our father was involved in the PNI [Nationalist Party of Indonesia] when he was young.[9]

There is an intense physicality in Aida's retelling of her first encounter with political struggle and what were known as the *aparat* (security forces).[10] Burning books, panic on hearing what had happened, and the shock of seeing her brother's wounds constituted perhaps a painful initiation ritual into membership of what would become the "1998" generation of students, who were later instrumental in securing the overthrow of the Suharto regime. Distancing herself in some ways from her parents' generation (she and her brother did not initially disclose their activism), Aida identifies herself as anti-Suharto but nationalist. She favours peaceful demonstration yet nevertheless links

8 Pramoedya was the pre-eminent novelist of post-colonial Indonesia, best known for his quartet of novels about the rise of Indonesian nationalism. The first two volumes in the series, *This Earth of Mankind* and *Child of All Nations*, were published in Indonesia in 1980, shortly after his release from incarceration on Buru Island, to great acclaim, but their circulation was banned in 1981. The remaining volumes were published overseas.

9 Interview with Aida Milasari, Jakarta, 2 July 2015.

10 Karen Strassler quotes a student photographer as using this term. Her book, *Refracted Visions*, contains some compelling images that capture the brutality and emotional intensity of student protests in Yogyakarta leading up to the fall of Suharto (2010: 222–4).

herself, through her father, with the revolutionary PNI (Nationalist Party of Indonesia). Other students in Yogyakarta had already claimed legitimacy by comparing themselves with earlier generations of nationalist youth: in October 1988, a large group from UGM marched along Yogyakarta's main street to commemorate the ideals of the *Pemuda* (youth) Pledge of 1928, choosing this as a frame for demands for campus freedoms (Aspinall 2005: 208–49). Their action, and Aida's politicization, can be seen as part of a process of reclaiming the discursive power of the term *pemuda* from what one contemporary observer described as Suharto-era attempts to depoliticize and isolate students as *mahasiswa,* the general term for students in Indonesia, which lacked the historical and political overtones of *pemuda* (Ryter 1998: 57–8).

Other women associated with the domestic worker movement from the outset spoke of similar transformations. Yuni Satia Rahayu, who began her history degree at UGM in 1987, spoke to me for almost an hour, with nostalgia and wry humour, about her student years, so I use her story as an example. For Yuni, it was reading Soe Hok Gie's *Diary of a Demonstrator* that was life-changing.[11] If, following his death, Gie became the forever "ideal" *pemuda* (Lee 2011a: 319–26), Arief Budiman, his brother, became the most influential exponent of "moral force thinking", which stressed the responsibility of students and intellectuals to act as guardians of the nation's founding ideals (Aspinall 2012: 165–9). Totally inspired, Yuni accepted an invitation to go to Salatiga to meet Budiman. While she was there, she took part in her first demonstration, recounting to me that:

> It was about the Ombo dam project, in front of the office of the governor of Semarang. This must have been in 1989 when the case of the dam was very much in the news and a very hot issue. There were lots of police but only a few demonstrators, maybe a hundred demonstrators. I saw one of my friends crying; she hadn't imagined

11 In a memorial written in 1970 after Gie's early death in a climbing accident, Benedict Anderson praised him for his courage in "naming names", his denunciation of "the ruthless exploitation of the poor" and his insistence on "the moral role of students in Indonesian politics" (1970: 225). Gie's diary, which circulated widely amongst student activists of the 1988 generation, contains vivid descriptions of student demonstrations of the 1960s (Lee 2016: 110).

> we were going to be confronted by so many police and military like that.[12]

As was the case with Aida, what stands out in this testimony is the shock of coming face to face with the stark realities of the repressive Suharto regime. Perhaps this was a significant awakening, as Butler theorizes, forcing students to consider the previously "*unthinkable*" matter of their "own destructibility", and, in turn, further cement their commitment to a "universalizing of rights" (2016: 28–29, 47; italics in original). Certainly, Yuni recalled her vulnerability and the relief she experienced when soldiers held back during another protest, described to me with these words:

> Mary, you really need to understand that my father was in the military and my family didn't believe there could possibly be demonstrations as big as this. But we were still very young, and we didn't take any weapons to demonstrations but just spoke loudly through the loudhailers. But at that demo, the first line opposing us was the military and they had fixed bayonets, and the second line was the police and they had dogs. But in the end, we were just allowed to go home. But afterwards the police followed up, trying to find out more about who had been there through their intelligence officers.

Her words convey something of the fear that such exposure to force engendered and give a glimpse of how youthful naivety, moral rectitude, and the frisson of personal empowerment motivated students to continue protesting, evident danger notwithstanding.

Yuni and her friends had to grow up quickly and learn the practical politics of the street. Given the risks, students developed support networks centred on organizations such as the Yogyakarta Students Communication Forum and various *komite aksi* (protest action committees). Groups shared detailed plans for demonstrations known as *kronologi*, circulated leaflets, posters, and banners, and moved meeting places frequently. Between 1989 and 1992 these forms of *aksi* (street protest) became widely known and achieved a degree of legitimacy with the public (Lane 2008: 197, 126–8). There was also a strong sense of solidarity. Before the end of her first year, Yuni told me, she had gotten to know her fellow activists well, a development which

12 Interview with Yuni Satia Rahayu, Yogyakarta, 23 February 2016.

brought "tremendous benefits", not least a sense of "belonging to a small community". By working with other students from Yogyakarta and beyond on campaigns such as the Kedung Ombo Dam, the future leaders of the domestic workers' movement established personal and political connections with influential NGOs such as the Indonesian Legal Aid Institute (Lembaga Bantuan Hukum or LBH), the Indonesian Women's Association for Justice (Lembaga Bantuan Hukum Asosiasi Perempuan Indonesia untuk Keadilan or LBH APIK), the International NGO Forum on Indonesian Development (INFID) and the Indonesian Front for the Defence of Human Rights (INFIGHT). Such networks and friendships were to be an important source of advice and support when the domestic workers' movement began to grow.

The Yogyakarta Women's Discussion Forum 1989–1999

Friendships forged during the Kedung Ombo Dam campaign led a group of women to set themselves up as the Forum Diskusi Perempuan Yogyakarta (Yogyakarta Women's Discussion Forum), known as FDPY, in 1989. Such groups were not new; study groups held in spaces such as student boarding houses or on campus, with tacit support from university staff, had been one way for students to engage politically following the "Normalization" of campus life in the late 1970s.[13] Indeed, *Tempo* magazine estimated that there were at least twenty such groups in Yogyakarta by 1987 (cited in Aspinall 2005: 121). During interviews, former members of the FDPY emphasized the intellectual excitement and personal and political commitment generated by sharing knowledge of modernist thinking and discussing texts, mainly by northern scholars, brought home by those who had studied or travelled overseas.

One of the founders of FDPY was Maria Pakpahan.[14] I met Maria – who started at UGM in 1988 and became the executive director of Rumpun Tjoet Njak Dien in 1995 – in Edinburgh where she now lives, after I had written, and sent her a copy of, a draft of this chapter.[15]

13 This term refers to a raft of regulations imposed on universities, such as the suspension of student-elected councils and the banning of student publications and campus-based political activity, known as NKK/BKK or the "Normalization of Campus Life/Bodies for the Coordination of Student Affairs" (Aspinall 2005: 120–21).

14 Lita Anggraini mentioned Damairia Pakpahan, Aida Milasari, Yuni Satia Rahayu, Hening Tyas Sutji, Siti Noor Laila and Rebeka Harsono as the other founders in an interview given to *Jurnal Perempuan* in 2019.

15 Interview with Maria Pakpahan, Edinburgh, 9 August 2017.

This proved revealing and constituted a challenge, as Maria pointed out places in the narrative where her recollections differed from those of some other informants or archival sources, reminding me that while oral history can constitute a "weapon of evidence against historical erasure", it also complicates in its propensity to be "subjective" and "partial" (Ramirez 2005: 124, 114). Reflecting on student study groups, for example, Maria pointed out the gendered inequality embedded in the mixed groups that proliferated in Jakarta and Salatiga where "the women were doing the teas and coffees", complicating accounts of these groups as unproblematically pro-democracy. Already a feminist while at school in Jakarta, where she had held an exhibition on women's double burden and interviewed leading activists and politicians (and was warned by her headteacher not to interview people disliked by the state), Maria took a leading role in relation to recruitment. The group began by inviting Arief Budiman, by then a popular and radical lecturer at Satya Wacana Christian University in Salatiga, Java (Suryadinata 2012: 44). Keen to learn from international students and leading intellectuals, the group rented a suburban house and held regular meetings "maybe twice a week".[16]

Maria described herself at that time as being "sort of fluid", "attending many groups" – including "more confrontational" ones – and building a web of contacts and allies. Interviewed for a piece in *Inside Indonesia* in 1996, she reflected on the "really exciting atmosphere in the Yogyakarta student groups at that time – we discussed feminism, Marxism, anarchism, liberalisms – all the isms. This gave us a strong grounding in theory." She went on to comment that:

> Feminism is a struggle of your whole life. I think feminism is more revolutionary than anything else, because you aim at changing not only society, but also human beings, the relations between men and women, getting them to accept each other. [...] It's not a trend, it's a choice of life, an ideology. (Pakpahan 1996: n.p.)

Maria was not the only member of the group who testified to the lasting impact of feminist thinking on their lives. Lita Anggraini, who also started her university studies at UGM in 1988 and shared a house with Maria in her first year, spoke in almost identical words when she explained, "our ideology becomes our perspective; it's

16 Interview with Maria Pakpahan, Edinburgh, 9 August 2017.

not just a job which needs to be done but an ideology that needs to be continually pursued. That's passion."[17] And while Maria had encountered feminist ideas at high school, for others, membership of FDPY marked the point at which they began to identify themselves publicly with feminism. Aida Milasari, for example, explained that "up until then, although I was becoming more politically aware, I didn't use the term [feminist] about myself because it had negative connotations already".[18] According to Heri Wardoyo, a journalist who published a book containing biographies of 100 prominent people in Lampung (South Sumatra) in 2008, Siti Noor Laila, the then chair of FDPY, confessed to being "electrified" by her encounters with feminism. After graduating, she moved to Lampung, founded a women's rights NGO, and went on have a long career in feminist and human rights activism, serving as a member of Indonesia's National Commission for Human Rights from 2012 to 2017. For her, grappling with ideas is how feminists maintain the "precision, suppleness and firmness of mind" necessary to deal with "a sometimes brutal and masochistic culture dominated by men" (Wardoyo 2008). Feminist thinking, out of all the "isms" the students discussed, not only lent the FDPY its core identity but seems to have steered the direction of the future working lives of several of its members.

However, the FDPY did not remain a safe space for feminist theorizing for long. In March 1991, members of the FDPY agreed to put the group's name as one of nine organizations sponsoring a calendar called *Land for the People* (*Tanah Untuk Rakyat*). I have not seen a copy – Yuni Rahayu told me it was too dangerous to keep copies at the time – but since the calendar satirized members of the government including Suharto's wife, the government banned its circulation and arrested thirteen students, lecturers, journalists, and officials of the organizations concerned (Lucas 1992: 79–80).[19] Maria recounted her part in the story with remarkable equanimity when I met her. She had agreed to pick up some 2000 calendars for distribution

17 Interview with Lita Anggraini, Jakarta, 27 Aug 2014.

18 Interview with Aida Milasari, Jakarta, 2 July 2015.

19 Anton Lucas, a lecturer at Flinders University who worked at the Inter-University Centre at UGM from 1990 to 1992, remembered a student from FDPY bringing a copy of the calendar to the office where he was working and asking for a donation. According to Lucas, the calendar "attracted considerable comment in the office after she had left". Lucas recalled that the nine signatory organizations claimed collective responsibility to try to defend individuals against criminal charges being made (1992: 79–80).

with another supporter, but in the event had to go into the print shop on her own and had shown her student card to the staff who warned her that men were watching the shop. Leaving the calendars behind, she left the shop, but the next day she was followed by a man on a motorbike who appeared to be pointing a gun at her. Later, police came looking for her in her student house. Her friends and her sister urged her to hide, so, fearing torture and aware the police saw her as an "entry point" to get to members of the other organizations involved, she went into hiding. Eventually, friends helped her escape to the Netherlands to complete her studies; meanwhile the remaining members of the group had to decide what to do.[20]

In the event they decided that continuing to meet as the FDPY was too risky. They regrouped under a new name, and concentrated on trying to assist and empower poor women rather than on political campaigns to avoid the threat of interrogation or imprisonment.[21] The fact that the authorities thought it worthwhile to pursue the leaders of the FDPY in this way is one indication, perhaps, of how far the students had come, the potential of the persuasive power they could command, and the spread of the radical networks with which they were connected. In the short term, though, the group dispersed. Some, like Lita and Damairia, stayed in Yogyakarta to continue their studies and community work, while others, like Yuni and Aida, moved away, all continuing, however, to look for spaces and places in which to make their feminist, democratic, and human rights ideals come alive.

Activist Spaces: Rumpun Tjoet Nyak Dien, 1995–2009

On 19 April 1995, four former members of the Yogyakarta Women's Discussion Forum established an NGO they named Rumpun Tjoet Njak Dien (RTND).[22] Their intention was to apply the principles of "solidarity, caring and goodwill" to the task of solving the problems faced by domestic workers, initially in the Special Region of Yogyakarta, having identified a gap in the growing market of rights-oriented NGOs. They chose the group's name carefully, wanting

20 Interview with Maria Pakpahan, Edinburgh, 9 August 2017; interview with Damairia Pakpahan, Yogyakarta, 5 March 2016.

21 Interview with Aida Milasari, Jakarta, 2 July 2015.

22 There are various spellings of Tjoet Njak Dien including: Cut Nyak Dhien and Cut Nyak Dien. I use Tjoet Njak Dien, the spelling preferred by RTND.

something which would attest to their nationalist *pemuda* genealogy and affirm their feminist intent. *Rumpun* was an acronym of Forum Perempuan (Women's Forum) and the Indonesian term for a clump of bamboo. The name invoked, they felt, an image of women standing together, signalling sisterhood, the power of the collective, and a desire to "try to be close to the people".[23] Strongly associated with Indonesian nationalism, Tjoet Njak Dien (1848–1908) was feted as one of the leaders of Aceh's military resistance against the Dutch, and as such was arrested and exiled to Sumedang in West Java where she died in 1908. Her name had been much in the public eye in the late 1980s and early '90s when Eros Djarot's 1998 film of her life, *Tjoet Nja' Dhien* (a film in the tradition of *film nasional*, which ascribes filmmakers a central role in the "struggle to define and articulate the nation"), was awarded the H. Antemas Prize for box office popularity and subsequently won best international film at Cannes.[24] By comparison with Kartini (1879–1904), the other national heroine after whom the group considered naming themselves, Tjoet Njak Dien was a woman prepared to put her body on the line (as student activists had done every time they demonstrated during the Suharto regime) rather than a woman known as an intellectual or for her writing (Siapno 2002: 24–5). Linking themselves with an assertive Acehnese woman who "agreed to marry again only if she could keep fighting in battle against the Dutch" (Suryakusuma 2013: 234), RTND's founders hoped to turn domestic workers into spirited protestors. This was in line with their view that women's position in the national imaginary should go beyond the submissive wife and devoted, suffering, mother promoted in Kartini Day celebrations during the New Order. As one founder member expressed it: "We chose Tjoet Njak Dien in preference to Kartini because we felt she was a broader thinker, we felt she was a much stronger fighter (after all Kartini didn't begin any real fight) and we knew she had been a very good strategist."[25]

The organizers of RTND realized early on the significance of strategy; they knew that in targeting domestic workers they faced a greater than average challenge. Not only was there the same gap in class and educational experience between themselves and the disadvantaged that all middle-class activist groups encounter, but domestic workers

23 Interview with Yuni Satia Rahayu, Yogyakarta, 23 February 2016.
24 Djarot in fact refused the prize because a film not meeting *film nasional* requirements had achieved far larger audience figures (Barker 2010: 15).
25 Interview with Yuni Satia Rahayu, Yogyakarta, 23 February 2016.

had also already been identified as a particularly difficult group to organize and one about which few members of the Yogyakarta public appeared concerned. Reportedly, an American woman living in Yogyakarta had tried and failed to establish a domestic workers' union in the early 1980s, and a group known as the Yogyakarta Women's Joint Secretariat (Sekretariat Bersama Perempuan Yogyakarta or SBPY) had also had an unsuccessful attempt before deciding to concentrate on market traders and porters. In both cases, failure was in part attributed to a lack of time, energy, or interest amongst PRT, the fact that NGO staff had little knowledge of labour organizing, and the challenge of mobilizing support from middle- and upper-class employers reluctant to pay more for household staff.[26] In 1992, Solidaritas Perempuan (Women's Solidarity for Human Rights), an NGO with which the founders of RTND had close connections, began campaigning for the protection of migrant domestic workers, judging it "too soon" to focus on the PRT in Indonesian homes.[27]

On a more personal level, announcing to one's family one's intention of working with domestic workers could be difficult, especially as several of RTND's founders came from wealthy middle- or upper-middle-class homes where having servants was taken for granted. As Lita Anggraini explained, "the challenges were present even among our families and friends, when we brought them [domestic worker issues] up there as well", or as Yuni Rahayu expressed it:

> We came to understand we had a class problem inside our group, and that different people amongst ourselves had different perspectives. For most of us, though, it wasn't too difficult, we weren't married yet, we didn't need a full-time PRT. When we got married, then the problems began because if we wanted to continue our activism then we needed PRT. But, at that time, we still made our own rules, and we were still very idealistic.[28]

---

26 I use the word "reportedly" because Berninghausen and Kerstan (1992), who mention the American expatriate, do not reference their source. Hadiwinata, on the other hand, who learned about the failure of the SBPY initiative from the coordinator of the programme, discusses the two as one (2003: 175–6).

27 Interview with Ati Nurbaiti (founder member of Solidaritas Perempuan), Jakarta, 27 June 2012.

28 Interview with Yuni Satia Rahayu, Yogyakarta, 23 February 2016.

Spoken with hindsight, and a between-the-lines acknowledgement that as a full-time politician, activist, wife, and mother, her "grown-up" household depended on several domestic workers, Yuni's comments point to a tension, inherent in the movement from the beginning, stemming from the middle-class identities of its activist leaders. Here, too, is a recognition that changing the division of labour within families in Java would be, at best, a distant goal, given the likely attitudes of future spouses, in-laws, and the wider public. Rather, RTND activists focused on legal reform and the task of winning public recognition for the economic and social value of domestic work.

A story Maria Pakpahan recounted about a conversation she had with the future president of Indonesia, Gus Dur (Abdurrahman Wahid), gives a glimpse of the personal and professional challenges members of RTND could encounter even amongst avowed supporters of democratization and human rights. After her return from the Netherlands, Maria worked for INFID in Jakarta and in that capacity came to know Gus Dur, at that time a prominent member of Forum Demokrasi, a group comprised of members of Indonesia's elite including leaders of Nahdlatul Ulama (one of Indonesia's two mass-based Islamic organizations, of which Gus Dur was chair), liberal intellectuals, Catholics, and what Aspinall describes as "post-PNI nationalists" who shared a commitment to building more democratic, participatory politics in Indonesia (2012: 168). Writing in praise of Gus Dur after his death in 2010, Maria described his reaction when she told him of her plan to go back to Yogyakarta to work full-time for RTND. It is worth quoting in full because it demonstrates what we might call the "appellations of the domestic imagination" – the names with which the role and status of domestic workers were inscribed amongst Indonesia's elites. In Maria's words:

> One of the responses that I remember vividly from Gus Dur was, "So you want to be the president of the PBB?"
>
> "What do you mean, Gus?" I asked. He chuckled: "PBB is the abbreviation of *Persatuan Babu* (the Maids Association)." He was joking, I was aware, but then I debated him and said that this expression *Babu* was one of the issues that must be addressed by the organization I wanted to set up. Gus Dur listened attentively and cracked no more jokes. (Pakpahan 2010)

Gus Dur's "joke" here is a play on the Indonesian name for the United Nations – *Perserikatan Bangsa-Bangsa* – generally shortened to

PBB. However, as Maria reminded him, *babu* is a derogatory term for a female domestic worker, resisted, along with others, by the domestic worker movement in favour of the more assertive *pekerja* (worker). The outcome of this conversation, a challenging one perhaps for Maria given the age, gender, and status differences between herself and Gus Dur, was remarkably positive. Gus Dur called Maria back just as she was leaving the room and offered to fund the cost of renting a house in Yogyakarta to serve as office and base for RTND. Shortly after this, Maria left her job in Jakarta and returned to Yogyakarta in 1997 to become the first executive director of the organization, now with more time to formulate its first five-year plan and, as the result of a conversation, a space to work from.

Two years later, Maria was awarded an Ashoka Fellowship. Apart from giving her global recognition and access to an international network, the award offered a stipend sufficient to meet the costs of her working full-time. In an interview she gave to *Inside Indonesia* before she left INFID, Maria had spoken of her belief that Indonesian NGOs needed to be less cautious about naming themselves as feminist organizations, and more focused on developing grassroots support, remembering their accountability to society as well as to their overseas funders (Dibley 1996: 12). Securing the Ashoka award had entailed one-to-one and panel interviews and a capacity to demonstrate both the "social impact" of her ideas and her entrepreneurial skills (Ashoka 1999). This was a different milieu, perhaps, from that of the activist student: Doreen Lee in her study of anti-Suharto activism, for example, spoke of "the assertive, organized, and militaristic register" of the "battle speech" of the *posko* or command posts used during student protests (2016: 166). However, Maria queried this judgement when I met with her. "I'm not sure that militaristic language really was the norm. We were just students at the time", she reflected to me.[29]

Yet, as they began contacting domestic workers, the activists in RTND nevertheless reproduced some less militaristic aspects of the *posko*. They established "outposts" in areas where domestic workers lived and worked, providing material and emotional aid. In Badran this meant running a public kitchen providing cheap meals for women and children; in Gunung Kidul activists listened to domestic worker stories and put women with urgent problems or who had suffered abuse in contact with agencies that could help them. More generally, RTND activists encouraged the PRT neighbourhoods to gather in the late

29 Interview with Maria Pakpahan, Edinburgh, 9 August 2017.

afternoons to socialize. They ran an open house at the RTND office, modelling it on their own study group as a place where women could not only be given information but "relax, read newspapers and hold informal discussions" (Ashoka 1999). In this manner, RTND built relationships with groups of workers, gained the credentials needed to win overseas funding, and amassed experience enabling them to move on to the next stage.

The RTND School: Philosophy and Pedagogy

Recognizing that creating safe havens and supporting individual cases of abuse would not achieve structural and cultural change, RTND created a domestic workers school, which opened for its first cohort in 2003. In line with the teachings of Paulo Freire's classic *Pedagogy of the Oppressed* – one of the books brought home by Indonesian students travelling abroad and widely discussed in study groups – they believed education was the route to worker transformation and empowerment. One activist I interviewed, Asih Nur Candra (Candra), a former factory worker and experienced trade union organizer who became involved in supporting RTND in the early 1990s, discussed the school using words that could have come directly from Freire. As Candra explained:

> Before you get PRT going out on demonstrations, first you must educate them about human rights and women's rights so that they understand why there is going to be a protest or march. At that time, we felt we were the ones who must teach them, so we established the school, and had not only teaching about the skills they needed for their work but also political education. We wanted the women to understand their rights as women and as citizens of the Indonesian state.[30]

This account, with its emphasis on political education and protest, could perhaps be read as "inciting the exploited poor to rebellion" (Freire 1996: 75). Candra explained, however, that RTND organizers were aware of this danger. The only workers they encouraged to go on public protests were those with a critical feminist awareness who had come to realize "what is missing and what should be there" in their lives. In the same way that bell hooks had worked, as a Black professor in the US, to turn classrooms into "radical spaces of possibility"

30 Interview with Asih Nur Candra, Yogyakarta, 25 Feb 2016.

where students might "collectively imagine ways to move beyond the boundaries, to transgress" (hooks 1994: 12), so the organizers of the RTND school envisaged it as a place where women might learn to push against the parameters of domestic work and the constraints family and community placed around them.

Whether or not Candra herself had read *Pedagogy of the Oppressed* (and I did not think to ask her, having not made this connection in my mind when I interviewed her), Freire's ideas about education for the masses were circulating widely in the NGO circles in which RTND's founder members moved. *Pedagogy of the Oppressed* was first published in Brazilian Portuguese in 1968, in English in the United States in 1970, and had sold over 500,000 copies worldwide by 1990. Nunuk Murniati, featured earlier in this chapter and a teacher at the domestic workers school, drew on Freire when she argued in her book on gender equality that "raising women's awareness of their own potential and the potential of human liberation is the most effective means of pushing people towards freedom and the fight for justice" (2004: 94–5). Well-known intellectuals, including Arief Budiman and Ariel Heryanto, used Freire's work to argue that NGOs should bring a "dynamic force" to grassroots empowerment, supporting workers towards self-reliance as well as speaking on their behalf.[31] Feminist groups such as Yasanti – an NGO in Yogyakarta founded by former students in 1982 to work for the empowerment of poor women – incorporated Freire's thinking as they developed Participatory Action Research (PAR), a method introduced to the women's movement in Indonesia at a seminar in December 1987 and further disseminated in Yogyakarta at workshops and seminars including the conference *Political Education for Activists in NGOs* held in April 1994 (Hadiwinata 2003: 112–13).

Freire's philosophy was also influential in the emergence of an Indonesian model of feminist critical education. Darmiyanti Muchtar (Yanti), another of RTND's early and lifelong supporters, established an NGO known as Institut KAPAL Perempuan in March 2000. The group's name derived from the phrase *Lingkaran Pendidikan Alternatif untuk Perempuan* (Alternative Education Circle for Women). At the time, NGO's usually had acronyms; Yanti and her colleagues chose the word KAPAL (which means "ship" in Indonesian). To them, ships

31 Budiman and Heryanto, teachers at Satya Wacana Christian University, Salatiga in the late 1980s, were invited to speak at a conference examining the application of (largely northern) scholarship to democratization in Indonesia.

represented Indonesia as an archipelago joined by the transport of ideas and people while the circle reflected "a no-center spirit and describes a cycle of continuous reflection" (Institut KAPAL Perempuan 2019). Playing with words, they took the "KA" from *Lingkaran*, the "P" from *Pendidikan*, another "A" from *Alternatif* and then returned to use *Lingkaran* for the "L". Their logo includes a drawing of a traditional Indonesian sailing ship and the gender equality sign. Created at a time marked by violent ethnic and religious conflict and fears that the nation would break apart, KAPAL Perempuan's mission links Freire's reflective learning with the "one people, one nation" ideals of *Sumpah Pemuda* (the Youth Pledge). Darmiyanti acknowledged Freire's influence on the group's educational work in poor communities and in post-Tsunami Aceh but argued that "popular" critical education failed to recognize unique aspects of women's experience or challenge the "double burden" placed on them. Radical methods, such as encouraging women to "touch their bodies from top to toe" (in the spirit of *Our Bodies, Ourselves*) and participate in open discussion of domestic violence and reproductive health (Muchtar 2010: 63–4) would help women "dare to say and act in their own names" (Kartika 2016: n.p.) It was such a feminist interpellation of Freire's work that underpinned the pedagogy at the RTND school.

The imagery chosen to describe the school on the RTND website portrays it as a space of transition. An archetypal "room with a view", perhaps, the school was a space in which to challenge domestic workers (like Forster's yet to be awakened heroine, Lucy) to reconsider their perspectives on the world and move beyond gendered notions of propriety.[32] The school aimed to "open and expand access to education", provide a "gateway" for PRT to bargain for better pay and conditions, and constitute a "doorway" through which they could enter public space to campaign and organize for gender justice and legal protection (RTND n.d.). Photographs of the house and classrooms show a shady garden and tall windows bringing in light and air. Thus, attending the school brought domestic workers "out of the shadows" where they were hidden in the backyards of employers' houses (a common trope in domestic worker activist literature) and into a house of their own, with a proud sign outside for all to see (Astuti 2012). Indeed, residents noticed the school and knew it as part of the neighbourhood, as I was told by one of my language teachers in

32 For a commentary on Lucy's transformation in E. M. Forster's novel see Heath (1994: 396, 429).

Yogyakarta, when I explained my project to him. Such an environment spoke of quite different power relationships and imagined futures from the high fences, concrete walls, barbed wire, male security guards, confiscated phones, and constant surveillance in the "camps" that cut trainee domestic workers off from the outside world as part of their mandatory preparation for work overseas (Rudnyckyj 2004: 408; Killias 2018: 107–14). Far from facilitating forms of Foucauldian governmentality and control, RTND activists sought to create a space of feminist enlightenment and Freirean freedom.

The RTND School: Curriculum

The ambitious curriculum devised by RTND activists for domestic workers interwove elements of modernist technology, Marxist structuralism, feminist self-realization, and Freirean student-centred learning. The aim was to address the multiple axes of intersection shaping the everyday realities of a domestic worker's life. Three sources proved particularly helpful in building a picture of the school's teaching practices. First, a dissertation written by an undergraduate, Reni Astuti, who spent several weeks in 2011 interviewing PRT, activist staff, and employers (Astuti 2012). Second, a two-part video made by RTND (viewable on YouTube) to publicize the school, *Sekolah PRT RTND Part 1 and Part 2* (2011a, b). Third, a teachers' handbook written to accompany an education programme for child domestic workers devised with ILO and government support (Moeliona et al. 2010). Although not dating from the school's earliest years, these sources embody the school's principles, reflect what had come to be seen as best practice, and offer insights into the vocational, feminist, and personal/political strands of the education provided by the school.

Pei-Chia Lan, discussing the training provided for Indonesian domestic workers going overseas, suggests that teaching domestic workers how to use vacuum cleaners and washing machines can be read as a re-inscription of colonialism; part of "a process of modernizing and civilizing the savage" (2006: 87). However, Astuti's *skripsi* (dissertation) suggests that the courses the RTND school offered in baby and childcare, caring for the elderly, and general domestic work, were highly valued by attendees who wanted to increase their marketability and bargaining power and prove their professional status. Not only did the school's registers show that workers often chose to follow more than one course, but Lek Jumiyem (Jumiyem) who had attended the school in 2003 and gone on to co-found Tunas Mulia Domestic Workers' Union, confirmed that she and others had a real desire for such training. While there was an emphasis on cleanliness and technology, the school promoted up-to-date knowledge and skills as a means to personal satisfaction and agency rather than inculcating fear of displeasing future employers. The RTND films reinforce the attractions of modernity, contrasting "outdated" aspects of village life with the modern lifestyle students enjoy on arrival at the school. Shots of village women laboriously washing clothes in the river in Part 1 are set against earnest (if staged) encounters with electric ovens and irons, a shuddering spin dryer, a vacuum cleaner, and a blood pressure monitor in Part 2. Empty roads, woodlands and seashore are left behind for the bustling city, and, whereas in Part 1 the village head is consulted as to whether a young woman should be permitted to attend the school, at the close of Part 2, the camera shows her performing confidently and expressively in a drama class, claiming, as it were, the last word.

Lessons in gender awareness were compulsory. There was some debate about how much time students needed to reach a level of awareness that would enable them to become "empowered". Nunuk Murniati recalled that when Lita Anggraini asked her to develop a gender awareness programme for the school:

> I asked her if I could have sixteen three-hour sessions with them [the PRT] to teach gender theory, but they said that was too much. If I had been allowed to have three hours each time, the output would have been that they would have had sufficient awareness to organize themselves. It all depends on the methods, three hours isn't long if you have games, questions, and time for self-reflection.[33]

Looking back, Nunuk felt she had been right. Realizing that theoretical language might have little appeal for domestic workers, she began with the concrete:

> I didn't go straight in saying this is feminism, this is feminist language, but for example we talked about something special to do with women, like physical differences between men's and women's bodies, their feelings are different, and their experiences are different. So, from this to awareness-raising. For example, when there is a child crying, what's the difference in the reactions of the fathers and the mothers, I will ask the PRT.

33 Interview with Nunuk Murniati, Yogyakarta, 1 March 2016.

Rather than immediately challenging the idea that men and women are inherently different, Nunuk used familiar examples of differences in everyday behaviour to teach about cultural and social conditioning, moving from the known to the new.

Indeed, teaching about bodies, sex, and sexuality became a central part of the gender awareness programme. Very much in the tradition of *Our Bodies, Ourselves* the globally circulating, bestselling feminist handbook on women's bodies, health and sexuality published by the Boston Women's Health Book Collective in 1970 that had been translated into eighteen languages by the late 1990s – the school gave PRT the vocabulary and permission to talk about such things.[34] As Asih Nur Candra, already introduced in this chapter, told me,

> The PRT know little about how their bodies work, they don't understand the difference between gender and sexuality, they tend to think it's the same.
>
> We felt we needed to increase their critical awareness and help them understand that gender, that's a social construct, but sex refers to the physical make-up of the body, that's sex. They can talk about these things; they will talk about vaginas [...] maybe using a different name. Indonesian schools don't do sex education so if they didn't have the domestic workers school, they wouldn't learn these things. We have to teach them, otherwise they are very vulnerable to sexual exploitation and abuse.[35]

Nor did domestic worker educators shy away from sex and gender in courses developed for child domestic workers. With the help of teaching materials such as annotated anatomical drawings, a jigsaw puzzle of women's reproductive organs, sorting cards of examples of sex- and gender-based differences between men and women, and interactive question and answer sessions, child workers were encouraged to experiment with newly learned vocabulary and practice expressing

---

34 For a discussion of *Our Bodies, Ourselves* as an example of the globalization of feminist knowledge production see Davis (2007) and Yanco (1996). Indonesian representatives had attended workshops on the book at the 1995 *Fourth World Conference on Women* in Beijing and work was underway on an Indonesian adaptation/translation by 1996. American versions of the book continue to circulate: one feminist counsellor in Indonesia set up a "Sexuality and Reproductive Health School" in Yogyakarta in 2010 after being introduced to the book by an American friend (Hudaya 2011).

35 Interview with Asih Nur Candra, Yogyakarta, 25 February 2016.

their feelings and opinions in a safe setting (Moeliona et al.: 108–21). The handbook urges facilitators to avoid rote learning but to flow with the responses of the children, in Freirean style.

Political education at the school conferred legitimacy on domestic workers' feelings of unfairness and provided a rationale for RTND's focus on legal protection. All students passing through the school were taught about rights enshrined in international law; the specifics of national and regional legislation relating to them, and ways of seeking legal redress for grievances. Such teaching also provided a means of developing solidarity. The "socialization" module for child domestic workers, for example, allocated a full day to teaching about rights. The guidance tells facilitators to emphasize practical, political action, "but not in a dreamy or abstract way". They should help participants turn action plans into "slogans, speeches or posters", get children to sign a statement of commitment to future collective action, and encourage them to see themselves as members of a bigger political movement running "from upstream to downstream" (Moeliona et al. 2010: 41). The first of the two RTND films shows domestic workers visiting the then newly opened museum at the former Dutch fort of Vredeburg. The museum's main attraction was a diorama celebrating the independence movement in Yogyakarta. Vredeburg was also the place where Yogyakartans suspected of being PKI (Partai Komunist Indonesia, Indonesian Communist Party) supporters were held (Stroud 2015: 4). This and other field trips helped situate the PRT cause within the longer heroic narrative of Indonesian nationalism, adding local legitimacy to an international human rights frame.

In terms of personal education, students could opt into writing workshops or drama sessions. These offered not only a means of personal expression, but also the chance to incorporate individual histories into collective truth-telling. This was exactly what Ratna Sarumpaet had done in her shockingly powerful play, *Marsinah Menggugat* (*Marsinah Accuses*), first staged in September 1997. In the play Sarumpaet gave Marsinah, a factory girl from the village who was raped and killed for her union activity in May 1993, a voice after her death, making her a means of denouncing New Order oppression of women as well as the government's disregard for the injustices meted out on the poor (Sarumpaet and McGlynn 2000; Bodden 2010: 221–7). Partly because the play was banned after several performances resulting in national and international outrage, it came to represent the power of drama as a means of refusing silencing. The production and its aftermath contributed to Marsinah's elevation into an iconic figure: the young working-class woman who was not only a victim but agent, "protesting the injustices of the workplace" (Ford 2003: 106–7). She died in part because she spoke out and wrote letters to her employers documenting their illegal production of branded goods and denouncing military intervention in labour relations (Weix 2002). While Marsinah's voice continued to be silenced after her death – her murder has never been solved – drama and role play were seen by NGOs as an effective means of education and consciousness-raising for workers, more likely to engender confidence and stronger worker voices than mere lecturing (Bodden 2010).

Including writing and drama in the curriculum for PRT thus created a link between generations and served to incorporate domestic workers' voices into the nation's traditions of resistance. The two teachers involved in the school that I met both had personal memories of the politicide that brought Suharto to power. Nunuk Murniati opened her conversation with me by saying, "I'll finish being an activist when I go to my grave: when I can't talk any more, I'll write". Her determination to write and publish stemmed in part from witnessing the arrest of three women in her *kampung*, all members of the mass-membership left-wing organization Gerwani (Gerakan Wanita Indonesia or Indonesian Women's Movement), which was eradicated following the coup in 1965 that brought President Sukarno to power (see, for example, Wieringa 1993).[36] "I defended them, I even gave a statement in their defence, I said they weren't members of the PKI", Nunuk explained.[37] Nusya Kuswantin, a Yogyakarta-based writer and researcher who ran writing workshops for the school in 2003, told me that as a child she watched some of her neighbours being dragged away to be hanged. "This was the time", she told me, that "my mother taught me to keep my mouth shut and not ask questions, it was too dangerous."[38]

Writing thus could be a means of breaking the silences and denials about the realities of domestic work in Indonesia that had insulated

36 Dating back to the 1950s, Gerwani claimed a membership of five million women by 1965. The massacres, arbitrary imprisonments and torture meted out to Indonesian men and women suspected of being members or associates of the Communist Party were the subject of an International People's Tribunal held at The Hague in November 2017 (Wieringa et al. 2019).

37 Interview with Nunuk Murniati, Yogyakarta, 1 March 2016.

38 Interview with Nusya Kuswantin, Yogyakarta, 2 March 2016. In 2009, Nusya published *Lasmi,* a novel telling the story of a teacher who became a member of Gerwani.

the institution from scrutiny within the seemingly safe blanket of the family home. When I interviewed Nusya she was editing a book of domestic worker stories for JALA PRT. Feminist writing does not depend on having a "room of one's own": writing workshops in communal spaces can build self-confidence, solidarity, and sisterhood. Nor do stories need to be only of exploitation or loss: Nusya told me that Yuli Maiheni (Heni), a founder member of Tunas Mulia who was working as a babysitter in the house next door to her, writes wonderfully funny stories about domestic work, good enough to warrant a book of their own.

In sum then, the space of the domestic workers school constituted a new arena for democratic participation, albeit one that was, in Cornwall's categorization, an "invited space", framed and managed by RTND with the support of its external donors. Initially, those who raised the funds, hired the staff, devised the curriculum, and negotiated the recruitment of workers at neighbourhood and family levels were well-connected NGO activists from middle-class backgrounds. Over time, Tunas Mulia activists took on leadership roles, and the model, based on a liberationist pedagogy, has become one of the hallmarks of domestic worker organizing across Indonesia.

Domestic Worker Spaces: Tunas Mulia and OPERATA

Some of Yogyakarta's domestic workers, more rapidly than their activist mentors had anticipated, applied lessons learned at the RTND school and claimed material and discursive space for themselves. In this stage of the movement's development, women who became the leaders of Yogyakarta's domestic worker organizations became agents and actors of the "everyday", radically changing their patterns of living and working, influencing other workers around them, and constructing, or connecting with, an increasingly complex web of relationships. Their newly carved-out spaces for meeting and organizing became sites of contestation between NGOs and workers over the meaning and practice of sisterhood and solidarity. One outcome of this contestation was a shift in the locus of legitimacy for leadership of the movement away from RTND. The pattern of relationships between activists and workers that evolved in Yogyakarta, I argue here, is significant because it provided a model for the ensuing development of Indonesia's nationwide domestic worker campaign.

Personal Journeys

In the same way that the founders of RTND spoke of the seismic impact on their lives of being students in Yogyakarta in the late 1980s, so the women who set up and ran domestic-worker-led organizations saw their exposure to feminist and human rights ideologies at the RTND school as a catalyst for profound change. Here I focus on three women who were heavily involved in running Tunas Mulia when I met them in 2015 and 2016: Ririn Sulastri, Yuli Maiheni (Heni), and Lek Jumiyem (Jumiyem). I draw on fieldwork and interviews as well as published articles about them.[39] While their experiences – in the sense that their roles as pioneering leaders brought them into the public eye – could not be said to represent those of most union members, aspects of the way they responded to feminist and human rights teaching can be seen in other domestic workers' lives.[40]

Ririn's story exemplifies the life changes going to the school could precipitate. She grew up in Berbah, a subdistrict of Yogyakarta severely damaged by the May 2006 eruption of Merapi. Like many of her neighbours, Ririn, a single parent with an elderly father and children to care for, turned to domestic work out of necessity, but, in her case, she bridled against the treatment she received. When she reported to her agency that she had been sexually assaulted at work they dismissed her complaint with the comment, "Ah, I think it was you who teased him, was it not?" She lost her job and the salary owing to her was withheld (Irham and Andapita 2015a). As she explained when I met her:

> Before I went to classes at RTND and Tunas Mulia, I was a member of a *yayasan* (charitable foundation). As a PRT I had already experienced harassment but the *yayasan* didn't help me. In fact, it was the opposite: they wanted me to keep working for the employer who had assaulted me. I even had to give money to them. My pay was only Rp.175,000 per month, I couldn't even buy a pair of jeans. At that time, I was having a great many problems at my workplace

39 These include a profile of Heni published in *Jurnal Perempuan* in 2005, a summary of a Trade Union Rights Centre evaluation of an ILO project (Ernawati 2016), and a 2015 interview with Ririn carried out by two journalists who had attended ILO-sponsored training on PRT issues prior to writing their piece (Irham and Andapita 2015a).

40 See, for example, the story of Sayuti, profiled in an article on the Solidarity Center's website (Solidarity Center 2011). Sayuti went on to study English at college as well as working in a voluntary capacity for Tunas Mulia.

> but also within my family. But after I entered the school, I found friends I could talk to.[41]

At the school, PRT were encouraged to reflect on such negative experiences and practice negotiating skills. Consequently, Ririn "began to feel confident enough to change jobs if one workplace did not work out for me and my family"[42]. Ten years on, she no longer used an agency but negotiated her own terms and conditions, charging more for distinct kinds of work and agreeing only "a daily contract arrangement until I feel trust and that the chemistry with the family is right" (Irham and Andapita 2015a). For her, respect was as important as remuneration. Serving as the (unpaid) chairperson of Tunas Mulia at the time I met her, Ririn now coaches and cajoles other PRT to use employment contracts and softer skills to manage relationships with their employers. Beyond this, building on the public profile she had acquired as an effective union official, a frequent participant in street demonstrations and political lobbying, a celebrated performer in PRT-related theatre productions, and a national and international spokesperson for the domestic worker movement, Ririn put herself forward as a candidate in district elections in 2016 (Ernawati 2016).

Heni, too, speaks of undergoing a transformation from reticent domestic helper to articulate worker-with-rights. Born in Yogyakarta and raised by her grandmother after her parents' divorce, economic necessity had driven Heni to leave school early and take work as a PRT in Jakarta. Four years later her grandmother needed her home, so she found a job as a PRT in Yogyakarta, fortunately with an employer who allowed her time off to attend the RTND school. Listening to stories of women putting up with low wages and abuse, she decided her mission in life would be to improve the bargaining position of domestic workers (Subiyantoro 2005). At union meetings she shares data she has collected about the high demand for domestic workers in the locality to persuade women not to be afraid to negotiate, complain, or even leave unsatisfactory work situations, and frequently supports members in meetings with their employers when things are amiss. She no longer works as a live-in PRT, and her personal life was further transformed when she married a labour activist and trade union organizer.[43]

---

41 Interview with Ririn Sulastri, Chairperson of Tunas Mulia, Yogyakarta, 25 February 2016.

42 Interview with Ririn Sulastri, Yogyakarta, 25 February 2016.

43 Field notes, observation of OPERATA Berbah meeting, Yogyakarta, 28 February 2016.

Nusya Kuswantin (the author who taught writing at the RTND school) told me she had watched Heni and Ririn grow to become "assertive and self-confident women and workers".[44] She remembered meeting them in 2003 and was still in regular contact when I interviewed her; indeed, she regards Heni as a friend. As far as Heni, Ririn, and Jumiyem are concerned, Nusya told me, employer–employee relationships have almost been turned on their heads. Far from "the PRT being afraid of their bosses [...] it's the employers who are wary, not least because, as union leaders, they are often in the newspapers, appear on television, go on demonstrations and are not afraid of speaking in public about cases of unfair treatment". Laughing, she remarked that "Ririn makes all her employers afraid!" In less jocular mode, she argued that domestic workers like Ririn and Heni challenge the view Yogyakarta's middle classes have of their moral landscape. How paradoxical, she remarked, that

> a domestic worker like Heni, who [...] is active in the organization, disciplined, works hard and is full of dignity, fights like this, became secretary-general of the domestic workers' union and joins workshops in Bangkok, Nepal, and Uruguay, gets far less respect, and so little remuneration compared with employers who may be "super-rich" but by no means "egalitarian".

For Nusya, who grew up in Malang, East Java, one problem is that Central Javanese culture and language, contrary to the ideals of Indonesian nationalism, perpetuate feudal relationships. While employers embrace consumerist modernity, their unreformed attitudes and behaviours effectively debar domestic workers (and others) from their rights as workers and citizens in a democratic nation.[45] Carla Jones similarly found that although Yogyakarta housewives saw themselves as modern, moral, beings committed to equality and free expression in their marriages, they devalued the moral worth and emotional strength of the PRT they employed (2004: 520–23). As the number of families who are dependent on PRT in Yogyakarta increases, the status of domestic workers might be expected to rise. Yet, these witnesses suggest, Yogyakarta traditions and elite Javanese mores seem to resist change.

Ririn's reference to the "chemistry" of the workplace alludes to this affective dimension of domestic work. Gutiérrez-Rodríguez has

---

44 Interview with Nusya Kuswantin, Yogyakarta, 2 March 2016.

45 Interview with Nusya Kuswantin, Yogyakarta, 2 March 2016.

highlighted the problematic way in which the spaces of domestic work generate feelings of inferiority and worthlessness in workers while transmitting "positive affective energies" to household members; for her interviewees, challenging the denigration of their work, and by extension, the denigration of themselves, was as important as demanding higher wages (2014: 50–51). Similarly, when Indonesian women working as domestic workers in London joined "Justice for Domestic Workers" (an association for migrant domestic workers in the capital), they carried with them low self-esteem and a sense of themselves as servants rather than workers. Some expressed fear of being treated as "slaves", leading them to place having a "good employer" higher in their scales of reference than wages or time off (Jiang and Korczynski 2016: 822–4). While not constructed as alien outsiders in the way migrant domestic workers or Black women working for white employers in South Africa, for example, frequently are, domestic workers in Indonesia working in affluent middle-class homes still operate within "a dialectic of attachment and denigration" inflected by the ghosts of a colonial past where the white skin and implicit purity of the employer stand counterposed to the physical and assumed or ascribed moral dirtiness of a darker-skinned maid (Ally 2011a: 1). Whitening creams, whether metaphorical or real, do not possess sufficient alchemy to remove the emotional pain and strain that domestic work can entail.[46]

OPERATA

In Yogyakarta, finding spaces in which domestic workers could come together to share the painful (and amusing) experiences of domestic work other than in invited spaces provided by RTND, however, proved problematic. Some employers allowed small groups of women to gather in their homes, especially if the meetings were deemed to take the form of religious study groups. Once the women got together, though, conversations turned to issues facing them at work, a development that led some employers, fearing workers would spread gossip about their private affairs, to order their PRTs not to attend.[47] Some workers

46 This reference to whitening creams as a means of dealing with some of the affectual consequences of colonialism and consumerism is inspired by Ayu Saraswati's study of the circulation of ideas of beauty, colour, and race (2013).
47 Interview with Gita Nasution, Jakarta, 11 July 2016. Gita, an Indonesian student researching childcare arrangements in Jakarta for her PhD, told me that even though she identified herself as a middle-class mother, fellow parents at her daughter's nursery school were reluctant to discuss their domestic

proved resilient and continued to meet in mosques, markets, and even tennis courts, despite obstacles: "Never let failures be a hindrance – there must be a way out of the dungeon", they said (Papachan 2009: 10).

The use of the word "dungeon" here conveys the symbolic as well as material importance for Yogyakarta's domestic workers of finding spaces of their own. Committed to building a collective, a small group of domestic workers, perhaps ten in all, some of whom had attended courses together at the RTND school, set themselves up as an OPERATA on 27 April 2003, registering as a trade union with the government a year later under the name Tunas Mulia, a name they chose to emphasize the respect (*mulia*) they believed was due to them. The word *tunas* brings to mind budding shoots and new hope; hence, the Tunas Mulia emblem (which can be seen on the union's Instagram account), shows a house enclosed with a wreath of new buds and flowers. They then began the work of developing their union city-wide, using neighbourhood-based OPERATA as their unit of organization. Other workers in Yogyakarta responded positively: by 2006, union membership had risen to some 300 (Mather 2008: 20). Following a dip around 2008, the IUF (International Union of Food, Agricultural, Hotel, Restaurant, Catering, Tobacco, and Allied Workers' Associations) injected funding that allowed union and Kongres Operata Yogyakarta (KOY) leaders to revitalize the OPERATA and membership reached 500 by 2015 (IDWFED 2013; Irham and Andapita 2015a). For the ILO, Tunas Mulia represented an example of "spontaneous" action by domestic workers at the grassroots – in contrast to other unions more reliant on NGO resources (D'Souza 2010: 79). The choice of adjective reflects the sense of agency and control finding space of their own gave to workers previously kept, metaphorically at least, behind walls.

I saw something of the results of their efforts when Ririn invited me to join the monthly meeting of her local OPERATA in 2016. She collected me from my central Yogyakarta hotel and the twenty-five-minute journey on the back of her motorbike to her village in the district of Berbah brought home to me the significance for domestic worker activists of the motorbike and the mobile phone. Workers without access to either depend on the organizers of neighbourhood OPERATA to keep them in touch with union developments. Turning off the main road beyond the airport, the track into Ririn's *kampung*

worker arrangements with her as they feared she might intrude into private matters or pass on information to PRT or other parents.

became bumpy. Our slower progress, however, meant that I noticed how many women, dressed in vivid purple T-shirts emblazoned with "OPERATA Berbah" and "JALA PRT", waved and smiled at Ririn from their front yards. Domestic workers had established a visible presence and collective identity in their community. The meeting was held in the house of Ririn's father – a building in traditional style and one of the few in the village to have survived the devastation of 2006. Its advantage over modern concrete replacements was the large front room. With sofas and chairs pushed to one side and bamboo mats spread over the floor, the space easily accommodated the thirty or more women who assembled for the meeting, while small children and interested menfolk gathered outside. Plates of cassava, cold drinks, and baskets of rambutan had been laid out hospitably; this was clearly a social space as well as a business one.

In many ways the space, and the proceedings, mirrored arrangements in the RTND office and school. Flipchart pages were Blu-Tacked to the walls. Women of all ages greeted each other respectfully as they came in and began to gossip; a little later formal proceedings began with a prayer. Jumiyem chaired the meeting and began by reporting back on the training workshop for domestic workers from other regions of Indonesia she, Ririn, and Heni had attended at UGM the previous week. The second item on the agenda was a discussion of a book JALA PRT intended to publish to mark International Domestic Workers' Day, 2016, most of which was earmarked for domestic workers' own stories. Just as RTND activists ran writing workshops in the domestic workers school, so Jumiyem and Ririn sought to convince members of the OPERATA they could and should write something, otherwise, they said, the book would fail. Several women handed in stories and later, after the meeting ended, I watched Ririn, Heni, and Jumiyem sit together reviewing what the women had done. The main agenda item was a discussion about union dues. Heni's husband (the union organizer) had been invited to address the group and did so in dramatic style, using intensely expressive body language and radiating energy. His speech was remarkably robust and direct. As PRT and union members, he told the women, they needed to be less *malas* (lazy), and pay more in union dues. Otherwise, they would never be independent, escape poverty, or win their fight for legal recognition: collective action was the only way to a better future, he argued. Breaking into small groups, the workers discussed proposals for higher dues, and voices became raised. Women were worried about husbands discovering how much they were paying to the union and wondered whether they could afford to pay more. Eventually Ririn, Heni, and Jumiyem persuaded the women to compromise. Dues would go up a little, but more of the new money would go into their communal savings scheme than into a political fighting fund. Once the formal part of the meeting was over, food and drinks were shared. Ririn, Heni, and Jumiyem stayed behind to discuss the meeting and, some four and a half hours after our arrival, Ririn transported me safely back to the main road.[48] For the duration of the meeting, I realized later, a domestic dwelling had been reshaped into a space for the construction and affirmation of a particular version of collectivity, solidarity, and sisterhood.

Sisterhood and Solidarity Redefined

In the Tunas Mulia OPERATA, domestic workers formulated a vision of sisterhood different from the one underpinning the work of their "parent" NGO. The differences are spelt out in *A Manual for Domestic Worker Organizing*, a handbook published by the Committee for Asian Women (Papachan 2009). The *Manual* was one outcome of a week-long workshop held in Yogyakarta in 2007, which brought together domestic workers from Indonesia, India, Hong Kong, and South Korea. Several members of Tunas Mulia attended, and the fact that the *Manual* includes numerous examples from Indonesia suggests they played an influential role. The then chair of Tunas Mulia, Susi Apriyanti, was one of several attendees interviewed after the workshop ended to provide more detail to fill out the handbook.[49]

The section in the *Manual* on "sisterhood", then, is likely to reflect some of the principles and practices developed in Yogyakarta's OPERATA. Five key points stand out. First, to become a "sister", you need to be, have been, or intend to become, a domestic worker. Second, sisterhood should be non-hierarchical; workers should "never call each other Mrs XX" but "directly use their own names or 'sisters' in general", and all group members should be involved in running the group's affairs. Third, sisterhood is cultivated by caring. Caring could be shown by sharing such things as "women's knowledge" of healing, massage, food, and recipes, and by making the meeting place a "cosy, friendly, supportive […] place away from home" where workers could just be, rest, talk, and learn. Fourth, sisters need to build their own "knowledge for action" by going door to door, rather

48 Field notes, Yogyakarta, 28 February 2016.

49 The *Manual* is dedicated to Susi Apriyanti, who died in a road accident on 11 August 2007.

than relying on "papers for academics by academics". Fifth and most importantly, sisterhood is not subservient. Leaders must come from the grassroots, since "a leader having her roots from among domestic workers understands their situation because she is one of them and can articulate and share what their needs are with the public and concerned authorities" (Papachan 2009: 9–12). While there are points in common with the sisterhood espoused by RTND, for example the emphasis on gender, participation, and the need for caring and supportive spaces away from work or home, the *Manual* emphasizes the places where the models diverge. Intellectual workers such as activists do not have sisterhood or leadership rights, nor is academic knowledge privileged.

The *Manual* also included advice on building solidarity. Worker solidarity is presented as a tougher proposition than sisterhood; achieving it demands a "systematized and well-planned", "organized, disciplined and determined" coming together of workers into an effective campaigning engine and international political force. Even though, in the end "it is the solidarity of workers, their interactions with one another, which would bring changes to the position of domestic workers", the *Manual* points out that "solidarity between the upper and lower classes of society could prove [more] useful in broadening the reach of the DW campaign". However, in such cross-class alliances, workers needed to be seen as equal partners with NGOs, and differences discussed and negotiated openly, around the table (Papachan 2009: 10–11). The need for leaders who can operate confidently both within and beyond the spatial boundaries of the OPERATA is thus seen as important to the union's success. Union leaders see themselves as social and political agents ready to take on many of the roles middle-class activists had previously played.

Indeed, running through the *Manual* is a note of distrust of NGOs. NGOs are answerable not to the "collective will" of domestic workers per se, but to their own members. NGOs may be "unaware of union and worker issues" or even "tend to control domestic worker organizations and use them to gain funding" (Papachan 2009: 10–11). In this vein, the later pages of the document make detailed reference to difficult relationships between activists and workers in Yogyakarta, where, in the 1990s, the author states:

> There was a huge fall out between the NGOs and domestic workers' organizations (DWOs) and unions in Yogyakarta. The ripple effect of this fall out is still felt among the unions, NGOs and DWOs [...]. In 1999 in Yogyakarta, Indonesia, an NGO, Rumpun

> Tjoet Nyak Dien [...] formulated a draft without involving domestic workers.[50] When they started to organize domestic workers, the domestic workers themselves sat together and reformulated the draft. (Papachan 2009: 36)

Having read versions of the origins of Tunas Mulia that suggested a smooth evolution from NGO to domestic worker organization, this was quite shocking to read. In sharing such information publicly, Yogyakarta's domestic workers were participating in their own "naming of names". They believed that their situated knowledge was crucial if any draft law was going to represent their demands and meet their needs.

At the end of the *Manual*, another piece of evidence surprises. Apparently, even though several years had passed, feelings were still running so high that at one point during the workshop, "some of the workers of the union refused to enter the office of the NGO they were previously part of" (Papachan 2009: 37). Such an action seems the more shocking since Yogyakarta was acting as host city, and Indonesia as host nation. Not only does this story reveal the intensity of workers' struggles to ensure their voices were heard, but it also explains why creating a network of independent OPERATA was so important to them. It explains, too, the fact that the workers and activists I interviewed seemed reluctant to go into detail about the circumstances surrounding the union's separation from RTND, merely hinting at, or glossing over, tensions between the workers and their middle-class mentors. One domestic worker involved in the union at that time, for example, spoke of the process as akin to "adolescent children growing up and reaching for independence",[51] while one founder member of RTND simply commented that the move to a separate union "happened a bit sooner than we might have planned".[52]

---

50 An article written by three members of Tunas Mulia published in *Jurnal Perempuan* in 2017 recounted that in 1997, RTND and the Yogyakarta Women's Joint Secretariat had worked together to submit a draft *Perda* (*Peraturan Daerah*, regional law) on the Protection of Domestic Workers to the Provincial DPR. This is likely to be the draft law referred to in Papachan's account, since, by 1997, draft laws were being submitted to local authorities in Yogyakarta by an umbrella network that included Tunas Mulia (Sargini et al. 2017: 130–34).

51 Meeting with Sargini, Yuli Maiheni, Lek Jumiyem, and Ririn Sulastri, Yogyakarta, 26 February 2016.

52 Interview with Damairia Pakpahan, Yogyakarta, 5 March 2016.

One reason workers and activists may have glossed over this discordance in the movement's history was that they had, as they said, "struggled" to rebuild relationships and create new structures following the rift between them. At the outset, while middle-class activists at the core of the movement had multiple contacts and were linked into networks dating back to their student days, the domestic worker organizations were tethered to RTND by an invisible umbilical cord. RTND provided enlightenment in the form of domestic worker education, and fuel for growth through its access to resources, expertise, and leadership. After Tunas Mulia departed to set up as an independent union, the movement needed to be reshaped. One crucial step was establishing the national advocacy network JALA PRT in July 2004 in cooperation with Jakarta-based feminist NGOs, following a piece of research into the conditions of domestic workers in ten cities in Indonesia (Eddyono, Fanani, and Maurice 2015: 10). Membership was open to a whole range of organizations; as Maria Pakpahan put it, "it was set up by many people, all the people who attended that workshop were the founders".[53] Those who joined included women's rights and feminist NGOs, domestic worker organizations, trade unions, children's rights groups, and a small number of individuals (Pratiwi 2017: 203). RTND and Tunas Mulia both joined as independent organizations and JALA signalled the importance of unions by putting domestic worker organizations first on its membership list.[54] The then executive director of RTND, Lita Anggraini, took on the coordination role and began dividing her time between Yogyakarta and the capital. Gradually, JALA PRT, rather than RTND, became the lodestar for the movement as it spread across the archipelago.

In Yogyakarta, activists and domestic workers made further organizational changes to strengthen collective solidarity. Blog entries on the RTND and KOY websites give a picture of these. An umbrella group known as the Network for the Protection of Domestic Workers (Jaringan Perlindungan Pekerja Rumah Tangga or JPPRT) took on the task of organizing demonstrations and lobbying, continuing until the Domestic Workers Convention was adopted in Geneva in 2010. In April 2009 some OPERATA expressed their feelings of solidarity

53 Interview with Maria Pakpahan, Edinburgh, 9 August 2017. During the interview, Maria mentioned that there might be some notes of the meeting. However, when I asked Lita Anggraini about these, she explained that keeping records had been difficult at that time.

54 The membership list was available to view on the JALA PRT website; the last print out I have is dated May 2015.

and set up their own umbrella group by establishing a Congress, the Kongres Operata Yogyakarta or KOY, so that workers could build their own "joint organization". KOY thus enabled PRT to unite and choose representatives without needing to join an official trade union. By December 2009, the Network encompassed eighteen OPERATA (Kongres Operata Yogyakarta 2009).

Despite the fragmentation and complications involved, the arrangements proved workable. In 2009, for example, KOY collaborated with RTND and the Joint Theatres of Yogyakarta to stage a two-day drama festival at Taman Budaya Yogyakarta, Yogyakarta's premier public arts space. Sixteen OPERATA took part in self-scripted performances and the programme included presentations and awards involving the mayor of Yogyakarta, the Head of Social Affairs, and Rieke Diah Pitaloka, a former television personality and rising politician. The culmination of the festival was a production of *Vashti*, written and produced by prominent Yogyakarta writer and director, Wahyana Giri. Members of both Tunas Mulia and KOY have attended international conferences and workshops on a regular basis and the two groups continue to be important in organizing PRT and producing leaders who can, legitimately, represent the voices of their peers at local, national, and international levels.

2009: "*Mau Kemana Gerakan PRT?*"[55]

This chapter has shown how feminist and Freirean philosophies underpinned the processes of refashioning domestic workers' views of themselves and their place in Yogyakarta. Activists and domestic workers created new private spaces where, to use Bourdieu's frame of the habitus, new dispositions were acquired and rehearsed. Lee's analysis of student spaces (and the street) as places where the disposition to "occupy and adapt" fuelled *reformasi* politics, proved fruitful in pointing to a similar pattern in the Indonesian domestic worker movement, where the RTND office in a suburban street became a school and village houses became meeting places for OPERATA. But,

55 This is the title of a workshop held in Yogyakarta on 1 May 2009, the English translation being "Where Does the Domestic Worker Movement Go from Here?"

as this chapter has demonstrated, the PRT who set up Tunas Mulia did not want to assume roles sketched out for them by ostensibly knowledgeable others; they wanted to play a part in designing the movement's future and have it recognized that, as workers, they knew best what sort of "new clothes" they and their compatriots should wear. Thus, while the dual structure of RTND as hub in the city centre and OPERATA as satellites in the *kampungs* and villages of the surrounding region provided a model that enabled the movement to grow and shift the contours of the Yogyakarta's social, moral, and cultural landscape, it was insufficient to achieve the movement's political ends. Both workers and activists recognized that if they wanted legal recognition of domestic worker rights, they had to expand beyond the feminist activist circles and *kampung* communities from which the movement's founders had come.

The records of a workshop entitled "Where Does the Domestic Worker Movement Go from Here?" held on 1 May 2009 provide further evidence for how the issues of class difference and representation with which this chapter began were, at this point, both still extant and beginning to be resolved. Organized jointly by RTND and the newly formed KOY (but with Tunas Mulia apparently absent), the seminar reflected a hope that domestic worker rights, in the context of a proposed ILO Convention, would be mainstreamed. Speakers included a mediator from the Ministry of Manpower, the former chair of the region's private sector ombudsmen, a specialist on alternative education, a professor from UGM, and a trade unionist. Yet, a photograph of the event posted on the RTND website presents an arresting image (RTND 2009). It shows the top table in the conference room of a Yogyakarta hotel, the Matahari. The table is, as was customary, covered with a cloth, neatly pleated and draped as for a banquet or wedding, with bottles of water and wineglasses as well as papers and laptops on display. Two artificial fir trees stand decoratively at the front, and the chairs on which the seminar speakers are seated are elaborately carved, Javanese-style. So far, nothing is unexpected; this is the familiar activist space of the budget hotel. What does stand out, however, is that the two authoritative figures seated in the centre are male. The text accompanying the photograph explains that one is the facilitator, the head of RTND's advocacy division, and the other the silver-haired figure of Professor Damardjati Supajar, a respected teacher of philosophy and Javanese culture at UGM with personal and family links to the *Kraton* (RTND 2009). Both men thus lend their culturally ascribed legitimacy to the PRT cause, but their occupation of the central space highlights hierarchies of gender and class.

More significant to this discussion, perhaps, is the apparent discomfort of the slight figure of Murtini, the domestic worker representative. The only woman on the panel wearing Muslim clothing, dressed for the occasion in a bright fuchsia pink jacket, headdress, and scarf, Murtini, one might fairly surmise, had not wanted to be overlooked. Nevertheless, she is seated at the very end of the long table, her chair slightly behind the others, and is pictured looking sideways and apprehensively (in a somewhat Lady Diana-esque way) at the male speaker whose body is turned towards her. Reading further, we find that her nervousness – the writer of the blog comments on how "pale" she seemed to be – was understandable. Not only was she to be the first speaker, but, as she explained to her audience, it had only been a week or so earlier that KOY had been formed and she herself chosen as its secretary-general. Taking up her leadership position entailed occupying new space in an unaccustomed way. Domestic workers had a seat at the table, but not yet equal status.

Indeed, the creation and occupation of new spaces ranging from the RTND school and the domestic workers' OPERATA to the international conference setting of an impersonal hotel was crucial to the early development of Indonesia's domestic worker movement. Away from the public eye, globally circulating ideas of feminism, gender equality, and women's rights on the one hand, and of "decent work for domestic workers" on the other were adapted and used in context. In the process, contestations over the meaning and practice of "sisterhood" resulted in the emergence of a new, informally managed network-based collective, which allowed for, but did not neutralize or render invisible, differences in class and education. JALA PRT and JPPRT had room for middle-class activists and domestic workers to work together on equitable, if not always comfortable terms. The reframed relationships between NGO and domestic workers, worked for painfully in Yogyakarta, provided a springboard for the development of a domestic worker movement across the archipelago and tapped into an energy and creativity of domestic workers previously unrecognized. Realizing that getting legislation passed would depend on working with politicians, media, and influential NGOs, and on establishing a physical presence in the capital, JALA PRT turned its attention to Jakarta, the focus of what comes next.

CHAPTER

3

Jakarta, JALA PRT, and the Politics of Presence

Crammed underneath a side table in the JALA PRT office-cum-house in South Jakarta is a large cloth bundle. Someone pointed it out to me shortly after my first visit to JALA in the summer of 2015. I recognized it as the "giant napkin" or *Serbet Cinta PRT* (Love Napkin for domestic workers) that had been the centrepiece of celebrations in February 2010 on what JALA activists had named "National Domestic Workers' Day". The headline-grabbing part of that day had been the ceremonial sewing together of some 900 of the cheap cotton squares known as *serbet dapur* (kitchen cloths or napkins used as dishcloths and tea towels all over Indonesia). Stitching transformed them into a massive banner (or even tent) that, held aloft, offered a perfect photo opportunity. The napkins had been collected from across the archipelago; each carried a message to the House of Representatives – the Dewan Perwakilan Rakyat Republik Indonesia or DPR – and the Ministry of Manpower and Transmigration urging the passage of the Domestic Workers Bill. As a piece of PR, the *Serbet Cinta* made its point perfectly; the event gained extensive media coverage. The Love Napkin also points to this chapter's purpose, which is to uncover how the domestic worker movement made its material, political, and moral presence felt in the capital following the establishment of JALA PRT in 2004.

The Love Napkin

According to press releases sent out beforehand, the first stitches were to be made by the minister for women's empowerment and child protection, the deputy of Commission 1X in the DPR (the standing committee responsible for the preparation and oversight of bills relating to labour law), a representative from a domestic workers' organization, and a representative employer.[1] After that, four teams of workers and supporters, marshalled into groups named "bucket, mop, iron, and pan", completed the sewing. Later, a group of PRT paraded a four-metre-tall doll with multiple arms symbolizing the myriad tasks domestic workers do in a day. Yet more workers, some accompanied by their families, hung clothing or more *serbet* on improvised washing lines strung across the spaces of Proclamation Park, the site of the declaration of Indonesia's independence in 1945. On the same date, domestic worker groups in Yogyakarta and Surabaya staged similar – if smaller-scale – ceremonies with the *Serbet Cinta* theme. In the fortnight following the demonstrations, radio stations in ten cities around Indonesia broadcast programmes promoting domestic worker demands for their rights.[2]

Staging such a piece of performative politics was a complex operation. That such an event was possible raises the question that is central to this chapter: how did a handful of former students from Yogyakarta, with perhaps a few hundred, at most, domestic workers organized into OPERATA (domestic worker organizations) behind them, manage to create a national movement that could mount events on this scale and persuade at least some politicians to pay attention? Other questions ensue. Who were their allies, and how did they manage the logistics involved? How did they locate domestic workers in the city and prepare them to participate in politics? How did gender feature in the moral tales JALA activists and PRT played out in public, and what was it that enabled domestic workers – to draw on Engin Isin's paradigm of the "activist citizen" – to move beyond the boundaries of the habitus surrounding domestic work and "make a scene" (2009: 379)?

This chapter argues that seeing Indonesia's domestic worker movement as practising "a politics of presence" helps answer such questions. It concentrates on developments in Jakarta between 2004 when JALA was founded and 2016 when my fieldwork ended, just at the time the movement was refocusing on expanding grassroots membership. As a rapidly growing megacity with perhaps twenty-eight

1 The House of Representatives has eleven standing committees responsible for the preparation and oversight of legislation. Commission 1X deals with labour law and has thus been the key committee for JALA PRT to attempt to influence.

2 Account constructed from the instructions sent to supporters, press releases, and news reports published in February 2010.

million inhabitants across the Greater Jakarta/ Jabodetabek area by 2010, Jakarta presented geographically specific and historically contingent opportunities and challenges to JALA activists as they sought to apply their blueprint for organizing on a national scale.

Many of Jakarta's PRT were migrants from the regions, excluded from political processes or established trade unions. To make an impact, activists moved into the sorts of locations Isin identifies as crucial for the disenfranchised "outsider" to get heard: "bodies, courts, borders, streets, media, [and] networks" (2009: 368, 372, 384). As Saskia Sassen argues, expanding global cities needed low-wage labourers but denied them the benefits of economic growth and full citizenship. Yet the very concentration and indispensability of such workers, she suggests, means that if they band together and take to the streets or the internet they can gain "presence" with the authorities and in the process, engender a sense of "presence viz-a-viz each other" (2006: 315–17).

As citizens, Indonesia's PRT are not formally excluded like the *sans papiers* Isin discusses or Sassen's "undocumented immigrants". They can, in theory, make claims against national and sub-national laws and the International Conventions Indonesia has ratified (ILO 2006: 10–16). Indeed, Gastaldi, Jordhus-Lier, and Prabawati make a cogent case for viewing Indonesia's domestic worker movement as a matter of industrial citizenship and a "politics of membership" as PRT struggled to "establish themselves a place in their nation's labour movement" (2017: 163, 172). That struggle is an important part of the story. But, as Jennifer Fish's account of negotiations over Convention 189 in Geneva demonstrates, there is something powerful at play when domestic workers come face to face with the mighty, most of whom will employ domestic workers in their own homes. In Geneva domestic workers were seen "sitting at the table with the world's political leaders" and heard sharing their experiences of abuse. This made it difficult, Fish contends, for privileged politicians and conference delegates to disregard their demands for a universally applicable basic standard of rights and protections (2017: 83–5). Unlike organized workers in the formal sector, PRT could not use industrial action, official disputes management structures or collective bargaining mechanisms. They could, however, use their presence. Some PRT did just that when, during the 2014 election campaign, they journeyed from the private homes where they worked to sit at the table with future President Joko Widodo (Jokowi), then Governor of Jakarta, wearing *serbet* headscarves so as not to be forgotten.

This chapter draws heavily on interviews with representatives of fourteen of the nineteen Jakarta-based organizations affiliated with JALA by 2015 and my observations of events run by JALA or JALA supporters. Seven other informants were individual members of the network or had worked closely with it. Two messages came through repeatedly. First, interviewees expressed deep loyalty to and admiration for Lita Anggraini. Many told me the movement could not have achieved all it has without her extraordinary dedication and unstinting efforts.[3] The second was a sense of feminist solidarity. Narrating how they came to be involved with JALA, interviewees identified moments in their lives when they experienced what Clare Hemmings describes as "affective dissonance": moments when a sense of how things *are* for women and how they *should be* collided (2012: 154–8). Such experiences drew my interlocutors to feminism and, to use Hemmings's terminology again, engendered an "affective solidarity" which fuelled JALA's struggles for political presence. As one informant put it, feelings of feminist solidarity underpinned "the deep discussion and analysis that goes on at JALA before we do anything".[4]

The chapter unfolds in three stages. "Networks and Alliances" explains how JALA carved a space within Jakarta's complex constellation of NGOs, organized workers in neighbourhoods, lobbied parliament and found new allies. "Street Protests" examines the logistics and iconography of domestic worker demonstrations and investigates how activists fashioned PRT into political activists. "Santi's Story" focuses on one domestic worker-turned-organizer to exemplify how JALA encouraged workers to occupy new spaces in the city, capitalize on technological change, and establish themselves as *bona fide* trade unionists – members, if you will, of an emergent domestic worker class.[5]

Networks and Alliances

Interviewed for an article in Indonesia's feminist journal, *Jurnal Perempuan*, Lita Anggraini listed twelve organizations she remembered

3 Further evidence of that loyalty and the reasons behind it are described in an article published by Project Multatuli, a journalism initiative dating from 2021 with a focus on the interests of the marginalized (Andinda 2022).

4 Interview with Rina Satdewi, Jakarta, 27 July 2015.

5 Here I echo the closing words of Carolyn Steedman's *Labours Lost* (2009: 356), one of the texts discussed in the Introduction.

meeting in 2004 to form JALA PRT (Pratiwi 2017: 203). The list included national organizations with headquarters in Jakarta, such as the Indonesian Women's Coalition for Justice and Democracy (KPI) founded in May 1998, and NGOs in Yogyakarta, Semarang, Surabaya, Solo, and Bandung. Yogyakarta-based Rumpun Tjoet Nyak Dien (RTND) took the lead. The moment seemed opportune; several leading women's rights activists and trade unionists well-known to members of JALA had won seats in the 2004 parliamentary elections. Instead of "shouting from the outside", JALA could now lobby potential supporters sitting on committees that had the power to effect change (Meitzner 2013).

JALA PRT

Soon after I met her Lita Anggraini drew me a diagram showing how JALA operated (Figure 3.1).[6] The sketch highlights the simplicity of the network or *jaringan* model of organizing JALA adopted in 2004 and has retained ever since. Smaller circles represent the membership. There were no hierarchies; individuals or organizations could join at will and anyone could be called upon depending on the task at hand. Two groups named on the diagram – Jakarta's Legal Aid Institute, LBH Jakarta (Lembaga Bantuan Hukum Jakarta), and the Indonesian Women's Association for Justice, LBH APIK (Lembaga Bantuan Hukum Asosiasi Perempuan untuk Keadilan) – had recommended a simple structure. Compared with the commonly used mechanism of the foundation (*yayasan*) with a board of directors and executives, or the more democratic association (*asosiasi*), answerable to its members through an annual meeting (Anastasia et al. 2013), they believed a loose network offered "more flexibility for advocacy".[7]

The model also capitalized on the expansion of social movement activism that followed the end of the Suharto regime (Aspinall and Weiss 2014: 222–4). As Ratna Batara Munti, an activist from Yogyakarta who had joined LBH APIK when it was founded in 1995 and became its director in 2003, explained:

> The more organizations that join JALA, the more powerful it can be. We can all spread the ideas without complex structures because we have the same shared goal. So, if each organization brings the JALA vision into their organization, that will be our strength.[8]

6 Interview with Lita Anggraini, Jakarta, 30 July 2015.
7 Interview with Pratiwi Febry, Jakarta, 28 July 2015.
8 Interview with Ratna Batara Munti, Jakarta, 31 July 2015.

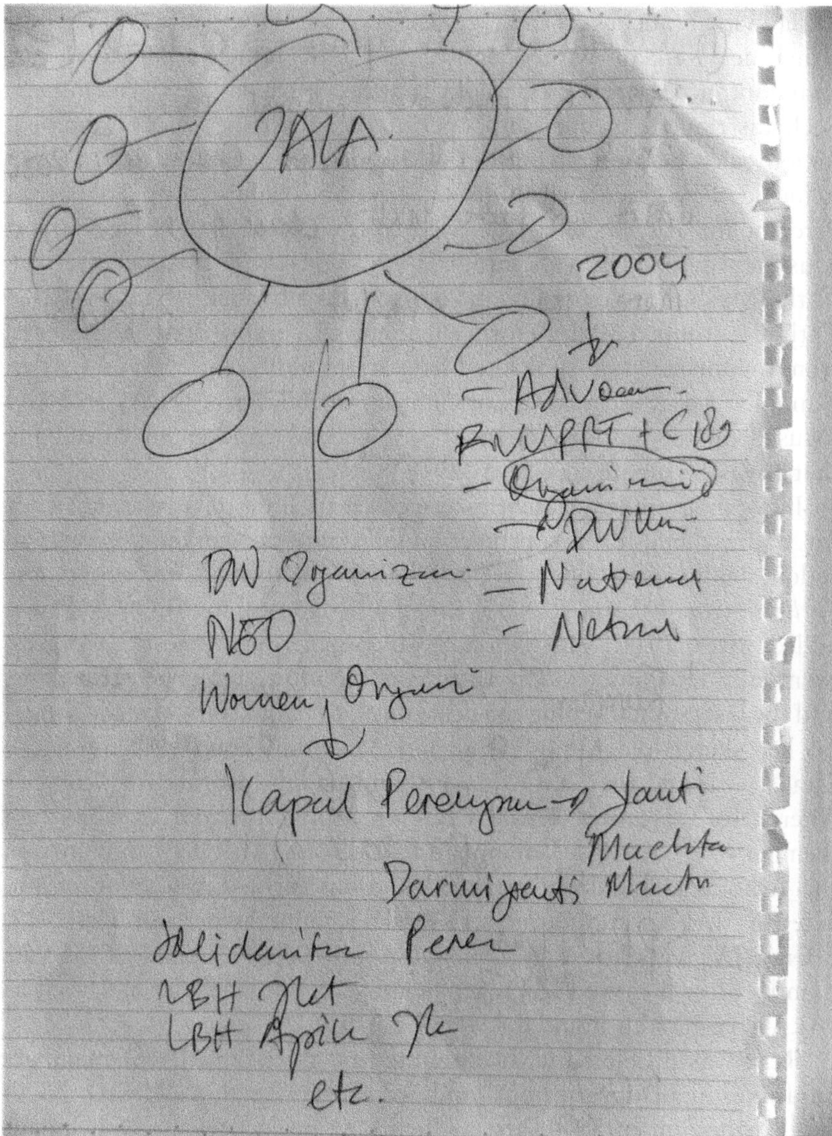

Fig. 3.1 Sketch diagram showing the structure of JALA PRT

The strategy was successful: membership grew from the original twelve to fifty-six by 2015.[9] Seventeen organizations were based in Jakarta

9 The membership list for May 2015 posted on the JALA website (jalaprt.org) is no longer accessible. The author has a paper copy.

(some with branches in the regions), six were in Yogyakarta, and the remainder were in West, Central, and East Java, Bali, Flores, East Kalimantan, Lampung, Lombok, Makassar, Medan, and Palembang. Such distributed membership opened the possibility of coordinated, nationwide "acts of citizenship". Membership was eclectic. In 2015 it included the secular feminist and human rights group Solidaritas Perempuan; Fatayat NU, the women's wing of Indonesia's largest Muslim organization Nahdlatul Ulama; KOHATI, the women's section of the Muslim Students Organization; Mitra Imadei, a Jakarta-based Catholic group; FSPSI Reformasi, the trade union that had seceded from the former state-sponsored federation, FSPSI, in 1999; and, as an example of a group with its orientation outside Java, ODA, an NGO focused on the empowerment of women and children in Palembang that I was fortunate to visit in 2015.[10]

Lita's diagram lists activities agreed on in 2004. First was advocacy for a draft bill for the protection of domestic workers, known in Indonesia by its acronym RUU PPRT (*Rancangan Undang-Undang Perlindungan Pekerja Rumah Tangga*). Advocacy for ILO C189 was added after 2011. The second was organizing domestic workers, eventually into unions. The third was mounting national campaigns, and the last, strengthening the network. Lita named only one individual on her sketch diagram, Darmiyanti Muchtar (Yanti). According to Lita, Yanti, and the NGO she co-founded, the Institute for Women's Alternative Education (KAPAL Perempuan), had played "a more than member role". KAPAL Perempuan had helped JALA get funding from the Ashoka Foundation, provided a room for JALA to work from, acted as JALA's secretariat and bank account holder, and in 2013, offered JALA its house in Kalibata, South Jakarta, rent-free for four months after it moved to bigger premises.[11] The house then served as JALA's base and a home for its coordinator.

Rent was problematic. It amounted to more than JALA members paid in annual subscriptions (and not everyone paid). A Dutch NGO funded the rent in 2014, after which ILO project resources helped.[12] Having a physical base in an area popular with NGOs and near a station underpinned JALA's political presence and allowed for

10 The FSPSI or Federation of All-Indonesia Workers' Unions was established in 1993. For an account of trade unions operating in Indonesia in 2004, see Ford (2014).

11 Interview with Lita Anggraini, Jakarta, 30 July 2015. Sadly, Yanti Muchtar died in November 2015 before I could meet her.

12 Interview with Lita Anggraini, Jakarta, 30 July 2015.

various activities. My observations in 2015 and 2016, by way of illustration, included the network's monthly planning and strategy meetings, training sessions and events for PRT, a communications team meeting, media interviews, visits by overseas researchers, a focus group, and a day-long celebration of International Domestic Workers' Day. All this was in addition to the report writing, communication, and administration needed to keep the network running. JALA also offered space to other groups, building goodwill. On two occasions, for example, I encountered members of the Urban Poor Consortium (UPC) gathered around JALA's large table for a meeting.[13] Food was always in evidence. The motorbikes and piles of shoes often seen outside JALA's front door testified to its location at the centre of a web of journeys across the city. Such journeys sustained, extended, and reshaped the relationships on which JALA's politics of presence relied.

Finally, the "etc." and the number of "member circles" on Lita's diagram point to the fact that, although cash-strapped, JALA had friends. Some were influential, internationally known, and conversant with political processes, Nursyahbani Katjasungkana being an outstanding example.[14] Some had detailed knowledge of domestic work; indeed, Nursyahbani told me that LBH (where she used to work) had embarked on research and advocacy on behalf of PRT in Jakarta in the 1980s and '90s when a new provincial regulation, "Local Ordinance No. 6/1993 on Improving the Welfare of Domestic Workers", was under discussion. She and Wiladi Budiharga, former director of LBH, had argued then that relationships between employer and domestic worker should be contractual.[15]

---

13 The Urban Poor Consortium (UPC) was a network of NGO activists, journalists, academics, and professionals formed in 1997. The UPC, like the domestic workers' movement, was inspired by the teaching of Paulo Freire. While UPC was not formally a member of JALA, there were close links between the organizations (Urban Poor Consortium 2016).

14 Nursyahbani Katjasungkana was amongst the feminist MPs elected to parliament in 2004. A founder member of Solidaritas Perempuan and one of seven human rights lawyers who founded LBH APIK in 1995, she served as a member of the DPR between 1999 and 2004.

15 Meeting with Nursyahbani Katjasungkana and Wiladi Budiharga, Jakarta, 4 August 2015. The ILO publication *Bunga di Atas Pedas* (Flowers on the Rock) (Putranto et al. 2004) cites a research paper by Katjasungkana written in 1997/8 and a seminar presentation by Budiharga in 2000, both related to child domestic work.

Additionally, by 2004, several of RTND's founders were in Jakarta: Maria Pakpahan was working for various NGOs and international organizations and in 2005 was appointed to the executive board of the National Awakening Party,[16] while Yuni Rahayu and Aida Milasari were running a domestic workers' organization modelled on RTND. And it was, I was told, through "two friends" that JALA got its first Draft Domestic Workers Bill onto the DPR's priority list of legislation in 2004. Just as had been the case in Yogyakarta, feminist networks and personal loyalties fostered through student and pro-democracy activism in the 1980s and '90s provided a platform for JALA's politics of presence in the capital after 2004.

Neighbourhoods

Two domestic worker organizations in Jakarta that joined JALA, Mitra Imadei (MI) and Rumpun Gema Perempuan (RGP), had neighbourhood work with PRT at the heart of their missions. MI, established in 2005, was built on an existing Catholic women's group (Mitra Imadei 2011). RGP shared the nomenclature *Rumpun* – a term that signified "standing together" – with its sister NGO in Yogyakarta, while *Gema Perempuan* ('the big voice of women') proclaimed its feminist stance.[17] Both organizations sought out domestic workers in poorer districts, renting premises that they made as much "like a house, like a home" as possible, with small kitchens and spaces for exhausted PRT to rest and socialize.[18] Both hired field staff or used volunteers to go door to door to locate PRT and encourage them to come to "learn to sew, bake a cake, use a computer" or "access the government's non-formal education scheme"[19] Both helped PRT resolve issues with employers or report abuse. Rina Satdewi (Satdewi), programme manager for MI, confessed that recruitment and retention were difficult: "it's a challenge, around fifteen PRT come along to monthly meetings [...] you have to reassure them it's going to be useful, but they will all come for something special like a writing class".[20] The two NGOs reached neighbourhoods in (at least) South Jakarta (Pasar Minggu, Kemuning),

16 Interview with Maria Pakpahan, Edinburgh, 9 August 2017. Gus Dur, whom we met in Chapter 2, was the leader of the National Awakening Party (Partai Kebangkitan Bangsa, PKB), founded at his home in Jakarta in June 1998.

17 Interview with Aida Milasari, Jakarta, 2 July 2015.

18 Fieldnotes, visit to domestic workers school, Jakarta, 19 February 2016.

19 Interview with Rina Satdewi, Jakarta, 22 June 2015.

20 Interview with Rina Satdewi, Jakarta, 22 June 2015.

Bekasi (Tambun and Babelan), Depok, Tangerang (Pamulang), and Bogor (Parung), acquiring expertise in supporting child domestic workers (Milasari 2005: 38; Mitra Imadei 2011). Focusing on children helped locate them (and JALA by association) on the moral high ground.

In addition to moral and political legitimacy, these neighbourhood groups provided data for advocacy. Aida Milasari, who had been RTND's programme director from 1997 to 1999, until she moved to Jakarta and began work with RGP (becoming its executive director in 2006), listed nine research projects she had been involved in between 1994 and 2009 on her online CV (Milasari 2009). International agencies criticized Indonesian government statistics as inaccurate, "designed to undercount" or hide issues behind "big national data" (Sheppard 2009: 41). They used groups like RGP with access to PRT, employers, and local officials to obtain vivid details and better estimates. Drawing on neighbourhood knowledge, JALA could ensure that "the reality of domestic work" featured in influential, internationally circulating reports such as those compiled by Human Rights Watch: *Always on Call* (2005), *Swept Under the Rug* (HRW 2006), and *Workers in the Shadows* (HRW 2009). While LBH and LBH APIK catalogued abuse cases that came to their notice, domestic worker NGOs in neighbourhoods brought information about everyday exploitation to international audiences. Lacking credible data of their own, it was difficult for Indonesian governments to dismiss such a "politics of presence" out of hand.

Both groups became testing grounds for education and awareness-raising programmes, developing the domestic workers school pioneered in Yogyakarta. The ILO and Indonesian governments funded some of this work, especially if child domestic workers were involved. Both RGP and MI advocated returning children to school wherever possible. To this end, activists spoke to religious leaders and parents about gender discrimination and the need for girls to finish high school.[21] Sofia Opie (Opi), recruited by Aida Milasari (her neighbour), described how lessons for child domestic workers operated in practice. When they discussed gender, she recalled, "domestic workers reacted by saying '*oh, begitu*'" (oh, it's like that), they recognized what was being described and were "happy, but sometimes fearful" about sharing experiences. Organizers got to know their neighbourhoods. Opi, for example, visited one abuse victim in her home, spoke to neighbours

21 Interview with Aida Milasari, Jakarta, 6 July 2015.

and local security officers, built a dossier of evidence, and helped the victim take her case to the police (who, she remembered, "hated everything to do with LSM" (*Lembaga Sadaya Masyarakat*, people's self-supporting organizations). The case went successfully to court.[22] Diah Rofika, also recruited by Aida as a community organizer in 2009, told a similar story. "We went door to door recruiting domestic workers [...] our money came from the ILO [...] at the school we taught them [PRT] how to negotiate with employers", she said.[23] When I visited one RGP group in 2015, the meeting room walls were adorned with life-journey maps made by PRT. The informal "school" session dealt with the minimum wage in an exercise designed to support workers having tricky conversations with employers about pay.[24]

Awareness-raising could be a prelude to some PRT becoming involved politically. As Rina Satdewi explained:

> When there's an *aksi*, I choose two or three potential activists to join us. Going on such action is significant for them, so I talk with them beforehand to ensure they have the time. I feel that they must choose for themselves [...] if they do, that helps us develop them into activists for the future.[25]

As they shared experiences in safe, semi-private spaces, domestic workers became, in Sassen's language, more "present to each other". Valued by some PRT as a home-from-home, belonging to a neighbourhood group also prepared some PRT to operate in more overtly political fields.

Lobby Rooms

In February 2022, Lita Anggraini looked back on eighteen years of lobbying. Ruefully she reflected that, too often, parliamentarians had promised to promote a domestic worker law but had withdrawn support "in the middle of the road". Meanwhile, "rumours circulated" that PRT demands were "grandiose" (Luviana and Utami 2022). Other pro-women or pro-labour activists faced similar problems. Indonesian political parties are not policy-driven, and no single party represents

22 Interview with Sofia Opie, Jakarta, 22 June 2015. The term "LSM" was introduced in the Suharto era to overcome perceptions of NGOs as anti-government groups and later used somewhat interchangeably with "NGO" (Eldridge 1996: 20–21).

23 Interview with Diah Rofika, Jakarta, 16 November 2016.

24 Fieldnotes, Jakarta, 19 February 2016, 16 November 2016.

25 Interview with Rina Satdewi, Jakarta, 27 July 2015.

the interests of workers. Law-making is complex. Eleven parliamentary committees (*komisi*) can propose new laws to a Legislative Council (*Baleg*), which, in turn, decides on priorities and sends proposals to the president for approval. Once approved in principle, a special committee addresses issues raised by ministers, other commissions, or political parties and seeks the consent of all the main *fraksi* or party caucuses. Finally, another committee sends the bill to a Plenary for ratification.[26] Along this tortuous route, committee membership may alter, individual politicians may change their minds or government departments delay proceedings. Bills can be left in abeyance, and few MPs are likely to know much about legislation from committees other than their own (Sherlock 2012, 2020). To counter such challenges, forty-five feminist and women's rights organizations (including JALA PRT) had agreed in 2005 to support each other's advocacy, discovering, however, that joint working could engender disagreements about leadership, strategy or the content and wording of draft bills under discussion. When a Gender Equality Bill was mooted in 2011, for example, some groups within the alliance competed rather than cooperated. The result was that, initially, time and energy was wasted as groups drafted different responses. Some wanted to include overtly feminist language and radical demands, others took a more pragmatic line (Poerwandari et al. 2018).

Following the pattern established during a successful campaign for the Law on the Eradication of Domestic Violence, enacted in 2004, JALA took a proactive approach.[27] JALA PRT and the National Commission on Violence against Women (Komnas Perempuan) jointly researched the condition of domestic workers in ten cities. Lawyers and activists then wrote a draft law and persuaded "friends" in the DPR to propose it as a priority for the 2004 to 2009 parliament. After that, the movement kept up its advocacy and lobbying. Consequently, versions of the Bill have been under consideration in almost every parliament up to the time of writing (mid-2023). My discussions with some of the activists and workers involved give a sense of what keeping a bill on the agenda for so long has entailed.

First, established organizations used their connections to help JALA get through the doors of committee rooms or government offices. Rena

26 Some *fraksi* represent a single party; others bring smaller parties together. They are represented on all the parliamentary commissions. For a discussion of the relationship between parties, commissions, and *fraksi,* see Sherlock (2012).

27 For a detailed comparison of advocacy in relation to the anti-domestic violence law and the RUU PPRT up to 2016, see Eddyono et al. (2016).

Herdiyani, who has held several positions including that of executive director with Kalyanamitra, one of Indonesia's longest-established (since 2003) feminist organizations, explained to me that:

> Lobbying by NGOs often involves getting a hearing from the relevant commission or arranging a meeting with a particular *fraksi*. Success depends on having the right contact person; there is usually a poor response to letters, so activists must cultivate relationships with specific party members.[28]

While all NGOs used contacts to track a bill's progress and identify critical players (Sherlock 2012: 557), JALA faced specific challenges. Nisaa Yura from Solidaritas Perempuan remembered how uncooperative staff in the secretariat and public relations sections of parliament had been when she accompanied Lita Anggraini to the DPR in 2015. JALA representatives were only invited inside when the vice-chair of the Legislative Council happened to come into the waiting area and recognized them. Dewi Tjakrawinata, a member of Indonesia's CEDAW[29] working group, told me that when lobbying for a new citizenship law, she would "just phone ministers or MPs to fix a date for a meeting". When she went with JALA, on the other hand, officials were "not welcoming" and "even the security guys treated us differently, they discriminated".[30] To get heard, she reflected, JALA had to "go through bureaucratic channels", resort to "loud voices", or "get journalists to record what was going on".[31] In such circumstances, members of the network had to agree on "which body we should lobby and talk with" to ensure that precious contacts were kept onside.[32]

JALA's most precious contacts were MPs on Commission 1X or on the Legislative Council. JALA has worked with a succession of politicians, including, in the period up to 2016, Maria Ulfah Anshor (National Awakening Party), Rieke Diah Pitaloka (Indonesian Democratic Party of Struggle), and Okky Asokawati (United Development Party). These

---

28 Interview with Rena Herdiyani, Jakarta, 23 June 2015.

29 The UN Convention on the Elimination of All Forms of Discrimination Against Women.

30 For a discussion of the campaign to challenge gender-discriminatory aspects of Indonesia's citizenship laws see an article posted by the Global Campaign for Equal Nationality Rights (Listyowati and Herdiyani n.d.).

31 Interview with Dewi Tjakrawinata, Jakarta, 29 July 2015.

32 Interview with Pratiwi Febry, Jakarta, 28 July 2015.

MPs used their "loud voices" on JALA's behalf, capitalizing on their standing inside and outside the DPR. Having Pitaloka or Asokawati at press conferences or meetings guaranteed media interest. A student activist in the 1990s, Pitaloka was famous as a celebrity actor playing a housewife in the long-running sitcom *Bajaj Bajuri*. Entering parliament in 2009 and sitting on Commission 1X, she quickly won a reputation as an outspoken advocate for workers' rights and the Domestic Workers Bill, issues she said in 2010 that are "still far from her Commission's attention" (Kuswandini 2010). Asokawati had a successful career as a beauty queen and fashion model behind her before entering politics. Both developed expertise in PRT issues. In December 2014, trying to keep the RUU PPRT alive, Pitaloka quoted data JALA had given her about the incidence of violence against PRT during 2014 (Samodro 2014). A month later, when the then minister of manpower, Hanif Dhakiri, issued his regulation on domestic work, Asokawati suggested that he was more interested in building his public image than building on "good knowledge" to find workable, comprehensive, and enforceable arrangements to regulate the employment of PRT (Polindo 2012). However, political support could fluctuate. In 2013, for example, Pitaloka stood for election as governor of West Java. She missed a crucial meeting of the Legislative Council at which the Bill went into reverse and was sent back to Commission 1X (Ikhbal 2015a). In 2014, contrary to expectations, Jokowi did not appoint Pitaloka to the post of minister of manpower. Activists then had to build new links.

I was unable to meet Pitaloka and Asokawati during my fieldwork. I did meet Irma Suryani, elected to the DPR in 2014. She had been introduced to JALA PRT by Manna Nababan, a DPR staff member who had worked with Komnas Perempuan and knew Lita Anggraini well. Suryani became a vocal champion of the RUU PPRT.[33] When I interviewed her at the DPR, she told me that even supposedly informed members of Commission 1X "are not on the same page" as JALA in terms of wages, leave, or professionalization, all of which were deemed too costly for employers. Rather than responding to evidence of abuse, some MPs saw JALA as an impatient and overly pushy irritant.[34]

33 Suryani was still supporting the RUU PPRT in March 2023 when she accused DPR leaders who had just postponed deliberation on the Bill of "violating" the human rights and constitutional rights of PRT as citizens (VOI 2023).

34 Interview with Irma Suryani and Manna Nababan, Jakarta, 3 August 2015.

Second, experienced lobbyists judged that their presence helped project JALA's case persuasively. They ensured that JALA's draft bills and academic papers were of high quality. As one informant from LBH Jakarta put it:

> We push the advocacy by helping JALA with legal drafting; you see, you know, they are really brilliant feminists and have a good understanding of what they want in law. Still, sometimes when they put it into the draft, you know, we should admit that legal drafting is a skill not all people have.[35]

Since members of DPR committees often lacked detailed knowledge of their areas, specialist input from NGOs like LBH could be influential (Sherlock 2012: 562). Well-honed presentation skills were also invaluable. Dewi Tjakrawinata, for example, mentioned that as "the only person in JALA with an MBA", she was often the one to "open proceedings" at meetings with ministers or parliamentarians, providing "just the pointers" and "making it nice". Lita Anggraini would follow up "with all the data" when questions were asked.

While the change of name from helper to worker was a red line, experienced activists argued that a degree of fuzziness in the use of language would render JALA's messages more palatable. One informant reflected that it made sense to "moderate our language sometimes [...] in the spirit of compromise".[36] Another explained that:

> There is no need to bring up feminist terminology. We have Pancasila and, you know [...] when we mention "human rights", it doesn't make sense to people, but when we say that Pancasila ensures justice and humanity and that our constitution has many clauses protecting human rights [...] and we say that feminism is about fulfilling the rights of men and women [...] if people don't accept feminism, we use these terms.[37]

When they linked domestic worker claims with Pancasila, activists emphasized shared citizenship and national identity. Pancasila is Indonesia's state ideology, enshrined in the 1945 Constitution. It consists of five principles: consultative democracy, social justice,

35 Interview with Pratiwi Febry, Jakarta, 28 July 2015.

36 Interview with Ratna Batara Munti, Jakarta, 31 July 2015.

37 Interview with Pratiwi Febry, Jakarta, 28 July 2015.

humanitarianism, the unity of Indonesia, and belief in a single God. Looking for shared values in lobbying, JALA's leaders countered accusations from MPs that the notion of domestic worker rights had come from "the foreigners" and should be dismissed as "western" pontificating.[38]

Third, JALA lobbyists sought to show that they understood employers' perspectives. The tactic was deliberate, as Dewi Tjakrawinata explained:

> Lita put me in a meeting with the minister to show that it is not only PRT in the movement, but there are also employers of PRT like me who are also joining; they put me on that side. I have the experience and empathy for the employers; that's what I can contribute. We argue that the Bill will be good for employers and PRT.[39]

Dewi's presence and personage, as well as her words, were intended to reassure politicians that employment contracts could address employers' anxieties (such as those discussed in Chapter 1) and enhance domestic harmony. Yuniyanti Chuzaifah (Yuni), chair of Komnas Perempuan from 2010 to 2014 and later its vice-chair, believed such arguments might persuade "influential wives of high officials to support a domestic worker law". She felt that strategic compromise was called for; even if, as feminists, JALA disagreed with the gender politics practised by some women's organizations, activists needed to "accommodate them, embrace them, sit with them". Only this could counter an already apparent backlash, Yuni had warned.[40]

However, calls for compromise exposed differences. The minimum wage was one area of dispute. Anggraini's starting point was clear: a minimum wage was a crucial battleground. She understood that not everyone who needed a domestic worker earned high salaries, but argued this was no excuse for holding domestic workers' pay down. Governments should subsidize childcare and, at a tribunal meeting on the minimum wage, she warned that unless the annual calculations of the minimum wage included an element for childcare and domestic work, "companies will resist [...] and the last victim will be the domestic worker". Speaking out against the tradition of PRT being "one of the family", Lita went on:

38 Interview with Nisaa Yura, Jakarta, 29 July 2015.
39 Interview with Dewi Tjakrawinata, Jakarta, 29 July 2015.
40 Interview with Yuniyanti Chuzaifah, Jakarta, 12 August 2015.

> It is not a matter of becoming part of the employer's family; they [PRT] want to earn money for their own families and their children [...] when they go out to work, they are looking for a better life all round.[41]

Other network members shared these views. As one informant recalled, "we told Lita at the beginning, you have to have a standard [wage] because this is what is happening in Jakarta; some people are only paying Rp.300,000 (USD30) to their PRT".[42]

While such statements were unequivocal, some within the JALA network were concerned that MPs might become "very paranoid" or "feel frightened" about what it might cost their own households if PRT wages matched the minimum wage. Worries might make them "stop thinking about solutions but just talk about themselves".[43] As one activist told me:

> At least one MP has eight or ten maids. Can you imagine [...] it's an issue of class; they don't want to leave their comfort zones. [...] They become MPs for the money, get paid a lot, and get backsheesh from everybody who wants to pass a law.[44]

By choosing the word "backsheesh", this activist, a fluent English speaker, was reflecting a widely held view that individual MPs accepted bribes to advocate for and broker specific pieces of legislation (Meitzner 2007: 239–52; Reuters 2015: 15). Another long-time JALA member made the same point. "We simply don't have money behind us", she expostulated, "if you want a bill passed, you have to buy off members of the DPR to vote for your proposal; that's how it works". She believed that MPs "don't consider the reputation of Indonesia overseas"; for them, "money is what seems to matter".[45]

In such a context, the matter of the minimum wage became contentious.[46] Over time, according to a senior ILO adviser who had been involved with domestic worker projects in Indonesia for many years, JALA lobbyists became "a bit more flexible on this matter [...] before

41 Interview with Lita Anggraini, Jakarta, 27 August 2014.
42 Interview with Dewi Tjakrawinata, Jakarta, 29 July 2015.
43 Interview with Ratna Batara Munti, Jakarta, 31 July 2015.
44 Interview, Jakarta, 29 July 2015.
45 Interview, Jakarta, 6 July 2015.
46 For details on differences between Komnas Perempuan and JALA PRT over issues such as the minimum wage, see Eddyono et al. (2016: 82–4).

it was no, no, no, they must get the minimum wage".[47] Later, JALA pushed for what was termed a "standard wage" to be discussed in regional wages' councils – a short-term concession, perhaps – since precise figures could be negotiated later.[48] Such blurring of precision over critical elements of domestic worker rights was inherent in the transversal "politics of presence" with which the network had to engage in order to keep its legislative goals on the DPR's agenda.

Finally, a gender-based "affective solidarity" between network members enabled individuals to survive what could be traumatic experiences of lobbying. As Hemmings has elucidated, shared experiences of "rage, frustration, passion, pleasure" can be crucial in "building a sustainable feminist politics of transformation", even "against the odds" (2012: 148, 158). Nisaa Yura, from Solidaritas Perempuan, told me a story of a discussion about the sexual abuse of domestic workers that underscores Hemmings's point. She recalled a meeting with members of the DPR she had attended with Lita Anggraini in these words:

> Sometimes I feel low. For example, there was a moment when we did the hunger strike, and I went with Lita to a meeting [...] one member of Baleg accused domestic workers of being too aggressive. He said PRT claim to have been raped by their employers. But, he continued, when he asks, "How many times?" and they say, "It's six times", he will tell them, "It's not rape but a pleasure, you know."[49]

Appalled to hear this denial of women's experiences from a leading parliamentarian, Nisaa confessed that on this occasion:

> Lita really had to calm me down, you know it's usually Lita who is angry, but this time my young blood, I could not do anything [...] I felt like I could not move, I just wanted to sit in a corner, I was so shocked. But Lita told me that's what we face, and it's not only one person, but you will meet more like that, she said.[50]

As Gutiérrez-Rodríguez emphasizes in her discussion of domestic workers in Europe, "wounds and pain are thus not individually felt, but

47 Interview with Arum Ratnawati, Jakarta, 24 August 2014.
48 See Pratiwi (2017: 207–8) for the principles behind JALA's arguments for the minimum wage.
49 Interview with Nisaa Yura, Jakarta, 29 July 2015.
50 Interview with Nisaa Yura, Jakarta, 29 July 2015.

affectively sensed as a social moment of collective suffering", propelling workers to come out of hiding and become engaged politically, making their communal presence felt (2009: 147). Similarly, Fish argues in her study of the struggle for C189 that experiences of having their voices stifled by officialdom or being forced to "swallow" emotions boosted domestic workers' determination to make their collective political presence felt (2017: 95). For JALA, continued activism in the face of widespread opposition depended on building such resilience and deepening the bonds of affective solidarity across its membership.

Facing opposition in the DPR, JALA supporters intensified efforts to proselytize. In July 2015 I attended a workshop on domestic workers hosted by the National Commission on Violence against Women (Komnas Perempuan, KP). One of KP's vice chairs, Magdalena Sitorus, spoke at length. The official minutes of the discussion say that she urged women representing mass-membership groups such as Aisyiyah, KOWANI, Fatayat NU, and the PKK to "share the tasks so that the Bill can be a priority in 2016" and exhorted "women in every organization to socialize this and use their political connections" (Yuniasari 2015).[51] Not everyone in the room responded enthusiastically; one representative spoke nostalgically about PRT of the past who worked out of "dedication". She argued against the minimum wage and stated that while employers in Hong Kong might mistreat workers, "in this country, it is not so". Another attendee pleaded for pensioners who, she felt, could not possibly pay PRT more. One, I noted (though the comment did not appear in the official minutes), spoke of the rudeness of "modern" PRT; they even, she said, "sit on the chairs".[52]

Others were more encouraging. Some agreed to undertake "*sosialisasi*" of the Bill by discussing it within their home organizations and amongst influential friends.[53] Since Komnas Perempuan

---

51 Aisyiyah, established in 1971, is one of Indonesia's largest Islamic mass-membership organizations; KOWANI, an umbrella group founded in 1928, was the official Indonesian Women's Congress during the Suharto period which, post-1998, joined the campaign for an anti-domestic violence law; Fatayat NU is the young women's branch of Indonesia's largest Islamic organization, Nahdlatul Ulama; PKK (Pembinaan Kesejahteraan Keluarga) is the Family Welfare Movement, which had promulgated the state's gender ideology during the Suharto regime.

52 Field notes, Jakarta, 30 July 2015.

53 During the New Order, *sosialisasi* (socialization) referred to top-down processes of persuasion and information-giving used to persuade communities to accept new developments and policies (Gibbings 2017: 98).

enjoyed links with political parties, religious organizations, and regional governments, such offers were important. However, given entrenched attitudes, progress was likely to be slow. Street protests, as the next part of this chapter will show, could perhaps push legislators to act more speedily.

Street Protests, 2009–2015

Demonstrations were an everyday occurrence in post-Suharto Indonesia. Staging a protest, referred to as *unjuk rasa* (show of feeling), *aksi* (action), *demonstrasi* (demonstration), or *reli* (rally), could secure media coverage, exert political leverage, and win a degree of public buy-in (Juliawan 2011: 353–4). At the same time, as Mina Roces persuasively points out, women's rights organizations can use demonstrations as "feminist practice in fashioning women into militant activists" (Roces 2012: 159–60). As did *reformasi* activists, PRT who donned a JALA T-shirt or protest outfit and joined a protest helped establish "a visible and concrete presence" for their movement and, in dressing in a universally recognized activist style, referenced "democratic forces elsewhere" (Lee 2016: 103).

From 2009 onwards, JALA staged a series of set-piece performances and protests in different parts of the capital and other major cities, coming to a crescendo in 2015. Tracing the history of these protests and examining a selection in detail addresses this chapter's questions about alliances, logistics, and gendered moral tales. Through staging demonstrations, JALA cultivated new allies, achieved media prominence, kept their claims on the political agenda, and created a street style, collective history, and unique identity for Indonesia's PRT as activist citizens and members of an emergent domestic worker class.

New Allies

Staging demonstrations was neither cheap nor easy (Juliawan 2011: 360). Activists needed a reasonable number of bodies on the ground and eye-catching costumes, props, or banners to interest a public becoming inured to street action (Padawangi 2014: 38–9; Leitner and Sheppard 2018: 450). With few organized domestic workers in Jakarta to mobilize, JALA looked for new sources of support.

Initially JALA linked with migrant worker NGOs and unions in a grouping known as JAKERLA PRT (Jaringan Kerja Layak Pekerja

Rumah Tangga) (Front Perjuangan Rakyat 2009). JAKERLA members all wanted the government and unions to endorse proposals for an ILO Domestic Workers Convention. Amongst the organizations that joined JAKERLA was the Hong Kong-based Association of Indonesian Migrant Workers (ATKI). ATKI brought the experience of protesting against employment agency practices and underpayments, including organizing a rally of 200 people outside the Indonesian Consulate in 2001 that forced a change of policy (Sim 2009: 65–70). Migrant Care, another JAKERLA supporter, was noted for its strong media profile. A third partner, the Union of Indonesian Migrant Workers or SBMI (Serikat Buruh Migran Indonesia), had branches in several large cities (Ford 2006: 323–5). This accretion of experience increased JALA's capacity to make itself visible.

JAKERLA disbanded once it had secured government support for C189. JALA then turned to Indonesia's trade union confederations. Razian Agus Toniman (Agus), a veteran union organizer and vice-president of the Confederation of Indonesian Trade Unions or KSPI (Konfederasi Serikat Pekerja Indonesia) at the time I met him, explained how his union became involved:

> Lita Anggraini and I already knew each other as fellow activists: Bu [Ibu] Lita was the leader of one movement, and I was a leader of another. After some thought, we decided to come together in 2011 because, essentially, we are both concerned with PRT as workers.

He also outlined what he saw as the advantages for JALA in the alliance:

> Bu Lita was the one who offered this collaboration – she could see how strong KSPI had been in pushing the government on social security and recognized that as we had more power and more members, we could help pressurize the government to pass the Bill. But it was the fact that JALA PRT didn't have many [grassroots] members that drove Bu Lita to make the alliance.[54]

KSPI was the largest of Indonesia's four labour confederations. In theory, its members could swell the numbers at demonstrations. A public alliance with KSPI also countered accusations from politicians

54 Interview with Razian Agus Toniman, Jakarta, 16 February 2016.

that the movement was "just about JALA PRT".[55] Furthermore, as Agus mentioned, between 2010 and 2011, KSPI had played an essential role in a successful social security campaign.

That campaign had been coordinated by an action committee, the Komite Aksi Jaminan Sosial (KAJS). More than a labour union, KAJS was a "civil society alliance of unions, farmers, fisher people, and students", united in defence of the rights of the "Indonesian people" (Cole 2012). KAJS lobbied politicians, prepared "counter-concepts", conducted seminars and public meetings, and monitored parliamentary proceedings. It filed a citizens' lawsuit against the president, vice-president, and speaker of the DPR and bombarded legislators with text messages.[56] When it appeared that the government was not prioritizing the Social Security Implementation Bill, KAJS rallied thousands of workers, threatening to "besiege or, if necessary, occupy the House" (Tjandra 2014: 49–52). Bowing to pressure, parliament passed the Bill on 28 October 2011, proving to unions and NGOs that joint efforts and a presence on the streets could effect change.

Some established trade union leaders recognized the domestic worker movement as an opportunity to build on the success of the social security campaign and expand into the informal sector. A rapid expansion of contract labour and outsourcing in Indonesia had resulted in a decline in traditional union membership (Juliawan 2011). At the same time, the ILO expected unions to support C189.[57] Thus, in August 2012, KSPI and two other sizeable Indonesian trade union confederations, the Confederation of Indonesian Prosperous Labour Unions (KSBSI) and the Confederation of All-Indonesia Workers (KSPSI), joined with JALA, the Union of Indonesian Migrant Workers (SBMI), and JARAK (an NGO Network for the Elimination of Child Labour in Indonesia) and launched an "Action Committee for the Protection of Domestic and Migrant Workers" or KAPPRT-BM (Komite Aksi Perlindungan Pekerja Rumah Tangga-Buruh Migran).[58] Agus served as chair. The ILO encouraged this development and named the new

55 Interview with Arum Ratnawati, Jakarta, 9 July 2015; interview with Irma Suryani, Jakarta, 3 August 2015.

56 Following KAJS's example, in April 2011, JALA PRT submitted a lawsuit accusing members of the government and the DPR of failing to protect its domestic worker citizens (Forum-Pembaca-KOMPAS 2010; Faizal 2011).

57 Interview with Surya Tjandra, Jakarta, 16 February 2016.

58 The two confederations were the Confederation of Indonesian Prosperous Labour Unions (KSBSI) and the Confederation of All-Indonesia Workers (KSPSI).

group as a partner in its six-year project to promote decent work for domestic workers.

However, according to Agus and Sulistri (Sulis) – a senior officer in the Confederation of Indonesian Prosperous Labour Unions (KSBSI), which also joined KAPPRT-BM – it was a struggle to persuade grassroots union members to support the domestic workers' campaign because their own families relied on low-waged PRT. Even leading figures in KSBSI, Sulis told me, had been sceptical. They viewed domestic work as a "gender issue to be taken care of by women only" and felt that PRT were unlikely to pay union dues. Nevertheless, Sulis had become "good friends" with Lita Anggraini after meeting her at activist gatherings and had recruited some 70 PRT to the KSBSI and offered them training in organizing.[59] Meanwhile, Sulis used her position in the union to promote the RUU PPRT.

KAPPRT-BM took the lead in organizing demonstrations. As Agus explained:

> We are the planners, the organizers, and the executors. We estimate the budget depending on the properties needed for what's planned. The money comes from each member. We divide the tasks among all the members; one takes on the official licence, another handles publicity, and so on.[60]

From 2012 onwards, KAPPRT-BM members provided command vehicles, megaphones, marshals, props, large banners and flags, and drinks and snacks for participants. They communicated with political contacts behind the scenes and during parliamentary committee meetings. Their political acumen, muscle power, and material contributions as new allies enabled JALA PRT to build a stronger presence in parliament, on the streets, and in the media

JALA activists I met had vivid memories of protests. While they might mention megaphones, marching, the heat, or the rain, they did not always recall dates or link their recollections with a particular happening. To complement evidence from participants, I collected photographs and accounts of thirty demonstrations involving JALA between 2009 and 2016 using the search terms *unjuk rasa pekerja rumah tangga* (demonstration of domestic workers) and *mogok makan*

59 Within Indonesia, documents refer to Sulis simply as "Sulistri"; in the online records of her activities in regional or international settings, both "Sulistri Sulistri" and "Sulis Afrilestron" can be found.

60 Interview with Razian Agus Toniman, Jakarta, 16 February 2016.

PRT (PRT hunger strike). Though not comprehensive – my list did not include, for example, a protest on Women's Day 2016 when I photographed a JALA activist standing atop a command vehicle and wielding a megaphone at Monas, Indonesia's 132-metre-tall National Monument – the materials indicate what press and NGO photographers found arresting, document the evolution of a PRT activist style, and offer insights into the experience of participating.

Occupying different spaces in the city, JALA PRT used costumes, props, performance, and location to create a disruptive assemblage of the female domestic worker that brought the bandana and the dishcloth, laundry maid and loudhailer, *kampung* and gated suburb or high-rise superblock into conversation.[61]

Fashioning a PRT Street Style: 2009–2011

On 15 February 2009, 14 February 2010, and 14 February 2011, JALA and its allies staged demonstrations – including the one described at the beginning of this chapter – to publicize what they had dubbed National Domestic Workers' Day (NDWD). At these protests, activists used elements of a "maid's uniform" to establish an arresting visual identity and media-savvy street style for Indonesia's PRT. Incorporating the positive values ascribed to work uniforms in Indonesia and adding legitimacy through association with Indonesia's protest traditions (Austin 2022: 30–32), JALA depicted PRT as vulnerable, virtuous, disciplined, and self-sacrificing national heroines, but with a twist. PRT were also ready to make their collective presence felt on the streets.

JALA had chosen 15 February to commemorate the death of a fourteen-year-old child domestic worker named Sunarsih in 2001. Working in a household in Surabaya (the provincial capital of East Java), Sunarsih had been subject to sustained abuse: shockingly, the employer, who had a history of violence towards PRT, received a mere two-year prison sentence (Sheppard 2009: 16). PRT in East Java and Yogyakarta had held rallies on or around 15 February since 2007, but in 2009 JALA PRT seized the opportunity offered by consultations surrounding an ILO Convention to demonstrate in the capital. Establishing a pattern of annual remembrances reflected a tradition associated with Marsinah, the young woman factory worker who was

61 For the notion of city spaces being in conversation, see Kusno (2010). In using the idea of assemblage to understand the portrayals of domestic workers, I draw on Ally's (2013) discussion of domestic work and advertisements for soap powder in South Africa.

infamously tortured, raped and murdered in East Java in 1993 while taking a leading role in industrial action (Weix 2002). The Marsinah case had become a national scandal; for Lita Anggraini, speaking to assembled journalists, abuse of PRT was similarly scandalous – "our problem", she averred – since "so many Indonesian families" employ domestic workers in their homes (Sabarini 2009).

Costume Uniforms and Cut-outs: National Domestic Workers' Day 2009

The 2009 demonstration was held at the iconic Hotel Indonesia roundabout in central Jakarta. Constructed by President Sukarno when Indonesia hosted the Asian Games in 1962 and used by him for state-sponsored celebrations, the roundabout had been the site of some of the vast student-led pro-democracy demonstrations of May 1998 that led to Suharto's downfall. With fountains, trees, iconic buildings, and the unmistakable "Welcome Monument" as a backdrop, photojournalists could shoot arresting pictures of even small-scale *aksi* (Padawangi 2013: 858). For women's rights activists, the roundabout had additional resonance as the place of the feminist-led "Voice of Concerned Mothers" (*Suara Ibu Peduli*), or SIP demonstration staged in February 1998, the first of the protests presaging the end of authoritarian rule. That demonstration won extensive media coverage and public sympathy through its strategic emphasis on motherhood and its deployment of peaceful performative elements such as the reciting of prayers or distribution of flowers and milk powder to motorists and passers-by (Arivia and Subono 2017: 16–19).

National Domestic Workers' Day 2009 likewise focused on peaceful performativity. A *Jakarta Post* reporter estimated that around 100 PRT and 200 supporters attended (Sabarini 2009). Lita Anggraini presented the protestors' demands in press releases and interviews. First, they wanted the government to declare 15 February an official holiday for PRT and guarantee domestic workers one day off a week. Second, they wanted the DPR to resume debate on the draft Domestic Workers Bill that had not progressed significantly since JALA proposed it for discussion in 2004. Finally, they urged the public and employers to view PRT as essential workers entitled to state protection from workplace abuse. During the event, PRT posed for photographs, made speeches, paraded giant painted placards and banners, and performed a play about the life of a PRT. Throughout, supporters handed leaflets to motorists who slowed down to stare.

Figures 3.2 and 3.3 illustrate the attention-grabbing costumes some protestors wore. During the proceedings, eighteen PRT stood in line at the edge of the roundabout, open to public view. Their "uniforms" consisted of a white T-shirt, a white apron, and for some, a *serbet* headscarf that was simply one of the kitchen cloths used by millions of Indonesians every day for dusting, drying dishes, or wiping up spills. Cheap and easy to hand out to protestors, the *serbet* was eye-catching and instantly recognizable, I was told, as the badge of a "helper" because of its regular appearance in a TV comedy featuring a male domestic worker often seen with a *serbet* over his shoulder or in his pocket.[62] Answering journalists' questions about the headscarf gave Lita Anggraini and other spokespersons the chance to explain that the *serbet* is one of the PRT's "tools of the trade" and that domestic work is "as noble as" other occupations (Saragih 2010). Like an apron, the *serbet* was familiar yet startlingly out of place on the street.

Passers-by could hardly miss the crimson lettering on the brilliant white aprons. The letters spelt out "*15 Pebruari Hari PRT*" (15 February Domestic Workers' Day). On what seems to have been its first appearance (I found no photographs depicting a maid's uniform before this event), the professionalism of a white uniform was interposed with the heroic, sacrificial red of Indonesia's flag, reminding onlookers that PRT are citizens as well as "maids". Seeing PRT bodies dressed like this was likely to jolt the senses – domestic workers were not expected, after all, to move much beyond their employers' backyards (Amnesty International 2007: 26, 40).

Apart from their outfits, the women appear quite ordinary. Described as "*ibu*" (mothers), they were members of a women's school established in 2003 by one of JALA's closest allies, KAPAL Perempuan, in a densely packed neighbourhood on the banks of Jakarta's polluted River Ciliwung (Institut KAPAL Perempuan 2016). Few women living there had completed high school, and many worked as PRT. The women's sparkling outfits metaphorically brought them, and the hitherto hidden bodies of other PRT, to light. Modest napkin-headscarves (or other headgear including the fitted Islamic *jilbab*) over pulled-back hair and enveloping aprons repudiated any resemblances to "Inem the sexy maid", the eponymous heroine of an ever-popular Indonesian film. Rather, the image is of hardworking but vulnerable women, more akin to housemaids or nurses than traditional PRT who might wear old clothes to work, as a rule. The grave, perhaps diffident, looks on the faces of some of the women who stand with their arms

62 Interview with Ririn Sulastri, Yogyakarta, 24 February 2016.

Fig. 3.2 Headscarf and apron: Demonstration at the Hotel Indonesia roundabout, 15 February 2009 (Photo: TEMPO/Adi Irianto)

Fig. 3.3 In line at the Hotel Indonesia roundabout: Domestic Workers' Day, 2009 (Photo: TEMPO/Adi Irianto)

at their sides to allow the red letters to be seen help create an image of virtuous vulnerability.

The women from Ciliwung were not the only PRT attracting attention in 2009. Photographs on JALA PRT's Flickr pages show that during the afternoon, women and girls from groups convened by Mitra Imadei, one of the NGOs discussed earlier in this chapter, were amongst those who carried large cardboard cut-out images of male and female employers abusing PRT around the periphery of the roundabout. Painted in the comic strip style of the activist art that flourished in post-*reformasi* cities, the cut-outs were designed to disconcert. One, for example, carried the words "*Pelecehan Seksual*" (Sexual Abuse). It depicted an employer entering the room of a PRT who kneels before him wearing nothing except a bright red bra and pants. Her wrists are bound, her mouth gagged, and tears fall from her eyes. Another cut-out demanded that child domestic workers be given time to attend school.

Aprons, headscarves, and cardboard cut-outs created vivid images of PRT as victims, workers, and activists. Sayuti, a leading member of Tunas Mulia who had travelled from Yogyakarta to be there, encouraged PRT participants to affirm their worker identities during the speechmaking part of the protest. Turning to the crowd, she asked rhetorically, "Who calls themselves *pembantu* [helper] here?". The response was unequivocal: "We should stop calling ourselves *pembantu*. We are workers!", came the reply (Sabarini 2009).

The 2009 NDWD demonstration won extensive media coverage. Reporters noted the surprisingly large numbers present, the novel use of aprons, *serbet*, and kitchen utensils, retold the Sunarsih story, and mentioned motorists showing support. Though there was no overnight success, Indonesia's parliament placed the RUU PPRT on its list of legislation for 2010.

Activist Citizens: National Domestic Workers' Day 2010

In February 2010, NDWD was even more ambitious. Photographs and accounts of what transpired – already outlined at the beginning of this chapter – show that on this occasion, "work uniforms" and the *serbet* created an iconography that situated PRT as members of the "family" of the nation entitled to rights under the 1945 Constitution.

The notion of PRT as citizens was highlighted when the deputy minister for women's empowerment and child protection opened proceedings (the minister herself did not show) and by the appearance of Rieke Diah Pitaloka, acting on this occasion in her role as one of three goodwill ambassadors for migrant workers appointed by the ILO in December 2008. Further establishing the tone of a semi-official ceremony, the head of the ILO office in Jakarta also spoke. Around a hundred PRT or returned migrant domestic workers attended, together with 200 supporters (Saherman 2010). This was a similar turnout to that achieved in 2009. To maximize impact, participants had assembled at the National Monument, Monas, before marching along the highway to the main venue, Proclamation Park. Organizers provided lunches, and afterwards, some PRT were bussed to the HI Roundabout to unfurl the Love Napkin there.

Figure 3.4 shows the outfits worn by some of the PRT participants. All wear the *serbet* headscarf. Almost all wear an official T-shirt, although one group stands out in pink. Marshalled in front of the monumental statues of the nation's founding fathers, Sukarno and Hatta, the assembled PRT appear as a disciplined army ready to do the nation's bidding. Their "uniforms" resemble the company outfits worn by female factory workers or issued to migrant domestic workers by employment agencies in Malaysia or Singapore (Killias 2018; Warouw 2004). Those workers were recognized members of the nation's workforce whose uniforms placed them above the everyday Indonesian PRT. Stitching the Love Napkin, as Lita explained to a journalist, was "intentionally linked to Valentine's Day"; the hope was that it could be a symbol of a new "love and care in the community towards domestic workers" (Kompas 2010a).

However, the message of 2010 is not acceptance of the status quo. The PRT lined up demurely are wearing T-shirts printed with the ILO logo, pictures of the vital tasks PRT perform, and the slogan "PRT=Pekerja", not the logos of employment agencies. A cartoon-style image of a multi-armed PRT brandishing work tools takes up half the space on a stand-up banner propped in front of the plaque bearing the words of the Declaration of Independence. That image evokes stock representations – likely to have been familiar to all present – of the brave young Indonesian warriors, armed only with sharpened bamboo sticks, who fought against the Dutch between 1945 and 1949 (Strassler 2006: 58). Student protestors in the 1990s adopted a similar style, tying red and white bandanas around their heads to show their allegiance (Lee 2016: 91–4). Coincidentally perhaps, the speaker holding the microphone in Figure 3.4 has tied her *serbet* bandana style. Her appeal is not simply to the press or politicians but to the promises of equality and social justice made in 1945.

As in 2009, red played a role. The finished Love Napkin, a section of which is shown in Figure 3.5, was covered with blood-red letters spelling out the movement's demands, situating PRT as heirs to the "political and chromatic redness" of protests staged during *reformasi* (Lee 2016: 86–7). Red and white colourways, those of Indonesia's flag,

Fig. 3.4 National Domestic Workers' Day, 14 February 2010 (Photo: Saherman)

Fig. 3.5 Sewing the giant napkin together, 14 February 2010 (Photo: Saherman)

emphasized that PRT were citizens entitled to the state's protection. At the same time, with its emphasis on "love" and "community", the 2010 protest was not a "politics of pity". Nor did it echo what Lee describes as the "masculine heroics" of *pemuda* activism that tended to belittle women's abilities to network and organize (2011b: 943–6). Instead, on this occasion, with C189 due for discussion at the 100th ILO Conference the following June, the protest paralleled the argument of Aj-jen Poo, director of the National Domestic Workers Alliance in the US. She believed that "Organizing with Love" can command broad support if campaigners ask the public "to respect the work that makes all other work possible" (Poo 2011: 11) and remember "that everyone needs the care of others at one point or another in their lives" (Poo 2009: n.p.).

After the 2010 demonstration, the *Serbet Cinta* took on a life of its own. Feminist activist Rena Herdiyani, at that point vice-chair of Kalyanamitra, explained what happened at the end of one protest, held on 3 June 2010:

> After all the organizations had spoken, we managed to get inside the DPR precincts using taxis. We soon received a message that Commission 1X could not or would not meet us. So, we spread out the giant tablecloth on the grass in front of the DPR building. We had hidden the napkins in the cars so security couldn't see them as we went in. This was an unforgettable moment for me.[63]

Such an action was in keeping with activist tradition; in the wake of *reformasi*, demonstrators frequently gathered outside parliamentary and government buildings, occupying courtyards if they could, demanding that representatives or officers come out to meet them (Juliawan 2011: 361). For JALA, it was the duping of security staff that made the day memorable, as the following account suggests:

> You know, Mary, I want to tell you an interesting story about how we smuggled the napkins in. We had friends in the DPR, and one of them allowed us to put the napkins in her car. Then we opened the giant napkin out inside the DPR complex itself. Everybody could see. The guards approached us, asking, "How come you got this inside the complex?" They were angry, but *Mbak* [sister] Lita had

63 Interview with Rena Herdiyani, Jakarta, 26 June 2015.

> been the leader of everything and got the press there, so we just carried on.[64]

The *Serbet Cinta* had begun life as a symbol of consensus. Now transformed into an object of resistance, its presence inside the parliamentary complex linked the PRT cause with broader questions about the failure of the "House of the People" to live up to its name.

Washing Lines, Laundry Baskets, and Irons: National Domestic Workers' Day 2011

On 14 February 2011, a wet and grey Monday, JALA returned to the HI Roundabout. It was a weekday; numbers were down on previous years. Nevertheless, members of KAPPRT-BM had assembled an impressive range of props and costumes that won media attention, for example, from the popular online newspapers *detik.com* and *tribunnews*. Dubbed the "100 Washing Lines" protest, organizers had stationed five-foot-tall wooden racks hung with items of clothing printed with slogans all around the roundabout. An enormous orange banner demanded a domestic worker law and ratification of C189. Orange had become JALA PRT's signature shade; it represented, Lita Anggraini told me, the fiery spirit of the movement.[65] Another banner reminded employers and politicians that they only looked smart for work because PRT kept their clothes clean.

Figure 3.6 illustrates the costume uniforms worn by a dozen or so women who mimed the washing, drying, and ironing of laundry during the demonstration. Aprons featured, but with a note of urgency added through bold use of colour. Performers wore black T-shirts and aprons adorned with pin-on badges featuring a tiny orange T-shirt printed with the words "PRT=Pekerja". Loud black and yellow slogans on the aprons demanded: "*Wudjukan UU PRT!*" (Pass the Domestic Worker Law!). Some PRT had painted their faces white. Washing lines and white faces were part of Indonesia's protest and performance traditions. They conjured the clown-servants (*purnawakan*) of Javanese theatre thought to embody "the 'simple honesty' and 'deep wisdom' of the *rakyat* or the 'common people'" (Clark 2011: 218). *Purnawakan* had permission, appropriated here by the Action Committee, to criticize their betters in the interests of society. Reporters noted the pantomime element of

64 Interview with Aida Milasari, Jakarta, 6 July 2015.

65 Email communication to author, 22 August 2022.

Fig. 3.6 100 Washing lines protest, National Domestic Workers' Day 2011 (Photo: JALA PRT)

the demonstration and praised participants for their enthusiasm despite the rain (detik.com 2011).

Standing against one of the superblocks that dominate the HI Roundabout, the figures of the domestic workers in Figure 3.6 tell a moral tale. In a space where older and newer values jostle with each other (Kusno 2006: 87–9), and a city where the rich and powerful seek to replace the "*kampung* with the condo", the young PRT in the picture pose the question of what future there might be for the poor in Indonesia's rapidly expanding megalopolis (Leitner and Sheppard 2018: 450).

At the House of the People: 2012–2014

Between 2012 and 2014, domestic worker demonstrations became more adversarial. After a last-ditch vigil, the DPR included the Domestic Workers Bill on its list of priority legislation for 2012. Persuading politicians to support the Bill now mattered most. Hence, the Action Committee staged many of its protests in this period at the gates of parliament. Headscarves morphed into bandanas, laundry symbolized the "dirty washing" of political corruption, and brooms became a metaphor for the need to "sweep the House clean". Two examples illustrate how activists maximized the aesthetic and political potential of the DPR setting even though photographs suggest that PRT turnout at some demonstrations was small; sometimes there seemed to be more KAPPRT-BM trade unionists and NGO activists than domestic workers in attendance, a point also made by other observers (Gastaldi et al. 2017: 128). Given dramatic enough props and staging, however, small numbers did not prevent demonstrations from getting press coverage the next day.

One example of this is the "100 percent Workers" demonstration staged on 22 November 2012. A press photographer captured a moment of drama when protesters hoisted the "Love Napkin" onto the gates of parliament (Figure 3.7). His image highlighted five male figures atop the gates, the slogans scrawled on the Love Napkin and an improvised apron, and a *serbet*-wearing PRT moving towards the action. The scene resembles images circulated in student publications in 1998 (Lee 2016: 85). In a theatrically contentious manner, PRT claimed ownership of the "House of the People", a familiar refrain in post-1998 labour protests (Juliawan 2011). In 1998, students climbed the gates of the University of Indonesia and later occupied parliament for five days. At the "100 percent workers" protest, JALA's supporters symbolically stormed the DPR gates, positioning PRT as heirs to the pro-democracy movement (Sutradani 2012a).

The wording on the back of the PRT running towards the gates, however, was very much of its time. Corruption and "money politics" had become part of popular discourse and "politician" a by-word for decadence (Meitzner 2007: 390). Hence the handwritten slogans scrawled on the improvised paper apron that read:

> *Dibalik Pakaian bersisih, makanan tersadi, rumah rapi & bersih, anak terawat* [*dan*] *halaman bersih* [...] *PRT*. (Behind [your] clean clothes, prepared meals, clean and tidy houses, well-cared for children and clean yards [is a] PRT.)

The repeated word *bersih* (clean) castigates corrupt politicians hiding behind the closed gates of the parliamentary complex. A second photograph taken once the Love Napkin had been raised (not shown here) offers another example of apron-clad bodies acting as metaphorical megaphones (Sutradani 2012b). It shows a group of PRT from Bekasi, an important industrial area adjoining Jakarta with a history of union organization, standing with their feet planted resolutely in front of the

Fig. 3.7 Union supporters raise a banner of 1,000 napkins on the gates of the DPR, 22 November 2012 (Photo: Sutradani/Beritagar.id)

gates of the DPR. More confident protestors raise messages written on the women's aprons addressed to "*Ibu-Bapak Wakil Rakyat*" (DPR Representatives) and "SBY" (President Susilo Bambang Yudhoyono), demanding legislation.

Speaking to journalists during this protest, Lita Anggraini repeated the words "demand" (*menuntut*) and "not yet" (*belum*) frequently. She enumerated parliament's failings: no report published on fact-finding missions to South Africa and Argentina conducted earlier that year; no ratification of C189 despite the president's promises at Geneva, and no revision of legislation protecting domestic workers overseas. JALA PRT, she said, did not intend to go away: "we always bring these napkins to demand the realization of the Domestic Worker Law, which until now is still not being discussed", she said (Syafina 2012).

A second example of powerfully persuasive use of props and costume is the "Giant Toilet" protest held on 1 October 2014. JALA PRT and KA PPRT-BM had hoped for success the previous year when, after public consultations, Commission X1 had pushed forward a scaled-down version of the Bill. However, even this diluted version had not passed into law before sessions closed for the 2014 elections.

Activists, therefore, decided to greet new and returning members of parliament on inauguration day with a symbolic gift or *kado* calculated to ensure that the RUU PPRT was not forgotten. The gift was a giant replica toilet and broom (see Figure 3.8). Knowing that anti-corruption rhetoric had swayed results in the 2014 elections (Kramer 2015: 104–6, 111–12), JALA activists re-engineered the cleanliness/laundry allegory used in 2011 and blamed "dirty politicians" for blocking their Bill.

The wording on the toilet was succinct: "Inauguration gift for the New 2014–2019 Parliament, Stop Slavery towards PRT". As Lita Anggraini explained to journalists:

> The giant toilet symbolizes the need for the DPR to throw out any dirt – such as corruption, collusion, and nepotism (KKN), bribery, slavery, abuse of authority – and any extortion by members of the

Fig. 3.8 Greeting the new parliament, 1 October 2014 (Photo: JALA PRT)

> House. The giant broom is a tool for parliament to clean up all its obligations. (Wulandari 2014)

JALA believed that after many promises, the DPR was "obliged" to pass the RUU PPRT and ratify C189. Doing so would enable new politicians (and the new president, Joko Widodo) to prove they were different from the old. Those who witnessed the protest or saw images of it in the media could not miss the male bodies, trade union flags, and the familiar acronyms of well-known confederations printed along the bottom of the red and white banner. Together, these elements of the protest signalled that PRT were now accepted members of Indonesia's labour movement, marking another transition in the emergence of an Indonesian domestic worker class.

The giant toilet, broom, and array of pots, pans, and brushes foregrounded in Figure 3.8 provided good copy for journalists. So too did the *serbet* napkins, improvised paper aprons, and the female orator wielding the megaphone. *Serbet* tied bandana or commando style and the "communist red" of the banner created a more contentious tone than earlier iconography focused on virtuous victimhood. Indeed, one reporter described Lita Anggraini as a "field coordinator" (Hiz 2014), a term once part of the "militarized taxonomy" of *reformasi* (Lee 2016: 75). While in earlier demonstrations, costume uniforms had been coded female, here, male figures wear the *serbet* with aplomb. The *serbet* had become a synecdochal sign for a maid's uniform – and, in turn, for the movement's connections with student and workers' protests past and present.

Hunger Strikes: November 2014–March 2015

Promises notwithstanding, after the inauguration, committees tasked with proposing legislation were slow to start. No government minister promoted the RUU PPRT. With a sense of betrayal, Lita Anggraini and four members of Tunas Mulia – Lek Jumiyem, Sargini, Haryati, and Ririn Sulastri – began a hunger strike or *mogok makan* on 24 November 2014, International Day for the Elimination of Violence Against Women. Forty-five organizations affiliated with JALA and seven other groups, including three located overseas, supported the protest. Logos of the Urban Poor Consortium and its Jakarta offshoot, the Urban Poor Network, appeared on publicity materials (IDWFED 2014). Visible support from these associations linked JALA's demands with a vision of the urban poor as a "coherent group or class" with rights to the city and the potential to change clientelist politics (Wilson

2019: 105). During the *mogok makan*, the hunger-strikers posed for photographs. They adopted different poses, sometimes standing with clenched fists raised, sometimes standing stoically in the rain, and sometimes holding a megaphone. As shown in Figure 3.9, PRT bodies rather than impressive props provided the focal point for the protest.

Chained to the railings and leaning exhausted against the gates of the DPR, the hunger-strikers allied themselves with the suffragettes who fought for votes for women in the UK between 1906 and 1914 and went on hunger strike when they were imprisoned for their militancy. Framed by snapshots of PRT victims of abuse pegged up like washing, the staging was intended to suggest the suffering PRT for whom the strikers were going without food. Lita Anggraini dressed differently from the others. Her black T-shirt and beige trousers drew the eye less than the orange and white outfits of the PRT. Just as Annie Kenney, a mill worker from Lancashire, brought authenticity to suffragette claims to represent all women when she wore her clogs and shawl (Jenkins 2019: 480–5), restricting the "maid's costume" to PRT helped characterize the hunger strike as the workers' own.

The hunger strike holds a special place in the movement's collective history. In 2017 the ILO published a collection of stories written by domestic workers. Lek Jumiyem, introduced in Chapter 2 as one of the leaders of Tunas Mulia, contributed a piece entitled "The hunger strike and the spirit of our struggle" ("*Mogok makan dan nadi perjuangan kami*"). Her words convey the material and affective dimensions of the

Fig. 3.9 Hunger strike: Demonstrators urge the passage of the Domestic Workers Law (Photo: Hukumonline CR – 17)

strike: stinging morning air, intense humidity, heavy rain, exhaustion, fear of a fracas with the police who tried to clear them from the site at nightfall, and the buzz of mosquitoes that stopped them from sleeping. She spoke of spirituality – prayers and the lighting of candles – and the solidarity of fellow activists trying to communicate with MPs to get them a hearing. Spurred on by the sight of the women, a group of trade unionists demanding increases in the minimum wage collected donations to help pay the strikers' train fares back to Yogyakarta. For Jumiyem, the hunger strike was not just the routine "oration, carrying protest equipment, posters, and banners" she was used to. Deeply internalized, it constituted "one act in a life drama [...] a thing never imagined" and something "we loved to live" (Jumiyem 2017: 147–51).[66]

Towards the end of the second day, members of the Legislative Council invited the hunger-strikers into the DPR for a meeting. They sat in the committee room chairs in their mock uniforms. LBH Jakarta staff, who were not allowed into the session but heard what happened immediately afterwards, reported that the vice-chair and four other members agreed "there must be protection, there must be a law". They promised to push the Bill as a priority for 2015 (LBH Jakarta 2014). The strikers called off their action. On 19 January 2015, they celebrated a significant victory when the minister of manpower issued a "Regulation on the Protection of Domestic Workers" (*Permenaker No. 2/Tahun* 2015). While it did not meet all JALA's demands and was not legally binding, it was a step up from silenced invisibility.

Celebrations were short-lived. The RUU PPRT was not on the list of priority legislation announced in February 2015. At this, activists called for a second hunger strike. This time, Lita Anggraini fasted every day, beginning on 16 February. On International Women's Day, 8 March, after a big demonstration at the HI Roundabout and a meeting at Komnas Perempuan's Jakarta offices, the movement launched a campaign to get at least 100 women to join the hunger strike, fasting for twenty-four hours in turn. By 18 March, when demonstrators rallied outside the Ministry of Manpower, at least 500 women across the country, including female factory workers, students, and entrepreneurs, were reported to have participated (Falanta 2015). At one point, Lita was hospitalized. Throughout the strike, which lasted until 24 March when Commission 1X promised, again, to support the Bill, JALA staged rallies at different venues in the capital

66 For brief extracts from the text in Bahasa Indonesia, see Appendix 3.

and cities such as Semarang, Yogyakarta, Surabaya, Makassar, and Mataram. However, despite widespread support, the Bill was shelved again.

By 2016, street protests had not persuaded Indonesia's politicians to pass a domestic worker law. Nevertheless, media coverage of the demonstrations had established the presence of the domestic worker movement in the public sphere. A new assemblage of headscarf, apron, broom, banner, and giant napkin sat alongside images of domestic workers as victims, countering stereotypes. During demonstrations, PRT bodies, albeit few at some happenings, and their giant-sized tools of the trade, took centre stage.

Santi's Story: Testimony, Technology, and New Union

Compared with Jumiyem and her companions from Yogyakarta, who had been union organizers for over ten years when they went on hunger strike in November 2014, Santi Sunarti, whose story comprises this last section, was newer to union business when she fasted in 2015. The union she chaired, Sapu Lidi – the first domestic workers' union in Jakarta – was only eighteen months old. It had begun in 2013 when JALA had helped a group of PRT, including Santi, to form themselves into a union. As Sapu Lidi expanded, the presence of Santi and her fellow domestic worker organizers operating in and moving between sites across the city lent a human face to the notion of a new kind of domestic worker. When Sapu Lidi members told their stories in public and posted photographs on social media, their presence nudged hesitant members of women's rights and trade union organizations and some policymakers, politicians, and employers to respond. Sapu Lidi leaders recruited and mentored new members, adapting models of organization pioneered in Yogyakarta to the changing cartography of the capital.

I first saw Santi in action at the Bumbu Desa restaurant in Cikini Raya on a Sunday morning in June 2015.[67] Located in an upmarket central area where the restaurants and cafés are frequented by academics from the nearby University of Indonesia Salemba campus and researchers from the SMERU research institute where I began my fieldwork, this was not the obvious place to find a domestic worker from South Jakarta. Santi was the first speaker at a press conference to

67 Fieldnotes, Cikini, Jakarta, 14 February 2015.

publicize JALA's plans for 16 June – International Domestic Workers' Day, when domestic workers globally celebrate the adoption of C189. PRT were to the fore at the restaurant, wearing distinctive JALA T-shirts, registering guests, and visibly constituting a good part of the audience. Upstairs, the stage was set to project Santi and Diah Supriyadi (a second Sapu Lidi organizer on the panel) as figures representing a national and international movement. Piled in front of the platform were some of the 1606 green and yellow kitchen sponges-cum-scourers (known as *spon* in Indonesia) gathered from PRT organizations across the archipelago, the number 1606 referencing 16 June. Each sponge was enclosed in a polythene bag with a handwritten message from a PRT to a member of the House of Representatives demanding immediate ratification of C189 and the passage of the Domestic Workers Bill. The sponges were to be delivered to the DPR the next day. Following a short film featuring a domestic worker coming into view as she cleaned a smeary window and spoke of the liberating experience of joining a union, Santi got up to speak.

With conviction, she explained that the name Sapu Lidi expressed the belief that domestic workers are more potent as a collective. Just as the twigs used to make the brooms known as *sapu lidi* used throughout Indonesia for sweeping yards would be useless and easily broken alone, domestic workers gain strength by joining a union. Ludiah (Diah) followed, criticizing employers who refuse pay increases even as Jakarta's minimum wage (and the cost of living) rise rapidly. Workers who complain, Diah testified, are told to leave. The novelty of hearing and seeing domestic workers in such a space was underlined as more highly educated, experienced (and salaried) activists came to the table, placing the domestic workers' campaign in the context of national and international struggles for women's and workers' rights. Journalists responded positively, clustering around Santi and Diah after the speech to interview them and take photographs. The presence of PRT, as much as their words, provided novelty and authenticity.

Two days later, at the JALA base in Kalibata, Santi spoke again at a gathering where testimony took up much of the afternoon. Here her presence as a storyteller was part of a process described in the context of African American domestic worker organizing as a means of "self-definition" through which workers "tell their own stories and craft their own historical narratives" (Nadasen 2016: 157). Carrying her baby in a sling and introduced by Lita Anggraini, who explained that everyone – young and old – should feel free to share experiences with the group, Santi explained how being part of the union had given her the confidence to challenge employers and advocate for others. Her speech became a model for others to follow as, in turn, attendees explained what had led them to be sitting around the JALA table. An account of the event posted on the LBH Jakarta website reported that PRT participants spoke of belonging to a "community of hope" that taught them their rights and inspired them with a "spirit of struggle" (Alfin 2015).[68]

Less than a fortnight later, Santi was at JALA again for a Sunday afternoon workshop. A roomful of domestic workers had begun writing life histories as part of a nationwide effort to assemble enough stories of a publishable standard to make a book.[69] Some volunteers read their accounts aloud. When Santi stood up, participants cheered and clapped after her first few words. Playing to her audience, she got many laughs and evinced a broad smile from Lita Anggraini. Underlying the laughter, however, as others took their turns, was a palpable sadness as women revealed details of poverty, rifts with families, illness, or bereavement, and described discrimination and ill-treatment. All presented their tales as transformative, just as in the Philippines, where activists had published women's accounts of their lives before and after joining a collective as stories of *Moving On* (Roces 2012: 148–9). Sharing experiences in a semi-formal but familiar setting brought workers from different parts of the capital together and provided a rehearsal space where activists prepared PRT to testify elsewhere.

On these occasions, as at others I attended, emotions aroused by giving testimony were diffused when food and drinks were shared in a spirit of sisterhood. The JALA base was Lita Anggraini's home as well as office. After the writing workshop, for example, Lita served the sweet drinks with which people broke their fast (this was during the fasting month). Santi contributed to the family atmosphere on these sorts of occasions, bringing some of her children along, greeting friends and newcomers, talking to potential supporters about the union, and, on one occasion, half-jokingly asking me for a donation. In public and with journalists, Santi appeared more reserved. Commentators noted her nervous excitement when an interview was being filmed, her age (thirty-five), her role as a mother as well as a worker, and her "every day", perhaps faded or well-worn, T-shirt, but also remarked on her growing confidence (Budiari 2015; Irham and

68 Field notes, Jakarta, 16 June 2015.

69 Field notes, Jakarta, 28 June 2015.

Andapita 2015b). Her presence conveyed neither vulnerable victim nor "modern, consumerist, spoiled city girl" – a category of some suspicion in globalizing Asia (Mills 2017: 321–5). Instead, Santi seemed to represent an Indonesian ideal of the dutiful and hardworking mother who seeks paid work outside the home to support her family and contributes to her community. Her politics of presence is not that of anyone's daughter but anyone's hardworking wife.

I gained a more nuanced picture when I talked to Santi one-to-one. She described how she had challenged gender norms and encouraged others to do likewise. We spoke in a side office during the writing workshop. Hence the story she told was on its way to becoming, it seemed, Santi's script.[70] The child of migrants to Jakarta from Surabaya, her parents had insisted she leave school to be married immediately after she turned sixteen but had encouraged her brothers to continue studying. At the time, she accepted her lot as "the path that is mine to follow" (*jalan saya yang ada*). Later, with five children to support and finding her husband's wages as a labourer insufficient to keep them all, Santi defied family norms and, on the advice of friends, switched from part-time work selling *sate* to work as a PRT, first for an Indonesian household and then for a Korean expatriate family. Her husband and father objected; to them, it shamed the family for Santi to become a PRT.

Santi persisted, seeing the advantages of working for expatriate employers who did not want a live-in PRT. New apartments in South Jakarta are popular with expatriates as with PRT, who find work for several employers in the same block. PRT working in such a way could command higher wages, cut travel time, benefit from the standard of the labour-saving appliances in apartments, and meet other domestic workers in the corridors (Jordhus-Lier and Prabawati 2018 276–80). Indeed, it was by aiding a co-worker that Santi became involved in organizing. She encouraged a friend whose employer had withheld wages to describe her situation on Facebook. Alerted, Lita Anggraini contacted Santi and her friend, met them several times, and encouraged them to get together as a group of domestic workers. Santi then went door to door, inviting PRT in her neighbourhood to a meeting. Ten attended the first time, she remembered. Two months later, the number had risen to forty-five. They met at peoples' houses, bringing food for pot-luck dinners.[71] At this juncture, Santi's family renewed their

70 Interview with Santi Sunarti, Jakarta, 28 June 2015.

71 Jennifer Angarita (2017), who researched the formation of Sapu Lidi as

opposition. As Sapu Lidi members confirmed at a focus group held in July 2015, relatives were often anxious that joining a union could endanger a woman or her family. Men could resent the time wives or daughters spent away from home on union affairs.[72]

In such circumstances, activists from JALA PRT and experienced Sapu Lidi members would offer to intervene. They visited homes and reassured families, helping husbands and fathers adapt. As Santi told me, her husband "minds the baby sometimes now". Another union member reported that as she is busier, her husband "goes fishing if he has free time". Some families were won over by the fact that the union provided classes in English language, writing, and IT; one PRT explained that her husband and son, seeing her new-found love of writing, suggested she "become a writer now". Relatives recognized the benefit of a union that negotiated better pay and conditions. Membership continued to grow; Santi was proud to tell me that "we now have 185 members, all good members who are active in supporting the union and pay their dues".

Santi's first meeting with politicians in parliament was also a source of pride, but – at the same time – of disillusion, as she told me:

> One thing I am really proud of is that Lita invited me to go with her to meet with members of Commission 1X. But I was so disappointed about how they responded. They argued with us and said domestic workers are more like family members than workers. I remember speaking about my own experiences and those of my friends at that meeting, and Lita talking about our rights as women and workers.[73]

But after the lobbying and hunger strikes, when the DPR still failed to make the Bill a priority, Santi added "Lita was crying; she had hoped so much to get somewhere that time". Indeed, the continued obduracy of politicians towards the Bill, even after repeated hunger strikes, was a bitter blow. In conversation with me and others, Lita spoke of JALA PRT fighting on even if it took twenty years to get their law.

Santi told me that despite disappointments, she came away from

part of an Open Society Internship in 2016, describes the same process but includes slightly different details, reflecting her conversation with Santi's friend, Vitri, as well as with Santi herself.

72 Field notes, observation of focus group with Sapu Lidi members, Jakarta, 2 July 2015.

73 Interview with Santi Sunarti, Jakarta, 28 June 2015.

protests wanting to do more. Some members of the JALA network, however, had concluded that demonstrations were not cost-effective, even if they helped turn PRT into activists. Ani Widayani Soetjipto, a senior lecturer in the Faculty of Social and Political Sciences at UI who had first met Lita Anggraini when the university sent students on placements to work at JALA PRT and had acted as an adviser in terms of advocacy and lobbying since that time, gave me her analysis of potential internal divisions within the movement that needed resolution. Some supporters wanted more emphasis on migrant domestic workers, some gave priority to wage increases and unionization, and others wanted to limit demands to legal protection or health issues, for example. Such differences were difficult to resolve in a loose network model of organization, she suggested, and while going on demonstrations was "fun" and "helped keep people motivated", she had advised Lita to have a Plan B ready and look for new allies and recruit more "champions" to add to Lita's voice if demonstrations failed to achieve their goals.[74] Tiasri Wiandani, another strong JALA supporter who had met Lita at a meeting organized through KAPAL Perempuan and had struck up a "personal connection", also spoke of the need for the movement to evaluate its strategy.[75] She was amongst those who argued it would be best to emphasize protection and health and safety in the workplace, since in some areas, such as Yogyakarta for example, PRT did not feel that wages were the key issue. With extensive experience of union organizing and training amongst women workers in the textile and garment industries within the National Workers Union (SPN), Tiasri felt that PRT might consider joining a general union until they had built a large enough membership and capacity to create a strong union and confederation of their own. There was some discussion, too, I discovered, of changing the network model into a more formal association or *yayasan*, though this did not happen.[76] In the event, an internal review conducted in May 2015 with the help of the Urban Poor Consortium concluded that a priority was to expand and strengthen domestic worker organizations across the country with a new strategy that adapted the door-to-door recruitment used in the movement's early days to the new mobilities and technologies of the motorbike and mobile phone.[77]

---

74 Interview with Ani Soetjipto, Jakarta, 28 July 2015.

75 Interview with Tiasri Wiandani, Jakarta, 20 August 2015.

76 Informal conversation at JALA PRT office, Jakarta, July 2015.

77 The strategy was devised to be replicable across Indonesia; its implementation outside the capital lies beyond the scope of my research.

New Towns: New Technologies

Margherita Gastaldi, an Italian researcher–activist who began collaborating with JALA in 2014, has described this shift in strategy in detail (Gastaldi 2017). Dubbed "Rap" because of the "systematically repetitive steps" linking the process to rap music, the new approach involved setting targets for recruiting new members, moving into new geographical areas, and training PRT in leadership roles. JALA's experienced activists, meanwhile, would focus on education and mentoring. Guidelines encouraged "Rappers", the name given to domestic worker recruiters, to use Facebook, LINE, WhatsApp groups, and SMS to contact potential union members, publicize union activities, and keep in touch with PRT in their areas between meetings. They were given a list of points to discuss with potential members and trained to address doubts or scepticism. Such methods maximized working women's time and, indirectly, through Facebook, for example, spread news of the presence of a domestic workers' network in targeted areas. Using mobile phones could also, as Pei-Chia Lan found amongst migrant domestic workers in Taiwan, help counter surveillance and control (2006: 198). Sapu Lidi members told me that phones helped them frustrate attempts by building management companies and employers to restrict their movements within apartment blocks.[78]

I attended five events involving PRT in the final few weeks of my fieldwork in November and December 2016. Snapshots of moments at those illustrate what JALA's reshaped politics of presence looked like in practice and show the various sites and scales across which JALA sought to extend its reach during 2015 and 2016.

Scene one: OPERATA Pamulang, a group supported by Rumpun Gema Perempuan (RGP), meets in a community building in Pondok Cabe, Tangerang, an area of rapid population growth and upmarket private development two hours by public transport from central Jakarta (Firman and Fahmi 2017: 72–4). Aida Milasari, RGP's director, and community worker Diah Rofika update members on JALA's plans and then hand the meeting over to the PRT. Excitedly, the dozen or so there choose a chairperson, elect a committee, decide to design a brochure, and (prompted by Aida) discuss turning themselves into a trade union.[79]

Scene two: a large expatriate house in Kemang (an area described online as an "ex-pat paradise" which also caters for "the needs of

78 Informal conversation with group of workers, Jakarta, 30 July 2015.
79 Field notes, Pondok Cabe, Jakarta, 16 December 2016.

Jakarta's middle and upper classes"). A vast living room filled with ninety-nine domestic workers (according to the register) listening avidly while Lita Anggraini leads a two-hour interactive session, a reworked version of the domestic workers school so instrumental in building the movement in Yogyakarta. Piles of shoes and ranks of motorbikes and scooters announce the arrival of domestic workers in the neighbourhood, as do the handwritten signs pointing to "PRT meeting" posted along the road to help workers find their way. Diah, now chairperson of Sapu Lidi's Cipete-Kemang KOMPERATA (*Komunitas Pekerja Rumah Tangga*, an alternative term used for domestic worker-led organizations in Jakarta), collects monthly dues and urges newcomers to complete membership forms. Afterwards, workers stroll in the garden, taking photographs to post on social media accounts. Lita rests before running a second school session elsewhere later that afternoon.[80]

Scene three: Kalibata, the JALA base. I sit next to Santi in a room packed with domestic workers attending training in citizen journalism. Co-facilitated by a PRT who has become a noted online journalist, attendees learn to use their smartphones to tell their stories and build union membership.[81]

Scene four: The Hotel Sofyan in Menteng, back in the city centre. A high-profile ILO-sponsored prize-giving for journalists who have covered PRT stories that year. The new chair of OPERATA Pondok Cabe sits at a conference table with other PRT; later, she asks a question, enjoys the buffet, and takes photographs. Two PRT receive certificates for their online citizen journalism.[82]

The final scene, the day before my departure: a new high-rise hotel in a private development known as BSD (Bumi Serpong Dama or Peaceful Serpong) in the district of South Tangerang in Greater Jakarta. Domestic workers from Jakarta, Semarang, Lampung, Makassar, and Yogyakarta attend a two-day residential workshop supported by the International Domestic Workers Federation (IDWF), with global domestic workers' leader Elizabeth Tang (who had travelled from Hong Kong to be there) in attendance.[83] Urging PRT to see themselves as members of an international movement for change, Tang speaks

80 Field notes, Kemang, Jakarta, 20 November 2016.

81 Field notes, Jakarta, 27 November 2016.

82 Field notes, Jakarta, 22 November 2016.

83 Field notes, Tangerang, 3 December 2015. For information about the role played by Elizabeth Tang in the transnational domestic workers' movement, see Fish (2017: 183–6).

of forming Federations to tackle fragmentation and forging new mechanisms for global and local organizations to collaborate. "What's important", she concludes, "is that we do it together with you. If you don't do what's needed, then we can't do it either."[84]

In the space of three weeks, then, the new chair of the OPERATA Pamulang, who attended this workshop, had moved from being a novice member of a small neighbourhood group to a participant in a globally influential forum. This is what a politics of presence signified for one Jakarta resident, now a connected and activist PRT.

Conclusion

The snapshots of JALA activity in Jakarta between 2004 and 2016 collected here (though not inclusive of all the movement's areas of work) provide answers to some of the questions raised in this chapter's introduction.[85] First, the network depended on the personal relationships and political loyalties of a generation of feminist activists schooled in the pro-democracy and student movements of the 1980s and '90s and on the existence of a plethora of women's rights organizations in the *reformasi* political landscape. Second, JALA activists extended and adapted strategies for engaging with domestic workers devised in Yogyakarta, finding a new model, the "Rap", which placed more onus on PRT groups to organize themselves. Crucially, JALA fostered the formation and strengthening of Sapu Lidi, the first PRT-led domestic workers' union in the capital. The visible presence of a worker-led-union gave JALA PRT greater authenticity and heft in NGO circles, parliamentary debating chambers, and the public eye.

Third, the network invested heavily in staging demonstrations that helped craft a new domestic worker persona and public image; worker rather than helper, activist citizen rather than silenced "maid". Finally, the rapidly changing geographies and technologies of the megacity Jakarta allowed JALA to locate itself in a national politics of the urban poor and a transnational global domestic workers' movement making its claims against internationally recognized norms.

---

84 Field notes, Tangerang, 3 December 2016.

85 One area omitted is the production of video material in support of ending child domestic labour. Working with students in schools and universities, the aim was to influence upcoming generations of employers.

Despite well-informed and persistent lobbying, well-resourced street protests, a growing pool of supporters including powerful unions, and increasingly articulate PRT, progress on a domestic worker bill continued to be stymied. Politicians swayed by self-interest and the primacy of money politics had recourse to culture as a means of defending the *doxa* of domestic work and disregarding domestic worker claims.

In the following chapters, I explore the contributions of journalists and academics/researchers who found ways to investigate and challenge the orthodoxies and infelicities of Indonesia's unregulated system of paid domestic work.

CHAPTER

4

Challenging Disregard: Advocacy Journalism and the Domestic Workers' Campaign

In July 2011, renowned brand agency Ogilvy and Mather released a series of glossy advertising images featuring Indonesian domestic workers (Ogilvy 2012). Their client was JALA PRT. The three images – "Mop", "Dishes", and "Clothes" – depicted young female Indonesian domestic workers having the life squeezed out of them by affluent employers. The adverts received wide acclaim in the advertising world.[1] However, Lita Anggraini, JALA's national coordinator, told me that many Indonesians had dismissed the adverts as sensationalist, exaggerated, and unfair. Consequently, the campaign achieved neither the political impact nor the cultural resonance JALA and the media professionals working with them had desired.

This chapter charts the contribution made by feminist and advocacy journalists to advancing the domestic workers' cause. It examines the challenges media professionals faced if they pointed out inconsistencies between the public outrage evinced at news of the ill-treatment of migrant domestic workers and the frequent dismissal – as in the case of the Ogilvy adverts – of the idea of abuse in Indonesian homes. Critical media coverage, it turned out, evoked a troubling tension between presence and non-presence, knowing and not knowing, seeing and unseeingness.

One of the adverts, "Mop", plays on the notion of "unseeingness". A photograph shows the hands and arms of what appears to be a male

1 During 2011 and 2012, the adverts featured on the "Best of Ogilvy Asia" and "Best Ads on TV" listings, won Bronze in the prestigious New York-based Clio awards, were shortlisted by Singapore's "Spikes Asia" media award, and profiled in the global archive "The Inspiration Room".

member of a prosperous Indonesian family wearing an expensive gold watch while wringing out a mop in a bucket. The mop and bucket are unusually modern – sculpted from stainless steel. What is shocking about the image, apart from the fact that it shows a man mopping, is that entangled in the head of the mop is a miniaturized image of a tiny doll-like Indonesian domestic worker being twisted by the strong arms of her employer to the point of immense pain. The strapline across the top of the advert reads, "JALA PRT – when domestic helpers themselves need help". The young PRT is dressed in sacrificial white; her head is thrown back in a silent scream. Like the ghost in *Hamlet*, she is both seen and unseen, an indictment and a spur to action, a symbol of injustice and perhaps of an unfinished project of political modernity.

The wording of the strapline is revealing. It reverts to the term "helper", even though, in establishing a presence on the streets and in NGO and union circles, as described in the previous chapter, JALA had promoted *pekerja* (worker) as its preferred label. Moreover, in contrast to the countless and familiar media stories of migrant domestic workers subject to ill-treatment, the "Mop" advert names neither victim nor perpetrator of the abuse. The strategy is to jolt unexceptional employers out of complacency, not capitalize on "hot news" of a particular abuse. Instead, the advert underscores that abuse and exploitation can be hidden away even in affluent Indonesian homes.

In her deeply empirical (and theoretically complex) study of the Dutch colonial archive, *Along the Archival Grain*, Ann Stoler maps out very similar terrain. She talks of a "politics of disregard": a means whereby colonial administrators and their families coped with the cognitive dissonance between ideals of empire and the stark realities of colonial rule such as the brutal treatment of coolie labour (2009: 187–97). A "disposition of disregard" was an amalgam of "knowing and not knowing" and of "seeming" not to know, held together by "clunky, scripted stereotypes" of indigenous peoples and places, and by self-deception (Stoler 2009: 246–8, 256–7). Such "wilful ignorance" helps explain the outrage JALA's "Mop" advert evoked. However, as Stoler argues, "ignorance" and "ignoring" do not carry the same meaning. Colonial officers who "disregarded" the poor to whom they "were beholden for their comforts" learned to look away through a practice of "studied inattentiveness". Drawing parallels with the present, Stoler suggests that "tacit ambivalences and implicit ambiguities", not ignorance, prevent people from challenging hypocrisy and injustice (2009: 246, 249).

Remembering my ambivalence about employing domestic workers in Jakarta, Stoler's warning that the colonial politics of disregard casts "longer shadows still" is germane (2009: 278). New Order and *reformasi* Indonesia were riddled with disparities and discrepancies.[2] Post-1998, the media was freer to expose corruption, collusions between business and the military, and a growing gap in income between rich and poor. PRT were not so much unseen or invisible (though NGOs often chose to use such words) as subject to the self-deceptive "unseeingness" of employers, politicians, and reading, viewing, and voting publics. Ati Nurbaiti, a well-known feminist activist and *Jakarta Post* senior editor when I met her, once quoted an anonymous editor who believed the public only became outraged when a case involved "extreme physical abuse carried out by Chinese Indonesians" (Nurbaiti 2000). On other occasions, journalists downplayed abuse as being perpetrated by "bad women"[3] or the mentally unwell.[4]

Such framing, applying Stoler's analysis to post-Suharto Indonesia, was one means whereby "those with privilege and standing could excuse themselves [...] from wrought engagement" (2009: 256). In Stoler's "disregard", racism was "a paramount sentiment in the official colonial mind", shaping political and personal responses (Gouda et al. 2009: 559). In this chapter, along with racism, gender, class, political and professional identities, and media cultures come to the fore.

A degree of personal interest was usually at stake when journalists turned towards advocacy on behalf of PRT. As Endy Bayuni, editor-in-chief at the *Jakarta Post* told me, self-deprecatingly, "I cannot write as forcibly as I wish about ending modern-day slavery because, as my wife says, when that happens, I will have to do all the house chores."[5] Female journalists, subject to strong social expectations that women prioritize family, could not work late on deadlines, or stay away from

2 For an account of ambivalence and disregard in relation to the employment of women and children in the Dutch East Indies, see Meerkerk (2016).

3 For an example of how good women/bad women binaries divert attention away from structural issues see the discussion of media depictions of motherhood in Malaysia in "Good Mothers, Bad Mothers" (Niner et al. 2014).

4 For example, a story in the *Jakarta Post*, 24 July 2008, carried the headline "Mentally ill women beat maids to death" (Setiawati 2008). For a discussion of anti-Chinese sentiment and its role in diverting attention away from wider questions of gender-based violence or the role of the state, see Strassler (2004).

5 Personal communication (email), 26 November 2016.

home without employing PRT (Utari and Nilan 2004). Journalists' households would come under further pressure if domestic workers won higher wages or shorter hours. Challenging taken-for-granted practices of domestic work could ruffle domestic harmony.

Professional comfort zones also came into question. In a study based on interviews with 385 Indonesian journalists, communications scholar Thomas Hanitzsch (2005) found them, collectively, to be but "timid watchdogs". The majority preferred not to express personal opinions, influence political agendas, or take an adversarial stance toward governments. One-third of the 385 admitted to accepting "envelopes" from sources. Such a climate was not conducive to calling out wealthy employers or castigating parliamentarians and ministers for disregarding claims for legal recognition.[6] Later, in a study of journalism in twenty-one countries (including Indonesia), Hanitzsch, with Folker Hanusch and Corinna Lauerer, used the term "interventionist" to describe journalists who do not "stay apart from the flow of events" but "get involved and promote change". They concluded that the nature and extent of interventionist journalism depended on the interplay between national politics, local media operations, and the political orientation and professional ambitions of individual journalists (Hanitzsch et al. 2016: 3–7). In this chapter, in similar vein, I use the term "advocacy journalism" to explore that interplay. "Advocacy journalism", as construed in the influential *Handbook of Journalism Studies* published in 2009, includes situations where civil society groups like JALA PRT collaborate with journalists to affect public policy as well as examples of journalists openly espousing a cause (Waisbord 2009).

Notwithstanding their contributions to media studies, Hanitzsch and Hanusch have been criticized for "overlooking" the gendered nature of journalism as an institution and working within a male/female binary (Ruoho and Torkkola 2018: 68). Feminist media scholars, on the other hand, have explored tensions between feminist subjectivities and the professional and organizational identities and practices cultivated in most media fields (see, for example, van Zoonen 1998: 128–31). Journalists who undertake "feminist-informed inquiries" trouble journalism's supposed objectivity (Santos et al. 2018: 13). Reporting on rape raises questions about whether there can or should be "balanced reporting" (Barbosa and Varão 2018: 20–25).

---

6 On the norms of Indonesian journalism see Pintak and Setiyono (2011), Tapsell (2012), and Adiprasetio (2016).

Building on such insights, this chapter focuses as much on the process of getting (better) domestic worker stories published as it does on the words and pictures produced. Interweaving interview material with content analysis of articles and broadcasts, I trace the trajectories of feminist, human rights, and workers' rights discourses as some journalists engaged in advocacy journalism. As in other aspects of Indonesia's domestic worker movement, feminist and activist networks dating back to the 1980s and '90s proved pivotal.

The chapter begins by reviewing stories about domestic work (other than those about overseas workers) published in *Kompas* – Indonesia's most influential and widely circulating daily newspaper taken note of by politicians – in 2004, the year JALA was established, and 2008, when consultations began in earnest about the ILO's proposed Convention. Next, I focus on four feminist journalists whose interventions helped the domestic workers' campaign. Finally, moving from the individual to the institutional level, I discuss an ILO-sponsored project designed to engage journalists and media outlets in breaking the stasis that had befallen the Domestic Workers Bill. However, as journalists reported on reasons for the rejection of draft legislation, they gave space to the words of politicians and employers who did not accept the need for change or believe the country could afford to ensure decent conditions and pay for its PRT. Such arguments revealed a profound disregard for the social and economic value of domestic work.

Stock Stories of Domestic Work

In her analysis of the colonial East Indies, Stoler observed that the circulation of caricatures and stereotypes sustained disregard. One of the subjects of her investigations was an official named Frans Carl Valck. A member of the Dutch colonial civil service in the 1870s, Valck noted in a report intended for his successor that while he could rely on some individual Balinese known to him, the Balinese, in general, were untrustworthy liars liable to be overcome by passions. Each incoming generation of colonial civil servants passed on such negative stereotypes in the guise of "insights" into the nature of the indigenous population, reinforcing, Stoler argues, a skewed ethics that justified disregard (2009: 256).

Similarly, Indonesian journalists had recourse to a store of well-rehearsed frames for presenting PRT stories that, with few exceptions, diverted attention away from systemic gender and class inequalities and found moral weakness within individual citizens. A search of the *Kompas* archive starting with the terms PRT, *pembantu*, *pekerja rumah tangga*, and RUU PPRT (Draft Law for the Protection of Domestic Workers) produced sixty-eight relevant articles, thirty published in 2004 and thirty-eight in 2008 (see Appendix 4). In these, dominant themes of abuse, distrust, and dependency reflected unease but not a consistent sense of outrage or demand for change. Instead, stock stories reinforced notions that domestic workers are not always what they seem, are not to be trusted, and not what they once were. Such interpretations provided excuses for inattention to local, as opposed to migrant, domestic worker claims.

Abuse

Surprisingly, given widespread beliefs that domestic workers are treated as one of the family in Indonesian homes, PRT featured as victims of abuse, workplace accidents, suicide, deceit, or other misfortunes in over half the articles analyzed. Journalists portrayed perpetrators as exceptional and focused on extreme cases, thus rendering the everyday exploitation of domestic workers ordinary. Two examples illustrate this point. In June 2008, a nineteen-year-old domestic worker escaped from the residence of a prominent local politician – one of Lampung's thirteen elected regents – and accused him of raping her (Nababan 2008). At the time the employer was standing for election as governor of Lampung. The case became "hot news". The PRT, referred to in the media as "DE", fled to the offices of DAMAR, a women and children's rights NGO led by Siti Noor Laila (Lela), a close friend of Lita Anggraini and founder member of RTND. DAMAR staff supported "DE" to report the rape and other abuses to the police. They found her a "safe house" and helped her prepare her case, even though, reportedly, Lela was harassed by a group of men wanting to warn her off defending DE (Kompas 2008a). Members of the Balinese community in Lampung came out on the streets in support of the PRT (who was Balinese), fearing the alleged perpetrator would escape prosecution (Kompas 2008b). Indeed, press interest in this case revolved around the fact that the candidate for governor was a "big man", shifting attention away from the vulnerability of all domestic workers to sexual harassment.[7]

7 For other examples of the reporting on high-profile cases see the case involving the wife of a retired police general in Bogor (Sufa 2014) or one involving Ivan Haz, member of parliament and son of the ninth vice-president

A second example is *Kompas*'s coverage of the death of a domestic worker named Maryati in January 2004. On 10 January, under the headline "Buried in the Backyard", *Kompas* reported an extraordinary event in a surprisingly matter-of-fact way.[8] According to a version translated by the ILO and published several years later in a newsletter, matters had transpired as follows:

> Maryati used to work in a luxurious house in the Bumi Serpong Damai real estate complex in the district of Tangerang, Banten. During her employment she experienced serious physical abuse. For months, Maryati did not receive her salary. She did not have enough money to escape from the torture she experienced. The employment turned into bonded labour because the employer would not let her go until she finished paying off her "debt".
>
> One day, the family driver found out the employer had killed Maryati and buried her body in the backyard; he reported the case to the police. Maryati's employer claimed she killed her because she had stolen bread. (ILO Jakarta 2010b: 4)

According to the family driver, the employer and her son often hit and yelled at Maryati. A PRT who worked in the house next door said she had seen bruises on Maryati's face, arms, and legs and watched her put out the rubbish hurriedly, always looking scared. Since her employer watched her when she swept the front yard or cleaned the windows, Maryati never got a chance to talk to anybody.

Maryati is placed firmly in the category of innocent victim. Her employer confessed. Beaten, isolated, confined to the house and under surveillance, Maryati as an individual was little known, except that she lived in trepidation of her employer and was probably starving. As witnesses had testified to her ill-treatment and the employer had confessed, Maryati's virtuous victimhood did not seem in doubt.

However, a follow-up story published two days later complicated matters. With the headline "Hoping Maryati Case Will Be Completed Soon", a journalist reported that the vice-chair of the *Rukun Warga* (RW) where Maryati died had "sensed some oddities in Maryati's case" (*Kompas* 2004a).[9] In June 2003, Maryati's father had come to

of Indonesia, eventually imprisoned and dismissed from the DPR for abusing a twenty-year-old domestic worker, referred to as "T" (Anya 2016a).

8 The ILO translation/adaptation of the article misspelt "Buried" as "Burried", but I have assumed the ILO quoted the same headline.

9 The literal meaning of *rukun warga* is virtuous citizen. The RW is one of

take her home. At first, she had appeared willing. However, according to the RW, "after she [...] met her father again, she refused to go with him [...] suddenly she didn't want to acknowledge her father anymore". The journalist offers no explanation. The reader is left guessing, but the report raises doubt; perhaps Maryati is not all she seems? The RW's comments introduce moral uncertainty, the interjection of what Carol Chan, in her discussion of victim narratives of migrant domestic work, terms a "gendered moral hierarchy" that enables "incompatible notions of exploitation and development" to coexist (2014: 6).

Further on in the article, the journalist quotes another local official who described the case as "very unfortunate [and] [...] not supposed to happen in an area like this". This official differentiated the perpetrator's family from the rest of the community. He explained that although the family "looked normal from the outside", they did not socialize and "everyone knew this abuse case was not the first to happen in [that] household. Their past domestic worker was also abused and [...] escaped" (*Kompas* 2004a). What in some ways looks like professional journalistic practice – gathering comments from several sides – in this case steered attention away from politics. Readers could continue to disregard claims that all PRT need legal protection if such outrages could be explained as simply due to the abnormal psychology of single families.

Maryati, then, was not invisible. Neighbours knew her employer punished her for petty offences. They had seen her bruises and watched her putting out the rubbish "in a hurry". They knew something was wrong. Perhaps locals found it prudent not to interfere. A broad-based study of masculinity and violence against women in Indonesia found that harsh verbal reprimands were the norm inside households. Furthermore, a "discourse of denial" operated in cities where "the best tactic for maintaining neighbourhood harmony is not to notice" (Nilan et al. 2014: 12, 16).

Discomfort about Maryati's death, one might infer, was swiftly followed by disregard. Indeed, after the second article about her murder, she seems to disappear from the *Kompas* record; no further reports surfaced. Another domestic worker story, however, soon replaced last month's news.

two neighbourhood-level administrative units in Indonesia, its role variously viewed as reporting to the government, ensuring the neighbourhood resembles a "big family", looking after the welfare of vulnerable residents, or, at worst, a means for extortion over the issue of identity cards (Anya 2016b).

Distrust and Dependency

In the *Kompas* sample, employers grappled with tensions between wariness of PRT in general and utter dependence on the individual PRT they employed. Fifteen stories presented domestic workers as a source of angst. In contrast to the reminiscences of older Indonesians featured in Chapter 1, where the presence of trusted servants in the house signified security, these articles reflect fear and distrust of PRT. Seven headlines mentioned stealing or robbery: four reported cases of "murder", "kidnap", or "mutilation". Two articles featured "criminal hypnotists" who had had approached domestic workers to get them to steal, another focused on a PRT who had been persuaded by "a friend" to filch valuable property, and a fourth described an employment agency as acting as a front for criminal activity. It is not surprising then that two published "letters from readers" urged caution in using agencies and recommended ways to manage "difficult" staff. The tone of the letters and articles suggests that domestic workers have changed, and not for the better. This view was not singular to *Kompas* readers. A managing editor at the *Jakarta Post* told me that some of her readers complain that younger PRT no longer hold traditional values and that "nowadays" villages send lazy or morally lax workers, not "good and clever young women", to the city to do domestic work.[10]

Rehearsing employers' anxieties and crediting nostalgia, such reporting diverted attention from a public debate about what might constitute decent work for domestic workers in a "modern" Indonesia. In the same way, popular stories that discussed *mudik*, the annual return of city dwellers to their hometowns or villages for Lebaran, focused firmly on employers' needs. Lebaran is when the majority of PRT get their annual bonuses and brave traffic chaos to spend time in their hometowns or villages. For middle-class families remaining in the city, *mudik* means coping without the domestic workers on whom the smooth running of their households depends. Apart from covering traffic accidents and congestion – hundreds die on the roads during this holiday period each year – journalists recycle a repertoire of stories about the inconvenience of being without PRT.

Scripts follow a pattern. One storyline is the impossibility of managing city life without household help: middle-class wives anxious to meet cultural expectations are reluctant to ask husbands or sons to help. Another is the inflated price of *infal* (temporary domestic workers prepared to work during Lebaran). Agencies seek to justify

10 Interview with Ati Nurbaiti, Jakarta, 27 June 2012.

high rates and one-off fees, yet there remains a sense that workers are taking advantage. A common concern is that formerly trusted domestic workers may not return after the holiday. Two articles featured an employer who organizes return transportation, withholds salary, or gives "prizes" to those who report back promptly (*Kompas* 2008c, d). Indeed, prominent feminist journalist Julia Suryakusuma shared with me her experience of feeling "betrayed" when a PRT with whom she thought she had a "mutual" relationship failed to return after a holiday.[11] Such narratives emphasize the discomfort and inconvenience caused to employers by PRT not being there when they are most needed – a reluctant acceptance, not willing embrace, of domestic worker rights.

Indeed, across the sample of stories examined, what is striking is the amount of space given to the voices of employers, owners of employment agencies, or officials. By contrast, the few articles in the sample reporting on the domestic worker movement operate in a different register. Journalists introduce a new vocabulary – *memberdayakan* (empowerment), *hak-hak* (rights), and *keterampilan* (skills) – running counter to the more common use of words such as victim, abuse, torture, rape, theft, kidnap, robbery, and deception. Two articles describe how the police abused domestic workers who denied accusations of theft. One broke new ground with the headline *Pramuwisma Minta Diperhatikan Nasibnya* (Domestic Workers Asking for More Attention to their Fate) (*Kompas* 2004b). Such a headline recognizes the potential for (contentious) domestic worker voices to be heard.

Feminist Journalists Intervene

A few feminist journalists supported the domestic worker movement from the start. They challenged commonly held assumptions, spread the word across their networks, and advocated for legislative change. Behind the scenes they helped JALA PRT and other domestic worker organizations develop media strategies and skills. The next part of this chapter considers the contribution of four such individuals, all self-identified feminists. Each emphasized a particular dimension of domestic worker claims to legitimacy. Modelling modes of storytelling that disturbed established narratives, they encouraged readers to

11 Interview with Julia Suryakusuma, London, 24 October 2015.

imagine a politics of intervention and protection instead of having recourse to a politics of disregard.

Ati Nurbaiti

Ati Nurbaiti, the distinguished journalist I met as I researched my MA dissertation, has strong feminist credentials and connections. A graduate in politics from the University of Indonesia and active in student politics, she was one of the founders of the influential feminist NGO Solidaritas Perempuan (SP). After leaving university, she became SP's first chair (Solidaritas Perempuan n.d.). While aware of issues relating to domestic work at home, SP leaders had decided to concentrate on the regulation of overseas domestic work. As Ati recalled, "when I worked with Solidaritas Perempuan, in those days they were saying they couldn't take on the issue of domestic maids: they recognized it as the hardest task then".[12]

Ati started at the *Jakarta Post* in July 1992, quickly winning recognition as a courageous journalist. She was one of a handful of women who put their names to the Sirnagalih Declaration, a document named after the West Javanese village where journalists and their supporters had gathered on 7 August 1994 (Harsono 1994). Fifty-eight journalists and cultural figures signed the document condemning the Suharto government's withdrawal of licences to publish from three popular news sources: *Tempo*, *Editor*, and *DeTik*. At that time, journalists were required to join the PWI (Persatuan Wartawan Indonesia), the only officially recognized Indonesian Journalists' Association. Bill Tarrant, who was working for the *Jakarta Post* at the time, described the outrage journalists felt when the PWI ("that toady press union") refused to back calls for reinstatement of the magazines' publication permits. However, the Declaration not only rejected all forms of government censorship but also announced the formation of a new trade union, the Alliance of Independent Journalists or AJI (Aliansi Jurnalis Independen). Ati was co-chair. Her actions risked her professional career and personal freedom. Her editor protected her job by telling government officials who wanted her sacked that she was "no longer working in the newsroom". However, one *Jakarta Post* journalist was dismissed and two imprisoned for publishing AJI's unlicensed publication, *The Independen* (Tarrant 2008: 142–6).

12 Interview with Ati Nurbaiti, Jakarta, 27 June 2012.

A forthright role model for female journalists, Ati investigated reports of killings by pro-Indonesian militias in East Timor in 1999. Witness to what looked like a massacre, she reported that the Indonesian military must have been in a position to control the violence (Tarrant 2008: 208–9). Such reporting was even more striking because, at that time, male journalists and editors frequently expressed the view that journalism was "too hard for women" and refused them contentious frontline work (Romano 2003: 109). Later, accepting one of several international awards for rights-oriented journalism, Ati explained that she had sustained her passion for advocacy by participating in feminist, student, and journalist networks dating back to the 1980s and found satisfaction in training journalists to provide "insightful coverage instead of merely sensational news" (Australia–Indonesia Partnership 2011: 9–10). Younger professionals found her inspiring. Prodita Sabarini, who covered the story of the first National Domestic Workers' Day demonstration in Jakarta described in the previous chapter, began at the *Jakarta Post* in 2005. When she was awarded a fellowship from the International Women's Media Foundation in 2013, Prodita credited her success to "senior female editors such Ati Nurbaiti" and expressed the hope that she might inspire the next generation "the way they have inspired me" (IWMF 2013).

In August 2000, Ati spoke on the theme of "Media and Labour Migration in Asia" (Nurbaiti 2000). Indonesia's First Lady, Sinta Nuriya, and several women's organizations had just called for a ban on sending domestic workers to Saudi Arabia. Fiercely critiquing current reporting practices as unprofessional, Ati argued that journalists should point out the futility of banning migration without reducing rural poverty. She urged journalists to worry less about political correctness, acquire specialist knowledge of the field, and write about policy – wrongly considered "too dry" for readers (and perhaps for journalists, too). In addition to reporting abuse cases, journalists should highlight the efforts PRT were making to establish support networks and fledgling unions, albeit on a small scale.

However, the crux of Ati's argument was that journalists are blind to the connection between Indonesia's gender order and the tide of women heading overseas. How, she asked, can women be expected to stay at home when they can earn around Rp.1 million a month (USD100) for household work abroad compared to "barely Rp.150,000" (USD15) in Indonesia? Why do stories about abuse of overseas workers, supposedly protected as part of employers' families, not "ring a bell" with Indonesian journalists who, most likely, describe their PRT as part of *their* families? Why do journalists repeat notions that mistreatment of domestic workers is a matter of "bad fate" or misjudgement? Answers to such questions, Ati argued, lie in the intersections of gender, class, and culture, resulting in too much focus on "agonizing" and too little on "organizing". Researching the latter can be "a long, gruelling process" that few journalists find interesting. Her words were an attempt to jolt journalists out of stasis into intervention. They offered a blueprint for advocacy journalism, a charter, perhaps, for a concerted media campaign against a politics of disregard.

In her management roles at the *Post*, Ati sought to get stories about domestic work inside Indonesia into the newspaper and keep them there. When I met her some twelve years after her Manila conference speech, she explained her thinking to me in this way:

> One aspect we are very interested in here at the *Post* is making the connection for our readers between the treatment of migrant workers overseas and the treatment of domestic workers here. We keep hammering on seeing the link.
>
> Our paper is trying to shift public opinion. People here tend to say that domestic workers are different from other workers because employers provide accommodation and food. They regard domestic work as "outside" the democracy sector and having nothing to do with politics.[13]

Ati's imagery suggests a weight of public opinion piled up against recognition of domestic worker rights. In her mind, the onus is on feminist journalists to challenge discriminatory divisions between public and private spheres and drive home the arguments for domestic worker rights.

Jakarta Post reporters in the provinces bridged gaps between feminist and international "rights talk" and regional custom and practice. They did so by acknowledging local values and Indonesia's national development. An article about the RTND domestic workers school in Yogyakarta portrayed the students as dutifully committed to Indonesia's development and Javanese ideals of harmony. Students so poor that they paid school fees (if at all) in rice, cassava, or vegetables were not "merely trained to do household chores" but "taught how to drive a car and a motorcycle, operate a computer, speak English, and

13 Interview with Ati Nurbaiti, Jakarta, 27 June 2012.

prepare a work contract" (Susanto 2004). Another journalist covered a public meeting to discuss a possible domestic worker law in Denpasar, Bali. She reassured readers that any new law would take account of "customary and religious rituals" and explained that local politicians and employers had endorsed reform on condition that "family-like" relationships were retained (Suriyani 2008). In Surabaya, describing a project for child domestic workers, a *Post* journalist lauded the region's strong family values and ethos of helping the poor, even while recounting the scandal of a seventeen-year-old PRT who gave birth unattended after being dismissed from her job (Harsaputra 2007). In Jakarta, reporters advocated for reform using frames familiar to their readers such as child domestic work, trafficking, and victim sagas (Setiogi 2003; Gunawan 2008; Yazid 2008). Editorial and opinion pieces "called" or "pushed" for legal protection, presented *mudik* stories in a feminist frame, or focused on Indonesia's international reputation, appealing to national pride.

Ati herself wrote articles incorporating a feminist analysis. "No Sense of Urgency to Help Indonesia's Heroes", for example, featured Weni, raped by her employer in Saudi Arabia and imprisoned for adultery (Nurbaiti 2008). The piece ends by making a more general, feminist-inspired reference to the disregard shown to Indonesian PRT, whether in the Middle East or Indonesia:

> Migrant workers earn much more abroad than they would in Indonesia, but back home, in a society that puts little value on women's rights or workers' rights, they are still just lowly maids.

In another piece, Ati argued that such a mindset perpetuates a damaging ideal of masculinity. Having low-waged domestic workers constantly on call produces children and "grown men", who see no reason to "take up even one cog of the household wheel". The result is a politics in which "Indonesian men and women [...] think they are so advanced while failing to notice how our meccas of modernity strive [unsuccessfully, my addition] to address the needs of household care" (Nurbaiti 2009).

Just as Stoler identified that a politics of disregard maintained a fiction of altruism in colonial times, Nurbaiti's journalism uncovered gendered fabrications and failures to take notice that sustained the comforts of twenty-first-century Indonesian modernities.

Luviana

If Ati Nurbaiti bolstered domestic workers by pointing to the self-deceptions – or what Stoler (2009: 259–60) refers to as "vital lies" – of the middle classes, Luviana Ariyanti (Luviana), a journalist with equally strong feminist credentials, is known for her outspoken defence of workers' rights. And if Ati was particularly valuable to the movement as a member of Jakarta's mainstream journalist establishment, with access to high-ranking civil servants, editors, and politicians, Luviana brought experience in community journalism. Her father had been a labourer on a sugar plantation in Central Java before winning a scholarship to university and becoming a civil servant. "We did not have a house or toilet then", she told me, "and I saw for myself that the life of the poor was very hard".[14] Studying communications at Atma Jaya University in Yogyakarta, she became part of the same student activism as the feminists who founded RTND and, in 1998, helped establish a branch of AJI in Yogyakarta (Tarida 2013b: 9).

After graduating, Luviana volunteered with LBH Yogyakarta and worked as a reporter for a fledgling community radio station. "We made the news then", she explained, "because there was only supposed to be one official radio. We decided to broadcast anyway." Having joined the radio arm of the Indonesian feminist journal *Jurnal Perempuan* in 1999, she became convinced that "journalism is supposed to work for the citizens, for the rights of citizens" (Wulandari and Thaniago 2012). Later, condemning business and political hijacking of press freedoms at a panel discussing "Women and the New Media" in Jakarta in 2016, Luviana urged journalists to use alternative media to "counter mainstream attitudes and media marginalization of women's issues" (Suryakusuma 2016).

Her status as something of a working-class heroine came, however, not from her work with feminist and human rights media outlets but her prolonged, high-profile dispute with Metro TV. Luviana joined the TV station as a reporter in 2002, becoming an assistant producer in 2007. However, the company dismissed her in June 2012, following disagreements over management practices and her attempt to organize an in-house union. Prominent businessman and politician Surya Paloh (described by at least one researcher in Indonesia as openly using the station to advance his political career and business interests) owned Metro TV (Haryanto 2011: 117).[15] Though the details of the dispute are complex

14 Interview with Luviana Ariyanti, Jakarta, 30 June 2015.

15 Surya Paloh was also chair of the National Democratic Party (Nasdem),

– eventually, three cases went to court – Luviana became a symbol of resistance to media owners' encroachment on editorial independence (Wulandari and Thaniago 2012: 6; Solidaritas Luviana 2016). One report of the drawn-out dispute with Metro TV couples Luviana's name with that of Marsinah, the young factory worker murdered for union activity in 1993 (Tarida 2013a). For Luviana, advocacy journalism on behalf of fellow workers, including PRT, was axiomatic, a matter of principle for a pro-democracy feminist campaigner.

Lita Anggraini was amongst a group of women who established "Women's Solidarity for Luviana" (Solidaritas Perempuan Untuk Luviana or SOVI). Lita served as the group's coordinator (Anggraini 2012). AJI, the International Federation of Journalists, the Press Legal Aid Society (LBH Pers), and a raft of other organizations including leading labour unions backed Luviana's campaign for reinstatement. SOVI framed the campaign as a continuation of the *permuda* idealism of the 1990s and an unfinished class struggle. A photograph on SOVI's Facebook page showed a very young Luviana with fellow members of the Youth Struggle Organization of Yogyakarta (Persatuan Perjuangan Pemuda Yogyakarta) taken on 21 May 1998, the day of President Suharto's resignation (Solidaritas Luviana 2016; see Tarida 2013b). Luviana won further international support when the 2012 Indonesian Film Festival held in Melbourne screened *The Frequency*, a film featuring her fight with Metro TV.

One consequence of Luviana's enforced absence from Metro TV was that she had time to become enmeshed in the domestic worker movement. She began to act as JALA's pro bono media consultant, writing and editing press releases and campaign materials and advising on media strategy. She counselled JALA to modernize, use Facebook and Twitter, and draw attention by other means than through demonstrations. To counter media recycling of stock stories, she suggested publishing a book of PRT testimonies as source material for journalists, a project that came to fruition with the help of ILO funding in 2017. Continuing the traditions of RTND's domestic workers school, she taught PRT how to produce good copy, improve their vocabulary, structure their prose, and participate in press conferences and online journalism.[16] Recognizing her expertise,

a party he founded after losing to Aburizal Bakrie, the owner of TVOne and ANTV, in a contest for the leadership of Golkar (Sudibyo and Patria 2013: 272–3).

16 Interview with Luviana Ariyanti, Jakarta, 30 June 2015; observation of writing workshops, Jakarta, 28 June 2015 and 27 November 2016.

the ILO employed Luviana to lead training for journalists and domestic workers as part of the PROMOTE project (discussed later in this chapter).

Along with domestic workers elsewhere, organized domestic workers in Indonesia have celebrated International Domestic Workers' Day (IDWD) on 16 June every year since the adoption of C189 on that date in Geneva in 2011. To mark IDWD 2013, Luviana posted an article on *Kompas*'s citizen journalism platform, *kompasiana.com* (Luviana 2013). Denouncing those who have failed to act on behalf of domestic workers, she spelt out the culprits clearly, as my edited translation shows:

> The government does not see it; the House [of Representatives] looks with only one eye. The country takes no heed of the struggles of the poor and remains silent every 16 June. This country claims to have fought for its workers but is too proud to accept the domestic workers as part of the workforce. They are still seen as *ngenger* [...] ignorant, job seekers, uneducated, and uninformed. While domestic workers contribute to society as workers, caregivers, and engaged and active citizens, those in power pay no attention and refuse to contemplate change.

Rather than depicting PRT as silent and silenced, Luviana reminds readers that they have been out on the streets protesting with "napkins, stoves, and pots". Castigating "the country" for its silences and refusals to pay attention, and casting politicians as the unseeing ones, she ends by addressing domestic workers with an invocation that reads like a prayer:

> Keep the dreams. May the president, the parliament, and the people listen to you because they cannot manage without you. They cannot go out without your help from morning till night, cleaning their homes, preparing their food, and nurturing their children.

To help reach "the dreams", in March 2016 Luviana and a group of feminist activists and journalists founded *Konde.co*, an online media platform to provide a critical public space for the views and voices of women and minorities. Designed to appeal to a new audience of younger feminists, radical journalists, and LGBTQI activists amongst others (Yoedtadi and Pribadi 2020), *Konde.co* frequently features PRT stories and articles championing the Domestic Workers Bill.

Dian Septi Trisnanti and Caecilia Mediana

Lita Anggraini introduced me to two other feminist journalists involved in advocacy, Dian Septi Trisnanti (Dian Septi) and Caecilia Mediana.[17] Dian is a left-wing, international feminist, while Caecilia's focus is women's rights and national development. Their stories illustrate how JALA PRT contains difference. Dian and Caecilia, along with many of JALA's supporters, have shared allegiances and histories. Both attended university in Yogyakarta, joining pro-democracy and feminist circles, both worked for the feminist *Jurnal Perempuan*, and both encountered JALA through NGO contacts.

Caecilia, a journalist at a prominent national newspaper, explained that in her case she met Lita Anggraini at a meeting in Jakarta in 2015. Impressed, she called a friend from *Jurnal Perempuan*, who advised her to contact JALA and learn more about PRT issues. She and Lita developed a "good relationship" and started meeting "quite often to discuss media coverage of PRT". This was even though Caecilia did not see being a PRT as a profession but more as a stopgap. Describing her contribution, Caecilia told me that:

> There are two things I prefer to write about PRT; first, about the neglect of their rights by their bosses, and second, about the success stories of domestic workers who go on to be brave and smart and start businesses and make their living that way instead of being a domestic worker.[18]

Betterment, in this reading, is about individual women improving themselves, not collective empowerment or getting domestic labour valued *per se*. Nor did Caecilia feel a need to "show it off about being feminist"; she preferred "to demonstrate it through action and writing". By contrast, Dian Septi, a member of the revolutionary socialist feminist organization Politik Rakyat and of the radical, worker-oriented feminist group, Perempuan Mahardhika, was working as a community radio journalist for Marsinah FM when I met her in 2015 (Septi and Ariane 2013).[19] Her focus was on supporting low-paid women workers to join unions and fight for better wages and conditions as members of Indonesia's working class.

17 Lita Anggraini mentioned a third journalist, Laeny Sulistywati, but I was unable to meet her or track down articles she had written.

18 Interview with Caecilia Mediana, Jakarta, 13 August 2015.

19 Interview with Dian Septi Trisnanti, Jakarta, 3 July 2015.

Dian was as impressed by Lita Anggraini as Caecilia. Having met Lita at a women's rights meeting in 2014, Dian built a relationship with her based on their "shared focus on gender and women's work" and a "feeling of solidarity". Believing that too many Indonesians have avoided "feminist discourse", resulting in the "relegation" of women's and LGBTQI issues, Dian aimed to use Marsinah FM to boost the "courage of women workers to speak, express, and protest" (Marsinah FM 2012). During one of my visits to JALA, I observed Dian patiently coaching PRTs as they rehearsed their "transformation" stories for a broadcast. Rather than seeking ways out of domestic work, Dian wants PRT to help build an anti-capitalist movement grounded in collective knowledge and solidarity (ILO 2013a; Perempuan Mahardhika 2014). Her advocacy journalism casts domestic workers as articulate and courageous members of an (adversarial) international socialist and feminist workers' movement, out on the streets of Jakarta and confident in using alternative media to promote their cause in trade union circles and on a global stage. Caecilia, in her turn, is well positioned to reach more conventional audiences and inform and influence a new generation of mainstream journalists, encouraging them to report on PRT optimism and organizational skills.

Individual journalists such as those profiled here did get the issue of domestic worker rights and more domestic worker voices into the news. However, as feminist media scholar Caroline Byerly points out, "the gender politics of media texts" resides in the often male-dominated work environments journalists inhabit (Byerly 2016: 18–21). In Indonesia, according to a report compiled by AJI, 94% of editors-in-chief were men who, in line with prevailing norms, were likely to leave their wives to manage domestic affairs (Luviana 2012). Recognizing that intervention was needed at the institutional level, AJI Jakarta, the ILO, and JALA PRT launched a scheme in June 2015 with the express intent of encouraging journalism that would "push policy change" and "influence public behaviour" (ILO 2008: 23).

Changing Newsroom Cultures: AJI and the ILO

The AJI/ILO journalism scheme was part of a well-funded, government-approved ILO project named PROMOTE. From 2012 to 2017, ILO officers sponsored initiatives co-designed with JALA PRT and other partners to help end child domestic labour and achieve the decent work standards set out in C189 for adult PRT (US Department of Labor

2012). As part of a drive to change public attitudes, AJI took the lead on a fellowship programme that offered journalists a residential training weekend, the opportunity to work with a mentor, and a cash award of Rp.5 million – a worthwhile sum given that journalists in Jakarta earned on average between Rp.3–4 million a month (around USD500). In return, the chosen fellows had to produce one or more items of innovative and well-informed journalism within a few weeks, and their editors had to agree to publish these (AJI Jakarta 2015; *Jakarta Post* 2016). The scheme also ran free training sessions for journalists, newsroom editors, NGOs, and domestic worker organizations in the provinces of Jakarta, East Java, Lampung (Sumatra), and South Sulawesi. Both the recollections of participants and an analysis of the journalism produced indicate that the scheme tackled backroom barriers to change, educated journalists about domestic worker issues and the politics of legal reform, and introduced reading and viewing publics to new versions of victimhood and new imaginaries of PRT as trusted professionals and contributing citizens.

Backroom Barriers

My journalist informants mentioned four aspects of newsroom culture that worked against engagement with PRT claims. First, editors believed domestic worker stories had scant news value. One journalist put the problem bluntly:

> Even if you feel you ought to write about domestic workers, stories about PRT just don't get enough clicks [...] so we can't run them. If we compare PRT stories with other news, such as, you name it, corruption, road accidents, eleven people killed, and so on, they do not do well, except maybe for exceptional cases where the PRT gets hit by her boss, then OK, it has good news value. Then we will grab it, take a photographer, and make a story of it.[20]

In other words, speed is of the essence and exceptionality wins. Online readers do not tire, it seems, of stories about political corruption or victimhood. These sell papers and arguably are grounded in Islamic ideals of justice and the obligation of individuals to protect the weak, promote good, and prevent evil (Steele 2011: 544). Unless victimhood is involved, one journalist from *Tempo* magazine told me, "Big newspaper editors are likely to be reluctant to cover such a

20 Interview with AJI member, Jakarta, 15 July 2015.

marginalized issue because there is always more important news".[21] Another, who did not want his newspaper named, described what happened when he tried to persuade his news desk to carry a story on a draft regulation to protect PRT. Things did not go well:

> Well, we held a meeting, blah blah, and it was just as I explained before, the reaction was that this was not a news story because nothing had happened, nothing has changed, so this is not news. Anyone can submit a draft regulation. [22]

After much argument, his article was published but "did not garner any response from readers" despite his enthusiasm.

Journalists attending training gave Arum Ratnawati, national chief technical adviser for the PROMOTE project (Ratnawati 2013), the same picture. They told her that "in the kitchens and boardrooms" of media offices they "find it very hard to get the issue of the RUU PPRT published [...] editors are not always ready to give us space".[23] Thwarted by editors and faced with unimpressed readers, there was little encouragement to do more.

The second barrier was that by 2015, managers and editors regarded domestic worker stories as "old news". As Luviana explained:

> I know what journalists need; they need something new. Truly, the PRT movement is something they have been getting information about so it's no longer new. Demonstrations are still important if the movement can build more support from below, but otherwise, demonstrations are boring [...] journalists won't come to press conferences unless the issue is new.[24]

Another committed journalist agreed. "JALA needs to change strategies", she said, "it's no longer about hunger strikes or demonstrations".[25] *Jakarta Post* journalist Sri Wahyuni was thrilled to make the national news with her coverage of a stage performance put on in Yogyakarta by PRT in 2004 (Wahyuni 2004). By 2016, however, she sensed a change. She reflected that PRT activism "was new then, workers were speaking with their own voice [...] but now the domestic worker story

21 Interview with *Tempo* journalist, Jakarta, 6 March 2016.
22 Interview with AJI members, Jakarta, 15 July 2015.
23 Interview with Arum Ratnawati, Jakarta, 10 July 2015.
24 Interview with Luviana Ariyanti, Jakarta, 30 June 2015.
25 Interview with *Kompas* journalists, Jakarta, 13 August 2015.

has been around a long time".[26] Political stalemate thus led editors to dismiss stories other than abuse sagas as non-events.

A third barrier was a skills and knowledge deficit. Journalists were unsure what or how to write other than by reproducing stock stories of PRT as victims or morally suspect. One AJI member, who had recently moved to Jakarta from Yogyakarta – where domestic worker organizing often featured in the local news – found his Jakarta colleagues ill-informed and "quite uncertain about where they should stand or what they should emphasize".[27] Another wanted up-to-date material, introductions to activist networks, and insight into different perspectives.[28] A third felt journalists needed guidance on how to report abuse "with a good angle".[29] A fourth confessed that even after talking with experts, she still hadn't decided "what side to take".[30] While indecision might reflect ambivalence as much as ignorance or timidity, an award-winning journalist told me that only specialist knowledge would enable journalists to move beyond writing about "flagrant abuse" or "the Lebaran moment" when housewives panic as PRT disappear.

Finally, some journalists believed that media owners with little regard for domestic workers influenced editorial decisions. One told me that editors deem migrant worker stories newsworthy "because government and big business make a lot of money out of them" and discount PRT news because "political parties are only interested if money is involved".[31] Three mainstream journalists I met early on shared this view. Confident that migrant workers get "top headlines" because they are "good business", they were hazy about the last time their paper carried a story about PRT. Indeed, one felt that few journalists would challenge editors by raising issues around domestic workers in Indonesia because "we have a patrilineal society, maybe [...] I must work and earn money; my wife must stay in the house and not do anything and take care of my kids." As far as PRT are concerned, he continued, "well, you cannot see them as other women workers, that's different in Indonesian terms, but it's not to do with gender, but with *budaya* or culture".[32] Journalists sharing his views, and

26 Interview with Sri Wahyuni, Yogyakarta, 1 March 2016.
27 Interview with journalist from *Tirto.id*, Jakarta, 23 November 2016.
28 Interview with journalist from BeritaSatuTV, Jakarta, 6 March 2016.
29 Interview with journalists from Reuters, Jakarta, 4 March 2016.
30 Interview with journalist from *Tempo*, Jakarta, 14 July 2015.
31 Interview with Monique Rijkers, Jakarta, 27 February 2017.
32 Meeting with three *Kompas* journalists, Jakarta, 27 June 2012.

facing uninterested editors were unlikely, perhaps, to join the AJI/ILO scheme.

Several senior journalists and editors, on the other hand, gave the project their blessing. Jajang Jamaludin, a senior editor at *Tempo* magazine and member of the management committee for AJI's school of journalism, and Monique Rijkers, an award-winning former Metro TV producer whose work on violence against women was well respected, acted as mentors to fellowship holders. Nurul Hamami, senior political editor at *Republika*, founded in 1993 by the Association of Indonesian Muslim Intellectuals (ICMI) and Indonesia's third most-read newspaper in 2012 (Steele 2013: 27), sponsored a journalist. Nurul found it "an honour to work with Lita Anggraini and see her dedication and commitment". He believed that *Republika* was duty bound to support PRT claims because of the paper's investment in democratization, "which makes it the right of every citizen to get a proper job in terms of benefit, health facility and others".[33] His views reflect what Janet Steele has called the "paraideology" of Islamic journalism – "the goal of justice" (2011: 5, 43).

Nine journalists won AJI/ILO fellowships in 2015. They came from a range of organizations including long-established print publications, radio and TV stations, and online media. Several were recent graduates in media and journalism, representing a new generation. The group was diverse in background and religion: the selection panel, pleased with the number and quality of applicants and the support from editors, was optimistic that the project would "change journalists' understanding and open their minds [...] for the long term". The then chair of AJI Jakarta, Ahmad Nurhasim, told me that the scheme was an expression of AJI's commitment to "give voice to the voiceless [...] the children, the poor and downtrodden" and an opportunity to change the minds of journalists who "just don't care" about legal protection for PRT. [34]

The Published Stories

Sixteen articles, four radio broadcasts and podcasts, and one TV news item produced by the AJI fellowship holders were published, posted, or aired, some in several formats, between 18 August and 19 September 2015. Editors had agreed to honour this publishing window. The ILO

33 Interview with Nurul Hamami, Jakarta, 21 August 2015.

34 Interview with Ahmad Nurhasim, Jakarta, 12 July 2015.

Jakarta office posted English-language versions of nine of the articles on its website.[35]

Support from editors was crucial in finding space for pro-PRT journalism. *Republika* placed hard-hitting features written by its journalist, Andi Mohammad Ikhbal (who, amongst other things, accused the DPR of "playing ping pong" with the draft Bill), on its front page for three consecutive days (Ikhbal 2015a, b, c). Carlos Michael Kodoati from BeritaSatu TV was thrilled when his eight-minute report, "Asa Anak Pantura" (Hopes of Children of the Pantura) – which exposed the coastal area of Indramayu in West Java as a regular source of child domestic workers for the capital – was screened as a news item "morning, noon and night" (BeritaSatu 2015).[36] The online news portal *CNN Indonesia* posted four features by its fellowship holders, Abraham Utama and Utami Diah Kusumawati. Their stories exposed the systematic and unscrupulous recruitment and exploitation of child domestic workers aged between fifteen and seventeen caught in "cycles of abuse" (Kusumawati 2015a, b; Utama 2015a, b; Utama and Kusumawati 2015a, b, c, and d). The business-oriented *Varia.id* sponsored two journalists, Muhammad Irham and Vela Andapita, and carried in-depth interviews with the leaders of the Tunas Mulia and Sapu Lidi domestic worker unions (Irham and Andapita 2015a, b) along with an investigative piece delving into prevarication and evasion amongst leading members of the DPR (Irham and Andapita 2015c).[37]

Other contributions included two radio broadcasts aired on KBR Saga (formerly KBR 68H, Indonesia's first independent radio broadcast agency).[38] *Kontan.co.id* ran Augustinus Da Costa's critique of government failures to formalize domestic work and introduce contracts (Da Costa 2015a, b). Mitra Tarigan's "Never Escaping from Modern Slavery" appeared in *Tempo*'s daily newspaper *Koran Tempo* (Tarigan 2015a), while the evening daily *Suara Pembaruan*, targeted

35 The list of references provides details of the Indonesian and English-language versions used. For simplicity, after the first mention and where appropriate, I have cited the English-language version.

36 Interview with Carlos Michael Kodoati, Jakarta, 27 November 2015.

37 The Indonesian-language versions I used for analysis are no longer available on the *Varia.id* website; all references are therefore to the ILO versions.

38 The same material was also published on the 68H News Portal. The ILO credited those articles to Quinawaty Pasaribu, a KBR staff member who edited Manan's broadcasts and was also part of the fellowship scheme (Pasaribu 2015a, b).

at Christian audiences, featured Ignatius Herjanjam's plea for the abolition of child domestic work (Herjanjam 2015). Only one AJI fellow expressed disappointment when her interviews with PRT about the health and safety hazards of domestic work did not make "headline news" but were placed elsewhere (Manan 2015a, b).[39]

The articles record a moment when journalists brought the views of PRT, NGO activists, employers, politicians, and the government into dialogue. They reveal discordant relationships but were also an exercise in re-inscription: a palimpsest, perhaps. The media fellows reworked tropes of victimhood, distrust, and dependency. Shifting focus from individual victims and perpetrators to structural deficits, and censuring parliament for its procrastination and the police and judiciary for apparent dereliction of duty, they portrayed PRT as trusted professionals and contributing citizens.

Rewriting Victimhood

Fifteen stories referred to abuse, but in ways that illustrate endemic disregard as much as episodic exceptionalism. As characterized by feminist media scholar Sally Munt, the AJI journalists supplied the names, places of origin, and the ages of victims to signal authenticity and "push towards a more redistributive social imaginary" (2016: 13–14). They used worker narratives to evince shame – shame that Indonesian employers (like those overseas) withhold or pay very low wages and shame that young women in poorer regions still have little choice of employment. They also illustrated agency and transformation. Thus, while the published articles record incidents of child trafficking, confinement, confiscation of phones, physical and sexual abuse, broken promises about wages and workloads, punishment for perceived mistakes, extreme overwork, and exposure to unsafe working conditions, in every case, victimhood occupied a small percentage of the article or broadcast. At least equal space was given to thematic analysis and advocacy.

Collectively, the victim narratives undermined myths of the mutual benefit and familial framing of the practice of sending young girls to the city to work as PRT. Readers met ordinary housewives who nonetheless treated the children they employed as PRT differently from their own. Just as Stoler introduced her readers to a broad swathe of "colonial actors [...] neither particularly malicious nor sympathetic",

39 Interview with Nurika Manan, Jakarta, 24 November 2015.

but (quoting W. E. B. Du Bois) "calm, good [women and] men" (2009: 249), so AJI fellows challenged the good women/bad women binary. Ratmi, a sixteen-year-old, called her employer "*majikan baik*" (a good employer) even though she failed to send her to school as promised (BeritaSatu 2015). Erly, an employer living in a housing complex in Bogor, took on a fifteen-year-old from a neighbour, knowing "she was still very young" because "she was already experienced, and submissive", yet later raised the young woman's salary and allowed her to visit family twice a month (Herjanjam 2015). In interviews, domestic workers did not describe themselves as belonging to their employers' families. Rather they spoke of the shame of returning to their villages sick, homesick, or unhappy (Utama and Kusumawati 2015c) and recounted how they had changed employers (and therefore moved home) several times before they were eighteen because of abuse or a desire for better pay (Herjanjam 2015).

Instead of blaming "bad" women, the AJI journalists implicated Indonesian society. Quoting the words of employers and brokers, they showed readers the profit-oriented and sometimes duplicitous practices involved in the recruitment and employment of PRT. One sponsor who recruited girls to work in cities as PRT or in karaoke bars admitted finding the fees from employers "very tempting [...] even higher than expected". This led the AJI journalist to describe such sponsors as "hunting" in unregulated hinterlands (Utama and Kusumawati 2015a). Another broker, who supplied child domestic workers to the affluent Menteng area of Jakarta, enticed young women from remote villages with such comments as "So how? You wanna be back or not? It's better than doing this?" – a question she put to a teenager pictured squatting over the task of breaking up the seeds of the melinjo tree (used to make highly valued crackers known as *emping*) with a stone (Kusumawati 2015b). Reports highlighted the recruitment of young women from East Nusa Tenggara and other notorious sending areas, noting the impact of rural poverty and the failures of police and judiciary to prosecute cases of confinement and trafficking (Herjanjam 2015; Utama and Kusumawati 2015a, b). One article featured Yantri, who started out as a vulnerable eighteen-year-old lured to Jakarta to find work as a PRT after being abused by her father, but later turned her victim tale around. She fled entrapment, trained as a babysitter, and then worked as a PRT to pay her younger siblings' school fees. In the meantime, Yantri kept busy "designing her future". She planned to return home, go back to school, and perhaps become a civil servant (Utama and Kusumawati 2015d).

Contributing Citizens and Trusted Professionals

Some of the articles turned employer dependency to the advantage of domestic workers. They showed how much the national economy and local communities depended on PRT. Whereas stock stories of domestic work made an implicit appeal to workers' loyalty and sense of duty, in the fellowship accounts the rhetorical appeal is towards justice for employees. Andi Ikhbal interviewed Ida Ruwaida Noor, a sociologist at the University of Indonesia whose research is discussed in the next chapter. He quoted her as saying that, although career families with children understand they save "millions of rupiahs" by hiring a PRT rather than using a child care centre, they fail to grasp that paying low wages perpetuates a system premised on exploitation (Ikhbal 2015a). In another article, Ikhbal describes Murtini (whom we encountered at the end of Chapter 2) as "an example of an ideal domestic worker" because she devotes her spare time to her role as deputy chair of Yogyakarta's Kongres Operata (KOY), attends evening meetings, and helps other PRT negotiate favourable contracts (2015a). Santi Sunarti (featured in Chapter 3) is similarly applauded for bringing domestic workers together to "build their own umbrella" of protection (Irham and Andapita 2015b). As was the case in Yogyakarta, where the names of activist PRT such as Ririn Sulastri and Yuli Maiheni became well-known through local media appearances, the AJI journalists introduced new names and characters into the repertoires of national media organizations.

Featuring PRT who contribute to their communities mobilized the Indonesian notion of *gotong royong*, a political and social construct that remains central in Indonesian imaginaries of nationhood. Powerfully invoked by President Sukarno to engender a spirit of togetherness and unity between government and people, the term was widely understood in the mid-1980s to refer to a tradition of mutual self-help and "a philosophy of life which takes the collective life as the most important" (Bowen 1986: 546). However, such a notion was, and is, open to co-option by government and state elites keen to control labour by linking *gotong royong* with familial harmony and a unified, quiescent Indonesian nation where poorer citizens will willingly work for free or at least conceal their discontent (Suwignyo 2019). Indeed, *gotong royong*, embraced by President Jokowi both pre- and post-pandemic, has been used against domestic workers.[40] A senior AJI official told

40 For example, a search of the Cabinet Secretariat website (https://setkab.go.id/) shows that Jokowi mentioned *gotong royong* four times in his

me, quietly, that he had heard ministers "use the argument that local wisdom in Indonesia, for example, *gotong royong*, is not totally in line with the ILO Convention, but is in fact preferable". Warned to be even-handed in the training provided by the ILO, the AJI fellowship journalists sought to persuade opponents of PRT reform by linking domestic worker rights and obligations with shared understandings of village values and collective struggles for social justice as well as for (national) or local development.

In addition to stressing the contributions of PRT as citizens, some of the AJI journalists took pains to portray domestic workers as modern employees. They replaced tropes of anxiety and distrust with examples of professional relationships underpinned by employment contracts. They provided examples showing that employers, as much as PRT, can benefit from more formal arrangements. Contracts are binding, so employers need no longer fear that workers will leave unexpectedly. Contracts specify duties and hours of work, removing concerns about paying workers "to do nothing all day". In place of anxiety about theft or the ignorant misuse of household equipment, workers trained in health and safety are shown to be willing and able to take more responsibility (Manan 2015a, b). In place of a belief that inexperienced, submissive, and low-paid workers are the most desirable, journalists demonstrate that contracts allow for flexibility and specialization and enable employers to secure and retain staff who offer reliable and professional housekeeping, child, or elder care (Da Costa 2015a).

When domestic workers were asked about contracts, they tended to describe them as being as much about trust, dignity, and empowerment as about wages and conditions. One informant from a "model" placement agency argued that a written contract "is made as a binder of trust" (Utama and Kusumawati 2015d). Workers recounted successful negotiations with pride. Santi described how she left one job where she was ordered to clean a toilet without gloves or a brush, telling her employer, "I am indeed a domestic worker, Sir, but I also have a sense of dignity". As a union member, she continued, "I learned to stand on my own, such as rejecting any job without adequate facilities and equipment" (Irham and Andapita 2015b). Workers wanted good relationships; "we don't demand a big salary",

inauguration speech in 2014 and six times in an opening speech to the National Working Meeting of the Indonesian Democratic Party of Struggle (PDI-P) in Jakarta on 6 June 2022.

they explained, but believed they deserved clean, safe, and modern working conditions (Manan 2015b). They wanted to feel comfortable in their "working culture" and viewed contracts as providing a basis for mutual understanding and respect (Ikhbal 2015a). In conversation with journalists, workers scripted new stories about themselves as "modern" domestic workers with rights. Yet being professional did not mean abandoning reciprocity. Rather than deleting the past, the activist PRT profiled in the AJI articles saw themselves as wanting to preserve the affective dimensions of domestic work.

Political Prevarication

Five journalists tackled the question of why Indonesia had not ratified C189 or passed a domestic worker law. Their writing was well-informed; at the three-day training for prospective fellows held in Bogor in early June 2015, Ariyanti, an expert member of the secretariat for Commission 1X at the DPR, had presented fifty-three slides giving an insider view of the content, processes, and (lack of) progress of draft legislation.[41] Her lecture highlighted six sticking points: wages, over-emphasis on workers rather than employers, a perceived attack on family values, difficulties with monitoring, underlying culture, and a lack of support from local governments (Ariyanti 2015). Capitalizing on access to insider information, the journalists who chose to focus on the Bill interviewed key MPs and top-level government officials, including some vocal opponents to change.

The oppositional voices told a story of politicians continuing to duck responsibility. Theirs was not a disregard arising from invisibility, but a matter of choice. Comments such as "not all employers are from the middle and upper classes", "we don't want this policy to burden the community", or "we beware of violating the rights of all components of the community" pitted the rights of workers against the interests of middle- and upper-class employers or more privileged formal workers earning at least the minimum wage (Irham and Andapita 2015c). Several politicians countered the call for comprehensive legislation. They told journalists that some employers need, or want, their PRT "to work 10 hours from the early morning to 5pm before they can take a rest". They insisted that work contracts would be "too rigid" as well as too "liberal, European or American" and would run counter to

41 Many thanks to Muhamad Nour for sending me a copy of the presentation following an interview with him at the ILO office, Jakarta, 10 July 2015.

Indonesian employment practices based on cooperation, kinship, and *ngenger* (Da Costa 2015; Ikhbal 2015a, b, c; Tarigan 2015a, b). One interviewee invoked the notion of *ibu-ibu rumah tangga* (wives and mothers who take care of the household), contending that the Bill must be delayed so that the voices of mothers who employ PRT could be heard (Ikhbal 2015a, c). Tarigan quoted a member of Commission 1X (the House committee that had sponsored the Bill) who argued that the relationship between the majority of domestic workers and employers could not – and should not – be considered a "professional" one, subject to legislation, but only a matter of private familial or *ngenger* practices (2015a).[42] Such comments imposed material and emotional binds on domestic workers and prioritized employers' wishes over domestic worker rights, ignoring the fact that many PRT needed time to care for their own households and children after work. No wonder, as one journalist recounted, that when Wina Ningsih, a member of the Sapu Lidi union, went with JALA to meet members of Commission 1X at the DPR and heard that the Bill would not be progressed, her smile shrank (*menyusut*) (Ikhbal 2015c).

Some of the politicians and officials interviewed blamed the political system (or each other) for stalling the Bill. Indonesia's legislative procedures, designed to achieve consensus, entail much toing and froing between government departments, party caucuses, standing committees, and a committee known as the Baleg which has the role of "harmonizing, unifying and consolidating" draft bills. However, a lack of transparency and an absence of party discipline can result in bills facing endless delays (Sherlock 2003: 31–3, 2012: 556–9). During his research, Andi Ikhbal secured an interview with a leading parliamentarian, Poempida Hidayatullah, who had supported the Bill as a member of Commission 1X between 2009 and 2014. Using Hidayatullah's testimony, Ikhbal (2015b) concluded that MPs, officials, and government ministers were "playing ping pong" with the draft

42 In 2017, the ILO published the results of a nationwide survey that effectively demolished many of these arguments. In 2015, only 1.3 percent of domestic workers were unpaid, child labour (defined as work by those under 18) was declining, and families employing domestic workers were of significantly higher economic status than families in general. Furthermore, domestic workers worked longer hours, more days a week, and received much lower wages than other workers. These findings suggest that "familial" relationships and "ngenger" practices, if taken to imply beneficence, were more imaginary than real (Suhaimi and Farid 2017).

Bill, rather than making "maximum effort" to bring the RUU PPRT to fruition.

Four points stand out in Ikhbal's analysis. First, party members in the Baleg did not necessarily support the position taken by fellow party members in Commission 1X. Consequently, progress at the final stages rested heavily on individuals such as Poempida and well-known actor-turned-politician Rieke Diah Pitaloka (featured in Chapter 3). Pitaloka had built a reputation for supporting the labour movement and had facilitated JALA PRT's meeting with Jokowi in May 2014.[43] Second, civil servants had failed to chase up on the Bill's progress. When challenged they covered themselves by saying that it had been "sent back to the Commission", or conversely, had been "sent to Baleg". Third, the Ministerial Regulation issued in January 2015 after the hunger strike provided an excuse for not championing a national law, even though senior civil servants admitted that a regulation carried no teeth at all. Last, in relation to C189, Ikhbal quoted one senior official who maintained that the government had not ratified the Convention for fear it would "overlap" with the RUU PPRT. Another averred that regulations were a better "match" with Indonesian society than C189. Such comments stood at odds with information I received in confidence from well-placed informants who told me that ministers wanted to delay ratification to avoid being criticized in public by ILO monitoring mechanisms. Setting one source against another, Iqbal's advocacy journalism revealed how intersecting aspects of disregard had systematically stalled the progress of successive bills.

Ikhbal ended his reports with comments from domestic workers and Lita Anggraini. Their words spoke of betrayal. They were caught in a cycle of raised hopes, broken promises, excuses, renewed efforts, and final disappointments. The ILO had urged AJI fellowship holders to find a balanced "middle way" so that "all sides could see something of their own viewpoint in any articles".[44] Journalists had indeed given proponents and opponents of the Bill space to speak. The message of their testimony, however, was bleak; even after giving domestic worker claims consideration in the DPR and ministerial offices, powerful voices still preferred to procrastinate.

---

43 I was unable to meet Rieke Pitaloka. For her comments on her role re the RUU PPRT in 2014–15, see an interview in *anataranews.com* (Samodro 2014).

44 Interview with Arum Ratnawati, Jakarta, 10 July 2015.

Beyond Disregard

In this chapter, disregard has provided a powerful tool for considering the contribution of advocacy journalism to the domestic workers' cause, moving the discussion beyond gendered invisibility or sensationalized victimhood (the problem of the "Mop"). Activists wanting to enlist journalists as champions of the domestic worker movement needed to take account of the affective, cultural, and institutional dimensions of the media world.

Individual journalists who supported PRT claims as part of a pro-democracy politics rooted in feminism were accustomed to risk. They set the stage for public debate about the place of paid domestic work in Indonesian modernity. With the support of the ILO and AJI, journalists and activists passed on *pemuda* values, activist experience, and professional expertise to a new generation of journalists. Upscaling advocacy presented challenges. ILO officials downplayed demands for a national law to retain government support. Journalists grappled with ambiguities arising from their personal dependence on PRT. Those wanting reform and those content with the status quo could experience the discomfort that disregard helped alleviate.

Nevertheless, advocacy journalism was a catalyst for change. In August 2016, to the organizers' surprise, eighty-two individuals or teams submitted entries to a competition offering generous cash awards for the best reporting about domestic work published or aired anywhere in Indonesia in the previous year. Senior figures – Endy Bayuni from the *Jakarta Post*, Burhan Solihin, executive editor of *Tempo.co*, and Mohamad Teguh, editor-in-chief of the large national private television company Surya Citra TV – judged the entries. I attended the awards ceremony, which took place at the upmarket Hotel Sofyan on the edge of Menteng in Jakarta. The room was crammed with enthusiastic young journalists. Buffet tables were piled with lunch. Domestic workers (including the group I had watched forming themselves into a union only a week earlier) occupied two large tables. Luviana presented a series of speakers endorsing the awards. Disappointment at the failure of the minister of manpower to appear as promised was replaced by delight as the award-winning teams received their cheques and attendees posed for the photoshoots that resulted in copious press coverage the next day.

Between September 2015 and September 2017, the ILO monitored press coverage of PRT issues to gauge the success of its interventions. They identified 480 articles and features in which journalists stated that they had contacted JALA PRT, domestic worker organizations, or other partners in the ILO/AJI project for information. An ILO-commissioned evaluation concluded that more journalists had written in depth on a wider range of topics, journalists beyond the Jakarta–Yogyakarta corridor were more aware of PRT issues, and younger journalists active on social media and working for online publications had reached new audiences (ILO 2018: 46–51). Qualitatively, the comparisons made in this chapter give substance to a new reporting repertoire and style which made material the presence of a new kind of professional and politically aware PRT. Advocacy journalism gave space to domestic worker agency. Reporters used PRT voices, testimony, and knowledge from experience to expose prevarication and excuse-making from recruiting agents, politicians, and civil servants. Journalists who joined the AJI scheme may have been motivated initially by cash payments and possible promotion, but were inspired by contact with PRT and NGO activists. As one put it to me, she was impressed "beyond expectations" on discovering how knowledgeable PRT informants were.

However, system-wide interventions also gave heightened visibility to influential opponents of the Bill. Indonesian governments and parliaments continued to disregard domestic worker claims. Such unresponsiveness in the face of marshalled arguments can breed cynicism and despair. Domestic workers in Kolkata, for example, asked researchers rhetorically, "if the employers read an article about us in the newspaper, do you think they would treat us with sympathy?" and continued, "no, they will beat us down more" (Qayum and Ray 2003: 546). Indeed, at a meeting for new members of a Jakarta domestic workers' union in December 2016, I heard Lita Anggraini, for the first time, say that getting a law passed might take twenty years.

The character at the centre of Ann Stoler's account of colonial disregard, Frans Carl Valck, lost his civil service job for writing reports of planter brutality that no one wanted to hear (2009: 199, 203). He disappeared from the (official) archive after being dismissed for outspokenness. At one level, this chapter tells a similar story – confirmed when a well-informed journalist told me, unobtrusively, that a minister had let him know the government had no intention of passing the Bill. However, the PRT profiled in many journalists' stories were not content with silent screams. Some have turned instead to citizen journalism. I watched Yuni Rahayu, a Sapu Lidi domestic workers' union member I had met several times, receive a certificate at the AJI journalism awards ceremony for her online advocacy. On 1 January 2018, a team of activist members from domestic worker unions in Jakarta, Yogyakarta, Semarang, Bandar Lampung, and Makassar launched an online newspaper to disseminate information and campaign tools to "their friends" – domestic workers across the JALA PRT network. Naming the paper *Tungku Menyala* (Burning Stove), and adding the strapline "once lit, will never be put out", the editorial team saw the online paper as a symbol of their struggle and an expression of their belief that "writing will inspire the hope of our movement" and, eventually, bring about change (*Tungku Menyala* 2018; Yuni 2019).

This chapter has demonstrated, as did Chapters 2 and 3, that feminist allegiances and shared personal histories of activism underlay the work of the journalists who advocated for domestic worker legislation and cultural change. In the next chapter, a companion piece as it were, I examine the contribution of some of Indonesia's feminist academics, researchers, and scholar-activists to changing mindsets governing domestic work.

CHAPTER

5

Contesting Certainties: Feminist Knowledge Production and Domestic Work

Early in my research journey, I outlined my ideas to an audience of Indonesian academics at a conference in Bandung.[1] The first comment from the floor struck a characteristic note. "In my experience", a female lecturer suggested, "whatever the activists may be saying, we will continue to use the term *pembantu* (helper) as we have always done. I think *pembantu* and employers are both fine with this." The second speaker was similarly implacable: "I think *pembantu* themselves prefer the term *pembantu* because they feel it gives them some respect, they are being seen as 'helping others' in this way."[2] The notes I made that day record that as the discussion continued (my topic proved controversial – I had to deal with ten questions in all), I was struck by three things: a sense that those who spoke were heavily dependent on having domestic workers at home; a sense of anxiety that "times were changing" and younger domestic workers were not as faithful or compliant as older ones; and a belief that activists overstate the problem. As one respondent put it, only Chinese Indonesians mistreat their workers; otherwise, the present arrangements work to everyone's advantage. Barely a month later, at a conference in Brighton, I encountered similar reports from some Southeast Asian

1 "From *Pembantu* to *Pekerja:* Changing representations of domestic workers in Indonesia", paper presented at the 7th International Indonesia Forum (IIF), State Islamic University of Sunan Gunung Djati, Bandung, 19–20 August 2014. Most participants were from Indonesian universities.

2 Field notes, Bandung, 20 August 2014.

scholars studying in the UK. My mention of Christine Chin's *In Service and Servitude* (1998), which exposed how low-paid domestic labour underpinned a middle-class modernity centred around a still patriarchal but dual-income nuclear family, caused a stir. Here was the same unshakeable belief I had met in Bandung; unregulated domestic work was an essentially benevolent institution.

What was I to make of such defensiveness? It tended to confirm comments I had already encountered, showing that middle-class professionals, including some describing themselves as feminists, had paid little attention to domestic work inside Indonesia because doing so would run counter to their class and gender interests and risk evoking deep discomfort (Blackburn 2004: 188; Irawaty 2011: 80–85). Academics in Indonesia, after all, have not commanded high salaries or had access to subsidized childcare and have therefore relied on low-paid domestic staff (Welch 2007: 673–4). Or were the views expressed at the conference evidence of the continuation of the "not sitting on chairs" culture considered in Chapter 1? In any event, it was with more disappointment than surprise that when Lita Anggraini gave me a list of people to contact on my next field trip, I saw only two names under the heading "academics". I began to fear that the answer to my question about the contribution of academics would be the negative one that they had contributed very little. I even considered shifting my focus elsewhere.

However, as I investigated further, a more nuanced picture emerged. The proposition that Indonesian scholars have neglected the study of paid domestic labour to protect class and gender privileges, I argue in this chapter, goes only so far. Such a viewpoint falls short in four respects. It underplays the structural constraints, cemented in the Suharto period and hard to dislodge post-1998, which operated around all Indonesian academics and social scientists who sought to develop unorthodox thinking. It overlooks gender-specific cultural practices and epistemic injustices feminist scholars faced (and continue to face). It telescopes the varied positioning of Indonesian scholars on a spectrum of academic to activist, ignoring the richness and dynamics of this continuum. Finally, I want to indicate how the position changed between 2011 – when C189 was adopted – and 2016, when I completed my fieldwork. By 2016, more individuals had embarked on higher-level studies in the field, and new collaborative research models had been trialled.

Yet, as feminist scholar Richa Nagar points out in her ethically challenging book, *Muddying the Waters*, politically engaged scholarship can be a risky venture, embroiled in uncomfortable questions of unequal power relations. Feminist research and writing "across borders", she argues, should be based on principles of "situated solidarities", an approach that attempts to share authority across researcher/researched binaries and acknowledges the possibilities of "distrust and epistemic violence" occurring in the context of "colonialist prioritizing" of scholarship from the global north (Nagar 2014: 5, 18). Describing her book as an "academic memoir", Nagar incorporates "stories, encounters and anecdotes" drawn from her excursions across the borders between academia and social movements, between academic and creative writing, and between her university in Minnesota and sites of resistance in Tanzania and India (2014: 6, 108–18). In her experience, challenging academic certainties and conventions comes at a cost. When she and eight NGO workers self-published a collective, self-reflexive critical analysis of NGO politics and practices in Uttar Pradesh in 2004, under the title *Sangtin Yatra* (Sangtin Journeys) for example, the village-based NGO staff whose life stories made up the body of the text were threatened with losing their jobs and Nagar was accused of conducting "unethical and exploitative research" (Anupamlata et al. 2004; Nagar 2014: 129–34). Later, Nagar's home US university press demurred at naming nine members of the collective as co-authors of an English edition of the book (eventually published as *Playing with Fire* [Sangtin Writers with Richa Nagar 2006]). The university press wanted Nagar – the "academic" – singled out as the "source of ideas" and provider of the "theoretical frame" (2014: 138–9). However, Nagar avers that feminist research can be more meaningful to those involved in struggles if scholars challenge those certainties of academia that distance research subjects from the production and dissemination of knowledge about them.

Similarly, this chapter draws on interviews, published reminiscences, "academic memoirs", and analyses produced by Indonesian scholars who sensed themselves to be living through critical times when boundaries between detached, seemingly objective scholarship and engaged solidarity needed to be breached. If earlier chapters considered the creation and occupation of social, political, and media spaces conducive to advancing domestic worker claims, this chapter traces the development of intellectual spaces where orthodox views of domestic life and work could be undermined. "Challenging Times" illustrates the obstacles in the path of feminist researchers in universities towards the close of the Suharto regime and during *reformasi*, highlighting two of the women's studies centres, known as *pusat studi wanita* (PSW) or *pusat studi gender* (PSG), that were a feature of that time. "Activist Researchers" examines an issue of Indonesia's first feminist journal, *Jurnal Perempuan* (*JP*), which was dedicated to the subject of paid domestic work and published in 2005 as a deliberate attempt to bridge the worlds of academia and activism. "Afterwards/ Afterword" reflects on my fieldwork encounters with researchers who investigated domestic work in Indonesia in the wake of C189.

Challenging Times: Women's Studies and Spaces for Feminism

Women's studies centres were well-placed, in principle, to research social issues such as domestic work. While fledgling centres had emerged from campus groups from the 1980s onwards, in November 1998, the ministries for women, religion, and education made a joint agreement to foster PSWs as research institutions "focused on creating gender justice". As a result, the number of PSWs grew from sixteen in 1988 to 132 by 2005 (Robinson 2009: 141; Qibtiyah 2012: 81–2). As expressed at a regional workshop in Bangkok in 2003, such centres could become "focal points for the monitoring and analyses of women's social and economic empowerment" (Bergstrom 2004: viii).

In practice, Indonesia's centres struggled. There was little demand for policy-oriented research, centres were underfunded, and bureaucracy was time-consuming. There were few career pathways for gender specialists inside universities, and three-quarters of the centres "became inactive" once the government withdrew seed funding (Cislowski and Purwadi 2011: 8–10; Poerwandari et al. 2011: 14–16). Furthermore, the interdisciplinarity and standpoint epistemologies of women's and gender studies came up against the Indonesian academy's positivism, disciplinary boundaries, and marketization.[3] Just as challenging were the personal criticisms that champions of women's and gender studies faced. As Sara Ahmed found when doing diversity work in the academy in the UK, feminists can be derided for talking about "unhappy subjects", "exposing how happiness is sustained", or seeking to "erase the signs of not getting along". In raising problematic issues, they risk

3 For a scathing analysis of the Indonesian academy from a social science perspective, see *Social Science and Power in Indonesia* (Hadiz and Dhakidae 2005).

being cast as the problem themselves (Ahmed 2010: 582, 2017: 96).[4] In an Indonesian context, feminists could be castigated (as I was reminded, gently, during my first visit to a PSW) for "thinking just about women, as perhaps feminists have done in the west". Pressure was on them to remember that "it is the harmony of the whole family that matters [...] women are but one part of the whole".[5]

Building on Ahmed's analysis, in what follows, I use two "academic memoirs" and draw on my interview material to illustrate the hurdles feminist academics in Indonesia encountered as they sought to change the architecture of the academy. Both memoirs were penned by scholars who wrote (albeit briefly) about domestic work. One chronicles the experiences of Konta Intan Damanik, a feminist scholar who established women's studies at Satya Wacana Christian University in Salatiga (Central Java). The other is an account by Saparinah Sadli reflecting on establishing a pioneering postgraduate programme in women's studies at the University of Indonesia. The Satya Wacana material tells a story of shocking pushbacks and blatant discrimination in terms of gender and ethnicity, while the UI narrative focuses on intellectual challenges and the counterweights of strategy and social capital.

Satya Wacana: Konta Intan Damanik

Konta Damanik's memoir of her journey to becoming chair of the PSW at Satya Wacana appears in a collection entitled *Changing Lives: Life Stories of Asian Pioneers in Women's Studies*, published in New York by The Feminist Press in 1994 (Committee on Women's Studies in Asia 1994). Calling her chapter "A Decade in Women's Studies", she covered the years between 1979, when she moved to Salatiga to take up a position as a professor of economics, and 1989, when the university established a unit for "Women's Studies and Roles". Her essay, shaped only by the brief to "write about your life and your interest in women's studies" (Karlekar and Lazarus 1994: 6), reveals the cultural challenge of resisting gender orthodoxy and the personal costs of feminist agency.

When Damanik died in 2015, students posted blogs about her in the student publication *Scientiarum*. She seems to have been respected and ridiculed in equal measure. Some judged her a ferociously impatient

4 In May 2016, Ahmed resigned her professorship in protest against her university's "failure to address sexual harassment" (2017: 198–9).
5 Interview, Yogyakarta, 2 July 2012.

teacher, prone to anger, while others found her inspirational – "courageous, pushy, smart, English-speaking and never afraid".[6] All agreed she demanded high standards of herself as much as of others.

Damanik begins by explaining how, under pressure from student organizations and the campus women's group, she agreed to speak at the university's Kartini Day commemorations on the subject of "The Role of Indonesian Women in Society" (1994: 93–4). Organizers felt she would command respect because she had recently returned from studying abroad and had worked in Jakarta. Yet, in the event, the accusations pitted against her when she gave her paper were vituperative. Her abiding memory of the occasion was this:

> My paper was strongly commented on and criticized. I was even accused of opening a new door for confrontation as far as the role of women is concerned. A major line of attack against my paper was that it contained provocative thoughts on how women should change established norms and values. (Damanik 1994: 95)

In threatening harmony and the status quo, Damanik unleashed a backlash. Some men in the audience scorned her talk of equality, finding it necessary (and acceptable in a university setting) to assert that "women should not think as men do or expect to be treated as men are" and argue that women are "born to be different" and "should always serve men". Their words hammered home the certainties surrounding ideas of women's *kodrat* or destiny (1994: 96). Barely two months into her job at Satya Wacana, having moved there from Sumatra, and, according to the student blogs already mentioned, a Batak woman possessed of a "loud" and "powerful" voice (in contrast to more softly spoken Javanese), Damanik risked opprobrium by "confidently" retorting that there was "no basis" for such assumptions (1994: 96). This was not how women in the academy were expected to behave.

Following this experience and feeling unable as a newcomer to raise her ideas for women's studies with policymakers, she set about building alliances, but opposition continued. Male colleagues were unhappy when she was appointed dean of her faculty, a position that had always gone to a man (Damanik 1994: 102). Even after the university conceded the need

---

6 See a selection of student comments in *Scientiarum: Critical Discourse Principles of SWCU & Salatiga Students*, http://scientiarum.com/2010/01/15/kindam/ (Accessed 13 January 2018).

for a women's research unit, some academics belittled the venture as a means for women to "hide their weaknesses" and get promoted. Better, opponents argued, to let "sleeping tigers" lie since "women, in general, are satisfied with their present conditions". Damanik herself criticized some of her female colleagues for accepting their fate too readily, "blinded and deafened", she opined, "by the status quo" (1994: 102–6).

Putting principles into practice, Damanik pioneered research in the local area on the socio-economic position of women, encountering further stumbling blocks. Satya Wacana is a Catholic university. Hence, when going into the field where most villagers were Muslim, she and her assistants had to be careful lest they be accused of proselytizing. While village women welcomed opportunities to participate, influential older men in the community wanted women kept at home. Questioning traditional norms "was seen as a betrayal of the forefathers", so much so that feelings aroused "could burst into hatred and revenge directed at us", Damanik remembered (1994: 99–100). Furthermore, while volunteers on her research team were unfamiliar with women's studies and lacked "a theoretical and methodological frame", Damanik found it impossible to acquire suitable teaching materials (1994: 102–3). Unrecognized, women's issues had been discounted as valid subjects for academic research.

Nevertheless, in 1984, Damanik chaired an interfaith project staffed by researchers from several universities. The project focused on female workers and included domestic workers in its sample. In her memoir, Damanik commented that meeting PRT as research subjects rather than subservient employees was eye-opening; she realized that they "are not weak but capable of determining what they believe is best for their own lives". However, due to a lack of expertise, funding, and time, no one wrote up or circulated the report (1994: 103–4).

Throughout Damanik's memoir, there is a sense of her battling alone. She never married and wrote of feelings of guilt and powerlessness when progress was blocked. She ended her testimony with a veiled complaint against her university authorities. Neither "the people in the university" nor "the system", she believed, had given the support needed to introduce gender studies successfully.

As a feminist scholar, Damanik had been disadvantaged by her gender, non-Javanese identity, and research interests. Yet, her persistent presence constituted a material and epistemological challenge to the seeming certainties constraining feminist knowledge production. At the same time, her testimony revealed the need for women to create and nurture supportive spaces within the academy from which to speak.

The University of Indonesia: Saparinah Sadli

A second "memoir", Professor Saparinah Sadli's reflections on establishing a postgraduate programme in women's studies at the University of Indonesia (UI), adds weight to my claim that feminist academics faced epistemic injustices. Sadli has spoken and written about the Women's Study Programme, officially referred to as the *Program Studi Kajian Wanita* but usually shortened to *Kajian Wanita*, several times. I draw on the edited version of a keynote address she gave at the annual "Indonesia Update" conference held in Melbourne in September 2001 (Sadli 2002). Her testimony shows that the task was complicated, despite having the support of the most senior university authorities and an established group of feminist academics working across diverse fields (Irawati 2006: 120–21). In contesting academic certainties, Sadli and her colleagues encountered structural bias and suspicion, even though they insisted that they were "applying" and not "importing" western ideas (Sadli and Porter 1999).

Sadli, and the co-founder of the programme, Professor Omas Ihromi, brought intellectual, political, and social kudos to Kajian Wanita. Professor of psychology and chair of the National Commission on Violence against Women, Sadli had taught at UI since 1958 and served as dean of her faculty. A well-known spokesperson for human rights, she had been one of the leaders of the group that had urged President Habibie to issue an apology to the Chinese Indonesian women raped in May 1998 (Ulung 2017). As a member of the Javanese upper class whose father had been regent of Kudus in Central Java and whose husband was a former minister and one of Indonesia's leading economists, Sadli possessed significant cultural capital. The same was true of Sadli's colleague, Omas Ihromi. A one-time Fulbright scholar and a specialist in legal anthropology, Ihromi was renowned in feminist circles as the "mother of Indonesian feminist studies", having established a women's study group on campus at UI in the late 1970s (Bachtiar 2010). Her husband was a UI professor and a senior member of Jakarta's oldest theological seminary. Yet, despite the status of the founders and the backing of officialdom, at the formal opening ceremony for Kajian Wanita, Sadli recalled, a senior lecturer in the Law faculty – a female lawyer – saw fit to counsel her not to be "overly influenced by Western feminism or feminist ideas" (2006: 82).

However, it was conservative beliefs in women's *kodrat* that Saparinah highlighted in her Melbourne speech. One challenge was developing a gender perspective in students because, as Saparinah elaborated:

> The programme challenged stereotypical thinking that saw feminine traits as a product of nature, biology and God's will rather than socially constructed. Once students had grasped some initial understanding of feminism and its various schools of thought, they often wanted to attach a fixed meaning to feminist concepts or find an immediate solution to overcome women's oppression and gender inequality. (Sadli 2002: 83–4)

Students found the tenets and internal controversies of feminism confusing. Indonesia's education system did not "stimulate students to develop critical thinking" and foregrounded "respect". This discouraged students from offering rejoinders to academic arguments (Sadli 2002: 83–4). There were no undergraduate courses in women's studies, so students came unprepared. Few lecturers possessed sufficient knowledge to deliver the curriculum, resources were scarce, and students could not progress to a doctorate in women's studies. Master's level theses produced empirical case studies but little theory. Such structural issues slowed progress towards building "a body of knowledge" on which to base "a distinctly Indonesian feminism" (Sadli: 2002: 81–3).

Indeed, energy had to be expended in working through contentious issues such as the relationship between western and non-western feminisms and the links between theory and activism. To avoid accusations of promulgating "non-indigenous values", "pro-lesbianism", or "anti-men" sentiments, Sadli and her colleagues used terms such as "women's studies" and "women's perspective" to mask the fact that they were "discussing the methodologies usually known as 'feminist'" Some leading activists criticized this stance, accusing Kajian Wanita staff of "not being feminist enough" (Sadli 2002: 83). According to Elizabeth Kristi Poerwandari (Kristi), the first scholar to graduate from the programme, who later joined the staff of the centre, some activists seemed "to want to control, to send messages such as 'I know better than you [...] you should be doing this'" (Aftab et al. 2003: 285, 297).

When I met Kristi, then head of Kajian Wanita, and Shelly Adelina (programme secretary) in 2015, I felt I was entering a nurturing, safe, well-loved and intellectually alive feminist space.[7] Lined with bookshelves holding feminist publications, much of the main room was

7 Meeting with Kristi Poerwandari and Shelly Adelina, Jakarta, 8 May 2015; follow-up interview with Shelly Adelina, conducted by Zahra Sakinatuzzahara, Jakarta, 25 January 2017.

given over to a large table where academics worked, held meetings, networked, hosted visitors, and, in Indonesian feminist fashion, shared food. Indeed, our discussion was interrupted by the unexpected arrival of a delicious lunch. When I discussed my interest in the role of academics in the domestic worker movement, Kristi and Shelly spoke of the issues PSW and PSG continue to face. In their experience, universities have not been good at supporting gender studies. Qualitative critical research remains suspect, universities denigrate gender studies as multi-disciplinary, and some rectors pay scant attention to expertise when deciding who should head up their PSW. Students and academics alike have found it "difficult academically"; hence, Kristi acknowledged, "we were not always as critical as we should have been".[8]

The stories recounted so far tend to tell a very similar feminist tale. I am not suggesting this is the only story. Indeed, when I met Alimatul Qibtiyah, then head of the PSW at the State Islamic University Sunan Kalijaga, she explained that a significant challenge for her centre had been developing gender perspectives within a framework of progressive Islam focused on "harmonious gender relations", rather than countering obstacles to multi-disciplinary studies.[9] Qibtiyah's research has demonstrated that for many Muslim feminist scholars and activists, "the smart discourse is not about transferring [western feminist] values into Indonesian" but showing how "what they have done in the West is also stated in the Qur'an" (2010: 167). Nor do I claim that scholars have not written about issues facing PSW in Indonesia before. Instead, my point is that when I met academics to discuss my research, they chose to tell me about the broader challenge of creating feminist intellectual space. This would seem to indicate that, in their estimation, the context within which all feminist academics worked was not one conducive to producing a corpus of scholarship on domestic work.

Despite the difficulties catalogued so far, some academics (including some of the scholars I have profiled) did undertake research on domestic workers during this time. In 1999, Saparinah Sadli wrote the introduction to a report on the social problems of domestic workers in Yogyakarta, commissioned by RTND (Sukendar 1999).[10] A student in the first cohort of Kajian Wanita, Siti Hawa N., wrote her thesis on "the rules that govern the employment relationship between women

8 Interview with Kristi Poerwandari, Jakarta, 8 May 2015.

9 Meeting with Alimatul Qibtiyah, Yogyakarta, 5 August 2014.

10 I have not been able to access a copy.

domestic servants and service users", as I discovered unexpectedly on an internet search (Kajian Gender 2012). Keppi Sukesi, head of the Centre for Gender and Population Studies at Brawijaya University, Malang, published a study of domestic workers in East Java carried out in 2005. The study concluded that returned migrant domestic workers were held in much higher esteem in their communities than women and girls who worked as PRT (Sukesi 2009: 121).

In June 2015, I interviewed Melani Budianta, professor of literature at UI, to sound out my research ideas.[11] She told me that in the 1990s, she had written and later published an article on the representation of Indonesian domestic workers in literature and film but confessed to not having a copy easily to hand. While I could not obtain the original, I did locate a summary of the article posted by a lecturer who had been taught by Melani at UI (Haryanti 2011). Haryanti's summary complements what Melani remembered of the article, her main point being that two plots predominated in the literature: the domestic worker as a victim of rape (the seduction story) and the domestic worker "in disguise", the middle-class girl who sets out to seek adventure and falls in love with, or is loved by, her employer.[12] Melani reflected that, for her, writing about domestic workers had been a way of dealing with ambivalence. She felt she owed a debt to a succession of domestic workers without whom she could not have pursued her career. While acknowledging power differentials, close relationships with domestic workers had been part of her "persona" since childhood and, she felt, "women very much need the work". Reflecting on my meeting with Melani, I realize that her conversation with me sowed the seeds of the argument I make in this chapter. She was adamant that I should eschew generalizations about middle-class women, or middle-class academics, a point she emphasized in her own academic "memoir" which interrogates difference, *Negotiating Boundaries and Alterity* (Budianta 2011).

Budianta's story, like those of other women in this chapter so far, suggests that dependence on domestic workers did not necessarily cause academics to avert their gaze. However, given the constraints around feminist work in the academy (and the vagaries of knowledge distribution at that time) individual academics could only contribute

---

11 Interview with Melani Budianta, Jakarta, 24 June 2015.

12 Later, Budianta worked on a project with colleagues in the psychology and humanities departments at UI, which interviewed some 150 returned migrant domestic workers and was linked with a theatre group in Yogyakarta who went on to produce a play.

fragments rather than build an accessible body of knowledge about domestic work. As the programme director of the Women [sic] Research Institute in Jakarta told me, from an activist perspective, when university students do their research "it's just small studies to be put on the library shelves".[13] Nevertheless, the work of the feminist academics in Indonesia who created PSW and PSG made a more indirect, but crucial contribution by introducing transnational feminisms and gender theory to new generations of students likely to go into activism, journalism, research, or national or local government. The discourses students encountered equipped them to be critical of the separation of the social into separate, gendered, spheres and the consequent devaluation of domestic and reproductive work.

Activist Researchers: *Jurnal Perempuan* Edition No. 39

In January 2005, *Jurnal Perempuan* published Edition No. 39, on domestic workers. It was the first time, to my knowledge, that an in-country journal had devoted an issue to the question of domestic work in Indonesia.[14] Crossing boundaries between academia and activism, *JP* 39 constituted a multi-pronged assault on the *doxa* of domestic work and on middle-class complacency. Through its content and presentation, the journal set out to lend the domestic worker movement its academic, feminist, and political legitimacy, elevate activists as knowledge producers, champion domestic worker agency, and expose myths surrounding child domestic labour.

Much of *JP*'s legitimacy rested on its origins as an academic venture. It was the brainchild of Gadis Arivia, the daughter of a diplomat who had received much of her education overseas. Gadis, fluent in French and English, returned from Paris in 1994 with a master's degree from the prestigious École des Hautes Études en Sciences Sociales to continue her studies at UI. When I met her, I heard what happened next:

> When I got home, my professor, Toeti Heraty, who was well-known as a prominent feminist, told me, "You know you have to teach, you have to teach feminism?" So, I did [...] but of course, we were not

---

13 Meeting with Edriana Noerdin and Siti Aripurnami, Jakarta, 22 November 2016.

14 As far as I know, it remained the only such example until August 2017, when *Jurnal Perempuan* revisited the topic.

> supposed to use the word feminism [...] we wanted to call our new course *Paradigma Feminisme*, but it was thought too empowering, so we called it *Paradigma Wanita* instead.[15]

Although many feminists in Indonesia disliked the word *wanita* (women) because of its associations with New Order gender ideologies, Gadis and Toeti changed the name of their proposed course in feminist philosophy to render it acceptable to university authorities. Resources were limited: "there was quite a lot on women in development, but that was not what I wanted; I was aiming at feminism, you know, feminist theories, the first wave, the second wave and so forth", Gadis explained.[16] To fill the gap, she began translating feminist texts into Indonesian, which were then sold at the students' cooperative (Sushartami 2012: 82). Students were expected to immerse themselves in the literature, as one alumna, Mariana Amiruddin, recalled:

> I finally passed the test in UI Women's Studies and there I was "forced" to spend all my time on books on feminist theory, directly reading the original author's publications, then writing and presenting it in front of classmates. Kate Millett, Karen Horney, Hélène Cixous, Deborah Cameron, Simone de Beauvoir are some of the books that led to the larger theories such as psychoanalysis, postmodernism, post colonialism, literature studies, and hermeneutic philosophy. (Amiruddin 2014)

No apologies were made for northern feminisms. The materials were highly theoretical. Yet for Mariana, such theory validated feelings she had had since childhood that sexual harassment "is something unjust, an injustice that happens because we are women" (Amiruddin 2014). In any event, the stapled copies of feminist texts proved popular; Gadis reported to a funder that 200 copies had been distributed in 1995, only a year after she returned from France (Hivos 2009). The audience for feminist texts was spreading beyond Kajian Wanita.

The shift from do-it-yourself bulletin to polished feminist magazine came about when the publishing conglomerate Gramedia offered to stock the translations in its bookshops. Asking herself "why not a journal, a feminist journal?", Gadis secured funding to further this idea from, amongst others, the Ford Foundation, which saw the

15 Interview with Gadis Arivia, Jakarta, 21 November 2016.

16 Interview with Gadis Arivia, Jakarta, 21 November 2016.

proposed magazine as likely to be welcomed by "highbrow academia" as a partial replacement for *Prisma*, the critical socio-political journal that had closed in October 1998 (Sushartami 2012: 82). Gadis, on the other hand, remembered the University of Indonesia at that time as "not open to the idea of critical journals, let alone feminist ones [...] not a place to come up with an idea but a place to turn new ideas off" (2016: 8). Hence a new intellectual space was required.

Some of Gadis's colleagues and students supported the journal, adding to its legitimacy. Three members of the philosophy department, including Toeti Heraty, joined forces to establish an NGO (Yayasan Jurnal Perempuan [YJP]) as a legal and organizational base for the magazine.[17] Heraty's support was substantial. A leading feminist, long-established professor, co-founder of UI's philosophy department, and internationally recognized poet, she was married to a professor at the Bandung Institute of Technology. She managed the intellectual property firm established by her father, eminent civil engineer Roosseno, who had served as a minister under Sukarno (Simanjuntak 2015). A succession of UI students and graduates joined the magazine's staff or wrote for the journal, including Karlina Supelli, well-known as Indonesia's first female astronomer. She had switched fields to philosophy after hearing Heraty lecture and gained a second PhD before becoming an editor with *JP* in 1997. Rocky Gerung, a teacher in the philosophy department, wrote for the journal and later taught on YJP's philosophy and feminism programme. Adriana Venny, then studying for a PhD in philosophy at UI, became chief editor in 2004. Mariana Amiruddin, already mentioned in this chapter as a Kajian Wanita graduate, became chief executive in 2007 (Ruzuar 2016: 18, 38, 132). When out fundraising, Amiruddin stressed the importance of "academicians" (*akademisi*) in *JP*'s development (2013). Gadis Arivia maintained a high-status profile as an academic alongside her role as the driving force behind *JP*; her career (and those of other scholars involved with *JP*) illustrates a pattern of movement across and along an academic–activist continuum in which contributing to the journal constituted a practical, and public, commitment to radical feminism.

However, it was the interventionist role played by Gadis Arivia and *JP* in 1998 that won the magazine political purchase. On 23 February 1998, at the height of Indonesia's economic crisis, Gadis was arrested at the Hotel Indonesia roundabout, along with Karlina Supelli and Wilarih Nophiana, an activist posing as "an ordinary mother". Gadis

17 Interview with Gadis Arivia, Jakarta, 21 November 2016.

has written about her arrest many times. One version of events (Arivia and Subono 2017) depicts her standing under a banner emblazoned with the words "The Voice of Concerned Mothers" (*Suara Ibu Peduli* or SIP) alongside twenty or so others, handing out flowers to passers-by and singing the patriotic, anti-colonial song "I saw our Motherland", a song which speaks of the "suffering, moaning, and praying" of Indonesian mothers unable to feed their children despite Indonesia's "stored wealth" (Sunindyo 1998: 4–6). While the protest was ostensibly about the price of milk and basic foodstuffs, Gadis has maintained that "motherism" was a camouflage for subversion: the movement's real aim being to bring the "silent" middle classes out against the regime (Arivia and Subono 2017: 14–18). This was risky. The protest defied a government ban.

National and international media covered the arrest and trial of the three women. Publicity fuelled the growth of the SIP movement, a movement which mobilized women across class divides to distribute powdered milk and other essentials to poor women, especially in rural areas. During the trial, SIP demonstrators used the "Motherland" song as a marching rally, in Melani Budianta's opinion turning the mother metaphor from that of dependent to that of an empowered rebel championing a moral cause (Budianta 2003: 157–8). The *JP* office became SIP's headquarters, and only two months later, SIP was supplying necessaries to the thousands of students whose demonstrations acted as a catalyst for the end of the New Order. After this, *JP* was no longer simply a feminist academic journal but a political, *Pemuda*-like presence associated with a nationalist vision of the caring, nurturing, and on occasion, combative woman.[18] The fact that *JP* had provided leadership and practical support to the anti-Suharto movement in 1998 cemented the journal into the *reformasi* political and intellectual landscape as a space where academics and activists could cross boundaries and collaborate.

In line with its genealogy, *JP* adopted a standpoint epistemology influenced by the work of Sandra Harding.[19] Such a standpoint

18 As described in Chapter 2, radical students in the 1980s and '90s framed their protests in relation to the Nationalist Youth Pledge of 1928.

19 Interview with Gadis Arivia, Jakarta, 21 November 2016. In the early period of *reformasi*, feminists in Jakarta were involved in discussion about feminist epistemology and standpoint theory, as evidenced in a column published in the Monday section of *Kompas*, *Kompas-Swara*, edited by leading Islamic feminist Lies Marcoes-Natsia in 2005 (Women Research Institute 2005).

privileges the experience of (marginalized) women and the importance of collaborative knowledge production (Stone-Mediatore 2016: 937). Hence, all editions of the journal published after 2001 included interviews with activists, profiles of key individuals and organizations, photographs, poems, and articles by "experts". This was unorthodox. Indeed, for twenty years, the Indonesian Institute of Sciences rejected *JP's* applications to become a registered academic journal on the grounds that it was not objective, pointing to the poetry found in every edition as proof of its profligate lack of academic professionalism.[20]

Edition No. 39: Domestic Workers.

What, then, could this new site of academic–activist collaboration offer the domestic workers' cause? Could the magazine's epistemology create new knowledge and understanding and change views? Analyzing the content of *JP* 39 indicates that by drawing on activist and domestic worker knowledge and by introducing themes that resonated with Indonesian readers, the special edition set global feminist and human rights agendas in the context of a modernizing and newly democratic Indonesia. The journal's editors also packaged their politics persuasively.

January 2005 was ostensibly an opportune moment to feature domestic work. By then, subscribers to the journal included potential influencers: "professionals, academics, women's study centres, libraries, members of parliament, government officials, NGO staff, and grassroots activists" (Sushartami 2012: 84–5; Amiruddin 2013). As outlined in earlier chapters, during 2004, activists had got a domestic worker bill onto the list of proposed parliamentary legislation. Optimism, however, was tempered by realism, as Gadis remembered:

> The activists were hopeful then of getting a law passed, but there was a great deal of pushback. We had a meeting concerning the issue and what came out was that the middle-class women always think that they have, in fact, treated their domestic workers very well.[21]

Here was the same reaction from middle-class employers that I had experienced in Bandung, a response Alison Bailey aptly dubbed

---

20 Interview with Gadis Arivia, Jakarta, 21 November 2016.

21 Interview with Gadis Arivia, Jakarta, 21 November 2016. Sri Eddyono, who had worked at LBH APIK from 1997 to 2003, later recalled the optimism felt by JALA PRT and others around the time of the 2004 draft Bill (Eddyono et al. 2015).

"privilege-preserving epistemic pushback" (or "wilful ignorance") in the context of her feminist and critical race philosophy classes. Such reactions, Bailey suggests, are common in conversations where some participants try to make injustices visible while others defensively seek to hold their ground (2017: 877–9).

Activists were buoyed, however, because assumed certainties ("myths" in activist parlance) about the benign nature of domestic work were beginning to be undermined. The plight of home and overseas domestic workers had figured in the media throughout 2004. In January, the story of the murder of Maryati by her employer (as recounted in the previous chapter) surfaced. In March, the ILO published *Flowers on the Rock*, an exposé of Indonesian child domestic labour (ILO-IPEC 2004), and in June it made domestic work the focus of its third "World Day Against Child Labour", utilizing the slogan "Behind Closed Doors". In September, women's rights organizations secured the passage of Indonesia's Anti-Domestic Violence Law, an encouragement to women to report abuse (Wieringa 2015: 33). In October, the government had (as one international agency put it) "eventually passed" a law on the placement and protection of migrant workers (IOM 2010: 9). While NGOs criticized the legislation for prioritizing the demands of placement agencies and imposing strict controls on workers, the formal recognition that paid domestic work is work was welcome. Activists immediately argued that the government should accept similar responsibilities for protecting PRT at home (Husni et al. 2017: 1).

Furthermore, despite doubts about whether parliamentarians would "really stand up for society and the people" (Wanandi 2004: 116–18), some prominent feminist activists won seats in the 2004 elections. Amongst them were Nursyahbani Katjasungkana and Eva Kusuma Sundari, both activists-turned-politicians who believed it was time to bring their "technical expertise" and "grassroots experience" to bear inside the DPR, adding to the pressure of NGOs "shouting from the outside" (Meitzner 2013: 37–8). More prosaically, *JP* editors, I was told, hoped the political climate would encourage international donors to contribute to the costs of their special edition.[22] Funding was crucial; the journal's reputation, reach, and retail success depended

---

22 Interview with M. B. Wijaksana, Jakarta, 5 December 2016; interview with Maria Pakpahan, Edinburgh, 9 August 2017. In the event, both informants suggested, some difficulties arose over external funding; in this case, Pakpahan intimated, around matters of editorial control.

on the professional quality of its design and its academic and editorial expertise.

Design

The cover of *JP* 39 challenges the certainties of domestic work in Indonesia head-on. The title, *Pekerja Rumah Tangga*, stands out. Printed in bold white capitals, it sits atop a colour photograph depicting the pristine, white-trousered leg of a young domestic worker sweeping a lawn. The reader's eye is drawn to the word for worker (*pekerja*) by the downwards sweep of an instantly recognizable, characteristically Indonesian *sapu lidi* broom made from the spine of the coconut palm. The image conjured is not the well-used one of (migrant) domestic workers as downtrodden, physically abused, "third world" victims, nor is domestic work portrayed as, by definition, dirty, dangerous, demanding, or demeaning, recurrent tropes in academic and activist discourse at that time. Instead, the message is that what appears ordinary and unproblematic – the employment of large numbers of women as "helpers" inside Indonesia – deserves attention from anyone concerned with women's rights.

JP's designer used (and continues to use – the layout of the front cover has scarcely changed since 2001) a large font for the word *Perempuan*, signalling the magazine's radical standpoint. *JP*'s strapline, "*untuk pencerahan dan keseteraan*" (for enlightenment and equality), is printed immediately underneath the words *Jurnal Perempuan*. The phrase locates *JP* in an international and national human rights frame.[23] The issue number, No. 39, is prominent. One effect of this packaging is to situate domestic work in a series alongside other gender injustices deemed worthy of attention. *JP* 38, published at the end of 2004, was entitled "*Pornografi*". That edition was produced to counter pressure from Islamic groups to bring forward an "Anti-pornography and Anti-pornographic Action Law" (Wichelen 2010: 99). Edition

23 Covers of editions of *JP* published between 2001 and 2005 can be viewed on the journal's website: https://www.jurnalperempuan.org/store/c8/Jurnal_Perempuan2001-2005.html. A complete collection of the covers of *JP* is on show in the magazine's office in South Jakarta. The front cover of *JP* 39 now posted online, however, differs from the original; *Pekerja Rumah Tangga* has been replaced by *Pekerja Domestik*. This change removes any link with the acronym PRT and its association with the idea of helper. For an international comparison, see the British Library collection of the groundbreaking feminist magazine, *Spare Rib*, which featured an article on female cleaners in its first edition in 1972.

Fig. 5.1 Original front cover,* Jurnal Perempuan *39 (author's collection, reproduced with permission)

No. 40 criticized the marginalization of women in reconstruction programmes in Aceh following the tsunami, while No. 41 "explored the issue of female sexuality which is still taboo". *JP* 39 thus lent legitimacy to Indonesia's domestic worker movement by presenting the topic as warranting a place on women's and the nation's reform agendas.

The journal's designers allowed copious white space, incorporated nine full-page photographs, and interspersed text with some thirty smaller illustrations and charts. This rendered the content more accessible and attractive to wider audiences than conventional academic publications (Amiruddin 2012; Sushartami 2012: 84–5). The design also challenged assumptions that academia was a world apart. As Chapter 2 of this book revealed, some PRT in Yogyakarta had dismissed academic research as irrelevant, preferring their own "knowledge for action". Meanwhile, some academics construed NGO research as under-theorized, oversimplified, or even "anti-science and anti-scholarship" (Ganie-Rochman and Achwan 2005: 214). To gain a hearing across their target audiences, the editors of *JP* 39 needed to challenge such certainties on both sides.

In line with its standpoint epistemology, *JP* put its activist mission upfront. The "Prologue" to *JP* 39 demands action. The editor urges the government to champion a domestic workers bill and asks readers to change their everyday practices and end "modern slavery" (Venny 2005: 5). However, *JP*'s standpoint was not a retreat from theory. Instead, as Harding had asserted, editors used the "situated knowledge" of the marginalized to "make visible a hidden phenomenon" (2004: 6–8). In so doing, they were breaching "the walls between theory and praxis, scholarship and activism" (Budianta 2011: 197–8). Not surprising, then, that the titles of several articles in *JP* 39 refer to "unveiling", the "marginalized", the "neglected", and "finding the true meaning of domestic work". Presenting the issue of domestic work as a matter of truth-telling increased its resonance with a readership that had previously purchased volumes with titles such as "Local Women Speak" (*JP* 17) or "Governments Standing on the Blood of Women" (*JP* 8).

Writers

Concerned with accuracy and legitimacy, *JP*'s editors expected its "expert" contributors to meet academic norms regarding originality, reliability, and references (Sushartami 2012: 84). The aim was not to platform individual scholars. *JP* 39 hides its brief author biographies amongst the adverts at the end of the volume. This contrasts with the upfront placing of the biographies of the contributors to Hadiz and Dhakidae's *Social Science and Power in Indonesia*, a collection of essays also published in 2005 that critiqued the limited contribution of Indonesian academics to social and political change. The authors of that volume were (almost exclusively) male, educated at elite overseas universities, and well-established in their careers. The authors of the six "*Topik Empu*" articles (articles by experts) in *JP* 39 were, in the main, female, young, Indonesian-educated, and not in high-status positions. Their credibility derived from their feminist standpoints and experience as activists in the field.

Five of the six "specialists" were graduates. Muryanti, Diah Irawaty, and Aida Milasari were working with RTND and RGP, founder groups in the JALA network. Aida Milasari and another specialist contributor, Andi Utami, had spent several years managing NGO projects and joining the internationally sponsored research teams that were beginning to map the contours of Indonesian domestic work and child domestic labour. As detailed in earlier chapters, Aida had been involved in the domestic worker movement from its beginnings and believed that activist interventions must be based on research.[24] Between 1994 and *JP* 39, she had worked on eight projects investigating domestic work, of which three were in collaboration with Atma Jaya University in Jakarta, and one with Duta Wacana University in Yogyakarta (Milasari 2009). Similarly, Andi, then working for the Indonesian Child Welfare Foundation (Yayasan Kesejahteraan Anak Indonesia [YKAI]), had published a study of child labour in India, worked as a principal investigator in a 2003 ILO-IPEC study of child trafficking, and was one of three co-authors of *Bunga di atas Padas* (*Flowers on the Rock*), an ILO study of child domestic work in Indonesia published in 2004. Moving between positions on the researcher–activist continuum, Andi observed wryly that she had to snatch writing up time "during the breaks" (Putranto et al. 2004).

In *JP* 39, Aida and Andi used their epistemically privileged vantage points to demonstrate that official figures underestimated the number of domestic and child domestic workers in Indonesia. They catalogued cases of abuse recorded by NGOs and taken up by organizations like LBH APIK and provided evidence that the police and judiciary frequently handled such cases unjustly (Milasari 2005: 36–7; Utami 2005: 51–2). Since both detailed the methods used to collect their data, their findings were not easily dismissed as scaremongering.

International agencies had already provided policymakers and politicians with data-rich reports of their investigations. However, their reports were lengthy and grounded in the universality of international norms. Authorship remained firmly in the hands of the originating agencies.[25] *JP* 39, on the other hand, could summarize

---

24 Interview with Aida Milasari, Jakarta, 2 July 2015.

25 See, for example, the acknowledgements page of the HRW (2005) report, *Always on Call: Abuse and Exploitation of Child Domestic Workers in Indonesia.*

key findings and frame domestic worker claims in an Indonesian context, translating a "global women's rights package" into messages more likely to resonate locally. Levitt and Merry call such translation processes "vernacularization" and suggested it works best when the actors involved range from "cosmopolitan elites" (such as Saparinah Sadli, Gadis Arivia, and Toeti Heraty) to field-based staff in NGOs (2009: 447–50).

Amongst the specialist contributors to *JP* 39, Diah Irawaty and Muryanti represent that second tier of NGO staff. Their knowledge claims rested on their close contact with domestic workers as organizers of OPERATA or as project leaders for externally funded initiatives. Irawaty describes how PRT internalize images of themselves as inferior beings worthy of punishment, develop inhibitions and depression, and find it hard to stand up for themselves. Yet, after joining a domestic worker organization, dispositions can change (Irawaty 2005: 29). Muryanti's article similarly foregrounds domestic workers' experiences. Recounting the stories of three PRT, Sutini, "N", and Jumiah, Muryanti applies her insider knowledge of child welfare to link abuse with failings of Indonesia's education system. Her main point, however, is that it is the mindsets and habits of the whole community – and the "shackles of social stratification" – that need demolishing (*perlu dibongkar*) (Muryanti 2005: 13).

One of the journal's staff editors, W. B. Wijaksana (Uung), filled a gap by contributing an article comparing domestic work in the Philippines and Indonesia (2005a). His undergraduate dissertation had been on gender in public administration. Taking a different stance from the pioneering radical feminist magazine *Spare Rib* first published in the UK in 1972, men were welcome to work at *JP*, providing they were "good" feminists.[26] When I met Wijaksana he recalled that at his job interview Gadis Arivia had asked more questions about his feminist credentials than anything else. A second *JP* editor, Eko Bambang Subiyantoro, contributed two pieces to *JP* 39: a profile of Yuli Maiheni, founder member of Tunas Mulia Domestic Workers' Union in Yogyakarta, and a discussion of the role of employment agencies. Introduced to feminism at Brawijaya University in Malang in the 1990s, Subiyantoro went on to establish the New Men's Alliance (Aliansi Laki-Laki Baru), dedicated to involving men in combatting violence against women and challenging patriarchal assumptions and practices.

26 Interview with W. B. Wijaksana (Uung), Jakarta, 15 November 2016.

Given these three contributions from *JP* staff editors, a straightforward explanation for the different profiles of contributors to *Social Science and Power* and *JP* 39 is that established academics did not respond to *JP*'s call for papers.[27] Yet, using "activist researchers" reflected *JP*'s commitment to standpoint theory, which validated knowledge from experience. In this sense, it was akin to the work of Kajian Wanita, where scholars sought to connect individual experiences to established feminist theory (Sadli 2002: 85–6).[28] While it may not have been planned, the contributors to *JP* 39 highlighted similar themes that collectively challenged taken-for-granted certainties and resonated with some of the recurrent refrains of *reformasi*.

Themes: Citizenship

One theme running through *JP* 39 was the denial of full citizenship rights to domestic workers despite democratization. Notions of obligation and reciprocity as a balance to individual rights reverberated in *reformasi* Indonesia. The words *hak* and *kewajiban* (rights and responsibilities) were frequently coupled in text and conversation (Blackburn 2004: 89; Gibbings 2017: 99; Ito 2017: 52). Hence, in *JP* 39, the authors accuse the government of failing to meet its obligations. According to Muryanti, legislators are "reluctant to discuss new regulations", and the judiciary never "side with the PRT" (2005: 12–14). Wijaksana concluded that Indonesia lags "far behind" the Philippines, where "the spirit of the law is that of protecting the rights of every subject it regulates". In Indonesia, he ventured, the absence of regulation favours "financial interests" (2005a: 39–40).

Other parts of the journal foreground reciprocity. A profile of Yuli Maiheni (Heni), one of the organizers of Tunas Mulia whose personal journey to activism featured in Chapter 2, presents her as an exemplary citizen who fights courageously for justice, works tirelessly for her community, and uses her store of experience to get a better balance of rights and obligations (*hak dan kewajiban*) for domestic workers (Subiyantoro 2007: 108–9). A section of *JP* 39 called "Tips" uses the *hak dan kewajiban* phrase again in relation to work contracts. Setting rights and obligations down, the piece contends, helps establish and maintain mutual relationships and "makes things easy for both sides"

27 Interview with W. B. Wijaksana (Uung) Jakarta, 15 November 2016.

28 Interview with Gadis Arivia, Jakarta, 21 November 2016. Interview with W. B. Wijaksana (Uung), Jakarta, 15 November 2016. Both Gadis and Uung mentioned the difficulties of finding writers. *JP* journalists wrote two of the main articles in *JP* 39, suggesting there may have been gaps to fill.

(*Jurnal Perempuan* 2005a: 82–5). Two articles focus on the economics of citizenship, stressing the need for governments to address poverty, land rights, and education (Irawaty 2005: 20; Milasari 2005: 32). Wijaksana argues that if labourers and civil servants had higher wages, they could fulfil their obligations to pay their PRT properly (2005b). In these ways, *JP* 39 inflects claims to universal and individual rights with a cadence of community, responsibility, and mutual obligation, challenging certainties that assume an offer of family membership to a PRT provides sufficient reciprocity. Such cultural framing sidesteps prejudices against claims based on "western" feminisms.

Indeed, though not explicit in *JP* 39, the discourse of *hak dan kewajiban* locates domestic worker claims in Islamic traditions. This point is amply illustrated in articles about domestic work published in the 2009 edition of *Swara Rahima*, the journal put out by Rahima (an NGO founded in 2001) with a mission to disseminate gender-egalitarian interpretations of Islam and promote women's rights by drawing on "transnational feminism and Islamic reformism" (Rinaldo 2013: 6). In this edition, with the theme of "The Spirit of Ramadan and the Rights of Domestic Workers", contributors laid out PRT claims to annual and menstruation leave, employment contracts, and fair wages paid on time by quoting from, and interpreting Islamic texts with an emphasis on the concept of *aqdu al-ijarah* glossed as "respective rights and obligations" between workers and employers (*Swara Rahima* 2009: 4).[29] Sumi Madhok, discussing the use of the term *haq* amongst grassroots activists in South Asia, argues that rights talk amongst the subaltern groups she studied should not be seen as simply a matter of vernacularizing western/northern concepts but as part of a process of creating new "vernacular rights cultures" (2017: 500–503). These blend place-specific claims, which draw on political, religious, and cultural contexts and histories, with the transnational, creating new social imaginaries that challenge the "epistemic centre" of "authorial global", US-led, and statist human rights thinking (Madhok 2017: 501–2). The language of *hak dan kewajiban* used in *JP* 39 strengthens domestic

---

29 For a justification of Indonesian domestic worker rights in Islamic texts, see Sofiani et al. (2012). Employing a broader frame, Bakker and Timmer (2014: 297) argue that notions of justice in Indonesia are rooted in "specific social processes and a changing culture shaped by local traditions and political realities". Manneke Budiman (2008: 88–91) discusses the importance of *Swara Rahima* in challenging "male-dominated readings of Islamic dogma" and promulgating Indonesian Muslim feminism.

worker rights-based citizenship claims with a place-based ethical and normative tradition and moral code.

Themes: Childhood

Childhood was much discussed in *reformasi* Indonesia. Karen Strassler suggests that in post-Suharto Indonesia, "children served as a symbol of the nation's future and as the objects of a struggle to render the violence of the reform movement meaningful within a teleology of national progress" (2006: 54). Her study of the iconography of a children's painting contest suggests that members of the public were preoccupied with the effects of trauma on children, seeing the child as an innocent victim, representative of the traditional village, and carrier of a vision of Indonesian unity (2006: 54–5). Jan Newberry studied early childhood education during *reformasi* and found that middle-class publics, NGOs, and government officials in Jakarta and Yogyakarta were taken up with a globally circulating notion of the autonomous, empowered, and "self-actualized" child (2010: 420). Strassler and Newberry's meticulous ethnographies detail how concerns were expressed through an emphasis on child psychology, play-centred education, children's creativity, and efforts to involve them in theatre and the arts. New notions of childhood could accommodate middle-class families' desires to advance their children's prospects and a communitarian ethic of shared responsibilities (Strassler 2006: 53, 61; Newberry 2017: 39–40).

The articles in *JP* 39 that examine child domestic labour derive legitimacy from mobilizing just these themes. Irawaty speaks of "severe psychological pressure", the internalization of negative stereotypes, learned helplessness, the trauma of violence, and the distress of not earning enough to meet families' needs and expectations (2005: 20–23). She sets these negative aspects of child domestic labour against an ideal of a childhood where children develop their potential, have opportunities for play and quiet study, and participate in "theatre, poetry, journalism, and computer courses" to "strengthen and empower themselves" (Irawaty 2005: 23–6). Milasari shocks readers with a graphic description of what can happen to child domestic workers (PRTA, *Pekerja Rumah Tangga Anak*):

> The forms of sexual harassment of PRT/PRTA are very diverse, such as requests for coin massage or *kerok* (treatment by rubbing someone's back with a coin) on the part of the body that leads to the top of the thighs of the naked employer who asks the PRTA

> to take off the towel, hugging and kissing abruptly; peeping at the PRTA while she is bathing, opening the bathroom door by force and inviting the PRTA to have sex. (Milasari 2005: 37)

Here shocking sexual abuse is pictured as happening within the everyday routines of Indonesian domestic life. Milasari describes abused children who are "very closed and anxious and resistant to any physical touch, even from fellow domestic workers [...] are very traumatized and cry spontaneously when considering the terrible things that have happened to them" (2005: 36). Not just the responsibility of their employers, Milasari and Irawaty argue, child domestic workers should be recognized as every "modern" Indonesian's child.

Themes: Cinderellas

Milasari also introduces the trope of the child domestic worker as Cinderella. In doing so, she subverts the traditional tale (and its Indonesian equivalents) in the manner of Margaret Attwood.[30] Disney versions of the Cinderella story circulated widely in Indonesia, reinforcing notions that young women demonstrate virtue through passivity, submission, forgiveness, and acceptance of their fate (Setiawan et al. 2013: 1). For Milasari, such beliefs leave child domestic workers as "*Cinderellas yang Terpenjara*" – a phrase she glosses as "The Invisible Cinderellas" but that also carries notions of imprisonment (2005: 39). The Cinderella comparison would have been familiar to Milasari. In June 2004, the ILO had released a video entitled *The Real Story of Cinderella: Children in Domestic Labour*, using stories from Guatemala to show that young girls in domestic work miss their mothers, are lonely, and are denied their right to play (ILO 2004). Delegates from five Latin American nations had used the term "Cinderellas among Cinderellas" when discussing the plight of poor rural women at the first UN world conference on women (cited in Olcott 2017: 144). Picking up the theme, Utami, in *JP* 39, depicts PRTA as cut off from their families and denied the chance to play or have a holiday. At the same time, Irawaty argues that young domestic workers, like other teenagers, should have time "to think about love, think about recreational life, think about achieving their dreams"(Irawaty 2005: 22; Utami 2005: 53).

---

30 For a discussion of an Indonesian folktale resembling Cinderella stories, see "Bias gender dalam cerita rakyat" (Setiawan et al. 2013). Attwood's treatment of the Cinderella story is considered in "Rejecting the glass slipper" by Rona May-Ron (2016).

Some of the photographs in *JP* 39 invoke the Cinderella story. Several show the slight figure of a young Indonesian girl left alone, sweeping, making the bed, or moving furniture in an empty house. One portrays a young PRT mopping the floor on hands and knees while her employer sits beside her, looking the other way (*Jurnal Perempuan* 2005b: 30, 39, 78, 102). Fairy godmothers come in the form of feminist organizers, exemplified in *JP* 39 by the smiling face of Tati Krisnawati, interviewed as a leading member of the National Commission on Violence against Women (Wijaksana 2005b: 90). However, alongside rescue by well-educated and more privileged "sisters", the sagas recounted in *JP* 39 reinforce the message that "real-life Cinderellas" can write their own stories and give them happy endings of their own. At a time of re-imaginings of the role of women in Indonesia, putting domestic worker agency in place of female dependency challenges middle-class employers to see, and treat, their Cinderella helpers differently.

I did not discover the immediate impact of *JP* 39 as no records of audience responses were available.[31] What became clear as my research progressed, however, was that this edition became a repository, an archive of extant knowledge of domestic work in Indonesia more accessible to wider audiences and perhaps more likely to be preserved for posterity than some of the scattered individual works of scholarship that had emanated from the academy until then.

Afterwards/Afterwords: New Knowledge Production Post-C189

Doing a part-time PhD has some advantages. Revisiting fieldwork sites over several years, I met researchers as they came on the scene in the context of C189. Not only did the Convention heighten interest in Indonesia's sizeable domestic worker workforce, the Research Network for Domestic Worker Rights (RN-DWR), established during the 2011 Geneva conference, raised questions about the ethics, accountability, and methodologies of researchers (Marchetti and Schwenken 2018). In May 2014, the RN-DWR published *We Want to Be the Protagonists of Our Own Stories!*, a handbook explaining how researchers and domestic workers "can jointly conduct research"

31 Personal communication with Anita Dhewey, Editor, *Jurnal Perempuan*, December 2016.

(Azzarello et al. 2014). The handbook lists seven authors.[32] As did the Sangtin Writers' (2006) *Playing with Fire*, which credited nine authors, it challenges academic orthodoxy, raising uncomfortable questions about hierarchies, partnerships, authorship, and, because many domestic workers are migrant workers involved in north–south or south–south patterns of population movement, the coloniality of knowledge production.

Encarnación Gutiérrez-Rodríguez (2009) and Louisa Acciari (2019) argue in their studies of domestic labour in Europe and Brazil, that the persistent universal devaluation of domestic work and the dominance of the global north in knowledge production are deeply rooted in colonial systems of racial classification and control. In that sense, studies of domestic worker movements which pay attention to "transnationalism from below" (Acciari 2019: 49–53) contribute to a process of decolonizing the academy. With this thinking in mind, I explore the contribution of Indonesian scholars who were involved in researching domestic work in Indonesia during the period 2011–2016, following the adoption of C189.

The discussion is based on conversations with seven Indonesian scholars I encountered during my fieldwork, which ended in December 2016. My research base is thus more of an assemblage than a sample; the points are illustrative but not definitive. Focusing on scholars I met through contacts was partly pragmatic: the sixteen researchers listed on the "Garuda Portal" as having published articles on domestic work in Indonesian journals between 2011 and 2016 were, in the main, based in cities outside my fieldwork sites, including Lampung, Malang, Semarang, Surabaya, and Denpasar. Often, only abstracts of their studies were accessible.[33] On the other hand, my assemblage is diverse, representing scholars placing themselves at different points on an academic–activist continuum, at different stages in their careers, and involved in projects of different scales, variously connected with the ILO and JALA PRT. Five of the seven were linked to large externally

32 The publisher's website names Helen Schwenken, who had been the project manager of a collaborative research project on which this handbook was based as the "editor", while the handbook itself names all seven members of the "authorial team".

33 *Portal Garuda* is a database of scholarship published in Indonesian journals previously known as the Indonesian Publication Index (IPI). In 2018 the portal was acquired by the Ministry of Research Technology and Higher Education (RISTEKDIKTI) and renamed GARUDA (Garba Rujukan Digital, which can be viewed at http://garuda.ristekdikti.go.id).

funded projects. Meeting the two individual scholars featured was serendipitous. I was asked to look through a conference paper Valentina Utari was preparing during my internship at SMERU, while Gita Nasution approached me directly, having heard about my research. Discussions revealed how far researchers saw their projects as praxis and how they dealt with the personal and professional challenges that arose in both north–south research partnerships and in projects that questioned the academy's taken-for-granted practices and relational hierarchies.

Sri Eddyono and the UN

I met Sri Wiyanti Eddyono in December 2016. She was the lead researcher for the Indonesian end of a UNRISD (United Nations Research Institute for Social Development) project researching government responses to gender-based claims in China, India and Indonesia.[34] A Law lecturer at UGM with a PhD from Monash University, Australia (where her supervisor was Susan Blackburn, noted for her research into women's movements in Indonesia), Sri describes herself on her LinkedIn profile as an "academician, feminist lawyer, researcher, and women [sic] activist", or more simply, to me, as "activist researcher". She undertook the UN research in a private capacity as an associate of SCN-CREST, a consultancy working for women's rights and social transformation she had joined in 2003 after spending six years as a lawyer with LBH APIK.

During our discussion, Sri reflected on the power relations between herself as a lead Indonesian researcher and the UN.[35] Before accepting the contract, she had raised some issues with her northern counterparts, challenging conventional hierarchies of knowledge production. This is what she said:

> Well, Mary, when we tried to deal with the United Nations, they wanted it to be very academic, strongly academic, with very conventional methods and methodology. Still, they were also very interested in our proposal [...] they needed someone to start and finish the project; they had to have someone.
>
> You see, they had worked out the framework, but [...] we said that we were not academicians per se, the way we like to

34 For an outline of the larger project see http://www.unrisd.org/unrisd/website/document.nsf/(httpPublications)/35CCB8F1110E6C02C1257C2E003DCFB6.

35 Interview with Sri Wiyanti Eddyono, Yogyakarta, 9 December 2016.

> do research, we think of it as being a way to empower ourselves through the research [...] we felt the framework was not really fit for the Indonesian context, it might fit India or different countries, but we needed to make our own.

The power dynamics were not all one way: the UN team could not operate without in-country researchers.

Finding her UN-assigned coordinator "very open-minded", Sri negotiated changes. The project fee intended for two researchers could be shared amongst seven in the interest of "supporting young researchers". The team could use "an active participation method, not just gather information". Feeling accountable to the domestic worker movement, Sri brought JALA PRT and the National Commission on Violence Against Women – "the main actors in our research" – together before discussing her findings with the UN, encouraging them to resolve differences she had uncovered between them. Testing out results with participants, Sri reflected, made for sounder conclusions – otherwise, "our analysis might not be right" – and helped those involved "see different views" and "the links one to another". As an activist researcher, she said, laughingly, "that's what I'd hoped for, and that's what I say research, academic research is for, you know". Working for a research consortium rather than a university allowed more leeway; the reason Indonesian academics have not done more research into domestic work, Sri surmised, is not so much class and gender self-interest as a feeling that academics "have to be careful in discussing everything [...] they are trying not to put a political point of view but be objective". In taking a stance with the UN and prioritizing interchanges with informants, Sri challenged assumptions that local researchers provide data while northern scholars develop theory and set research parameters – the accepted certainties of much transnational scholarship.

As she was new to her lectureship at UGM, however, colleagues questioned Sri's methodologies. They told her that "the faculty of law is very strict about boundaries", that "it's strange to study domestic work", and that "giving feedback to respondents" was unnecessary. Nevertheless, after completing the UNRISD research, she told me, the Dean has asked me to develop a paper; I will move slowly and then, who knows?"[36] In the meantime, when she and her colleagues

36 Interview with Sri Eddyono, Yogyakarta, 9 December 2016.

presented their findings in Geneva in July 2015, their paper engendered widespread interest.[37]

Ida Ruwaida Noor and the ILO

During 2015 and 2016, Ida Ruwaida Noor (Ida Ruwaida), chair of the laboratory for sociology research at the University of Indonesia, directed an ILO/UI collaborative research project exploring attitudes to domestic work across the archipelago. Her role was a delicate one. Officials were nervous lest the research raised expectations; at least, as Ida told me, "it took a long time to get government approval [...] they agreed that the focus would be on establishing a baseline, not on 'promoting' a new law or the ratification of Convention 189". This caveat was despite the fact the government-approved ILO project funding her research bore the name "PROMOTE".[38] In line with the ILO's tripartite structure, Ida involved government departments, employers, and JALA PRT. Managing such a partnership presented methodological challenges, as she explained:

> We wanted to involve all the stakeholders in preparing the research instrument, but this proved quite problematic; it was difficult to meet everyone's suggestions. Ibu Lita, for example, wanted to differentiate between PRT working in houses with land around them and those working in tall, new apartments, but to do this would have involved too many variables.[39]

For credibility, as project director, Ida needed to balance academic expertise with activist experience and "explore rights and responsibilities on both sides". Like Sri Eddyono, she felt she had "a double position, as an academic sociologist and a feminist with a responsibility to try to change the world". In each research site – Bandung, Surabaya, and Makassar – she trained twenty junior researchers drawn from local universities to assist in sampling some 450 households employing domestic workers in each locality. The research took twice as long as estimated; many employers refused to cooperate, fearing they were being checked up on. Others were resistant to change and to "ideas flowing from the ILO which they see as reflecting a western perspective". Researchers quickly learned to interview the

37 Personal communication from attendee at workshop, July 2015.
38 Interview with Ida Ruwaida Noor, Jakarta, 3 August 2015.
39 Interview with Ida Ruwaida Noor, Jakarta, 3 August 2015.

employer before the domestic worker in any household; workers were frightened to be interviewed without an employer's consent. This ILO/UI research represented a significant step; it moved beyond Jakarta and Yogyakarta, developed new research protocols, drew in new respondents not already linked with domestic worker NGOs, and introduced a new generation of researchers to the issues surrounding domestic work. The research found ambivalence and double standards amongst employers who were resistant to changing social relationships premised on "seeing and treating PRT [...] as servants or even slaves" even while recognizing domestic work as work (Ruwaida 2017: 48). Such *doxa*, Ida's team concluded, could only be undone through a combination of structural and cultural intervention: legal recognition and community-based work.

Debbie Prabawati, UGM and the Universities of Oslo and Ageder

Debbie Prabawati was the lead Indonesian researcher and coordinator of the domestic worker strand of a five-year collaborative project entitled "Power, Welfare and Democracy" (PWD) staged between UGM, the University of Oslo, and the University of Ageder, with the backing of the Norwegian Embassy. Her feminist journey resembled those of Ida Noor and Sri Eddyono; all three traced their activist bents back to involvement with student study groups, the student movement, and the early years of *reformasi*. Studying sociology at UGM, Debbie had participated in student protests in Yogyakarta and the capital in 1998. The harrowing experiences she had then stayed with her. She was sent to photograph the bodies of victims burnt in the Yogyakarta Mall. Some bodies had been unrecognizable, and, in Jakarta, "one victim, a street vendor [...] was shot in the back [...] I took him to the clinic, but it was a big bullet", she told me. Post-1998, Debbie worked with the Jakarta Social Institute, transferring to DEMOS in 2003.[40] There, she took the opportunity to go to Oslo with six others to study for her master's degree and became involved with designing the UGM/Oslo programme.[41]

Appointed project coordinator and joint lead researcher with Norwegian academic David Jordhus-Lier, Debbie worked on the domestic worker case-study element of the PWD project from October 2012 onwards. For reasons similar to those identified by Ida Noor, she found that "it was difficult to constitute a network between three different

40 DEMOS is the Indonesian Centre for Democracy and Human Rights.

41 Interview with Debbie Prabawati, Yogyakarta, 5 December 2016.

groups, people have their priorities, and it becomes hard to engage them in what other people want to do".[42] In facilitating the project, Debbie's expertise was indispensable; she was the person with links on the ground and a fluent English speaker accustomed to working with Indonesian NGOs. Nevertheless, the project presented personal and professional challenges: "feeling alive" in the fieldwork elements of the work. Debbie confessed that as a temporary staff member without tenure, she felt uncomfortable having to seek cooperation from more senior academics for whom the project was not central to their work. At the same time, working full-time on an externally funded project she experienced a sense of being both in the university and outside its walls.[43]

Notwithstanding the challenges, the project created opportunities to explore issues of co-authorship, co-publishing, and the recognition of knowledge coming from different regions. Jordhus-Lier and Prabawati negotiated differences in perceived status and academic standing to co-author papers (Gastaldi et al. 2017; Jordhus-Lier and Prabawati 2018). Debbie emphasized the importance of local knowledge production when she spoke to me. Having interviewed domestic workers in five cities – Jakarta, Kupang, Palembang, Medan, and Surabaya – she had realized "how different areas of Indonesia will create different knowledge and create new solutions". Her comment parallels Nagar's conclusion that paying attention to "new spaces and places" not "closely bound to the academy" can enhance activism by ensuring that strategy is grounded in locally produced knowledge, histories, and traditions (2014: 161).

Ade Indriani Zuchri, a second researcher involved in the UGM/Oslo project, likewise felt strongly that activists and researchers should "work with local traditions" and reconsider relationships between Jakarta and the rest of the nation, so much so that she invited me to go with her to Palembang in South Sumatra, which has a culturally specific history of protecting women and children.[44]. Otherwise, Ade warned, researchers can be faced with the riposte, "why do you [outsiders] try to protect our rights?" If outside researchers show that "they can learn from local wisdom", Ade averred, "people will listen more".[45] Her comment was not only about epistemology but ontology; "local wisdom" constitutes valid knowledge, and the decolonization

42 Interview with Debbie Prabawati, Yogyakarta, 5 December 2016.

43 Field notes of observation of focus group, Jakarta, 2 July 2015.

44 I accepted the invitation. Many thanks to Ade and her family for an amazing experience.

45 Interview with Ade Indriani Zuchri, Jakarta, 8 July 2015.

of knowledge production, in Indonesia, can entail changing power relationships between centre and periphery within the nation-state.

My interview with Ade also revealed the importance of local, NGO-based knowledge and of feminist connections that cross the archipelago in producing and distributing knowledge about domestic worker rights. Ade, whose family home was in Palembang, had been a member of JALA PRT since 2004, representing the local NGO she worked with, the Organization for Women's Advancement (OWA). She knew Lita Anggraini well. From 2014 onwards, Ade worked for the Institute for Research, Education, and Information (LP3ES) in Jakarta, returning to Sumatra at weekends. Debbie Prabawati knew Ade through DEMOS and invited Ade to join the research team on her return from Oslo. As Ade reflected, members of the UGM/Oslo research group knew about domestic worker organizations, especially in Yogyakarta, but "didn't know about JALA PRT". As a result, Ade facilitated links between Jakarta and Palembang and brought her local knowledge and connections to bear; as she said, "a good connection is good for everybody".[46] Responsible for the Palembang element of the UGM/Oslo research, Ade argued for situating domestic workers' claims in the context of the expansion of oil palm plantations, mining, and the sale of land rather than relying on appeals to the legitimacy of claims emanating from the ILO.

Along with the other multi-sited research exercises discussed so far, the UGM/Oslo collaboration offered opportunities for disseminating research findings from Indonesia to international audiences, filled in details of the domestic worker landscape in areas of the country little studied before, and provided opportunities for scholars to challenge northern hegemonies shaping research.

Individual Scholarship

Finally, individual scholars have broken new ground. Muryanti, the author of one of the *Topik Empu* pieces in *JP* 39, was the first Indonesian academic (to my knowledge) to gain a doctorate on domestic work inside Indonesia. She laughed when she told me that at her viva at the prestigious Institute of Agriculture in Bogor, her examiners knew

---

46 Interview with Ade Indriani Zuchri, Jakarta, 8 July 2015. For further insight into the importance of individuals in circuits of alternative knowledge production and distribution in cultural locations outside Java, see Evelyn Blackwood's account of the circulation of queer discourses as experienced by those identifying themselves as "lesbi" in the city of Padang, West Sumatra (2010: 181–90).

little of her topic and were amazed to find it a subject of interest.[47] When I contacted her, she invited me to co-present at a seminar at her university, Sunan Kalijaga, on the theme of the changing relations of domestic work. The event was attended, with due ceremony, by the dean and senior staff as well as by students on the sociology course.[48] Muryanti's work focuses on the social and economic background and cultural constructions of PRT that result in their exploitation and abuse, and on the continuation of kinship and *ngenger* traditions in employment patterns and employers' imaginations in the Yogyakarta region (Muryanti 2012, 2015). Valentina Utari, a researcher I met at the SMERU research institute during my internship there, opened a new field for investigation when she examined masculinity and domestic work for her master's degree. Changed attitudes amongst husbands who had taken on domestic duties while their wives studied in Australia, she discovered, did not generally transfer when families returned to Indonesia, where the *doxa* ran deep.[49] Gita Nasution, doing fieldwork in Jakarta for her PhD from Monash University, had been persuaded to study domestic work inside Indonesia by her supervisor, Katherine Robinson, a long-term researcher on women's rights in Indonesia, even though she had gone to Australia to study trafficking. Too well-worked a topic, Robinson had advised; better to use her position as a mother to examine the institution of domestic work in relation to the lifestyles of middle-class families in the capital. When I met Gita, she was reconsidering her research methods since neither her middle-class friends nor their domestic workers were keen to talk to her, each group nervous about what the other might say.

Do my encounters with these seven researchers justify my claim that C189 helped set new trends? In four respects – the emphasis on transnational partnerships, the inclusion of new research sites outside Java, a focus on training and methodology, and the appearance of Indonesian PhD students choosing domestic work as their theme – arguably so. Valentina Utari's interest in masculinities and Gita Nasution's in the changing lives of the middle classes indicate that future studies of domestic work will find new foci.

---

47 Interview with Muryanti Muryanti, Yogyakarta, 7 December 2016. A list of Muryanti's publications, including several relating to domestic workers in Yogyakarta, is available at https://scholar.google.co.id/citations?view_op=list_works&hl=en&hl=en&user=Arbfo9MAAAAJ&pagesize=80 (Accessed 28 August 2022).

48 Field note, Sunan Kalijaga, Yogyakarta, 6 December 2016.

49 Meeting with Valentina Utari, Jakarta, 2 December 2016.

Conclusion

In this chapter, I have examined the contribution of Indonesian scholars to the domestic workers' cause and argued that the structure of the Indonesian academy, as much as the defence of class privilege, accounts for the absence of substantial academic publications before C189. The creation of feminist spaces for knowledge production inside and outside universities made a difference: a few pioneer researchers placed domestic work in a feminist frame. At *JP*, activist researchers analyzed domestic work using a standpoint epistemology. Following C189, experienced researchers with feminist and activist roots dating back to the 1990s provided the leadership and expertise to support larger, externally funded projects. A sprinkling of a new generation of Indonesian researchers began to explore unresearched dimensions of domestic work. Collectively, the actors featured in this chapter extended the theorization of domestic worker issues beyond a victim/perpetrator paradigm and, by foregrounding knowledge produced by activist researchers and PRT and experimenting with new methodologies, entered debates over feminist knowledge production and the coloniality of both the academy and hegemonic western/northern feminist and rights-based discourses. Their evidence and arguments may not have demolished the certainties of domestic work but have lent legitimacy to the task of undermining them.

With Nagar as a starting point, I have paid attention to academic memoirs. One theme running through this chapter is the importance for domestic workers of rehearsing and recreating their "life scripts", to use Nicole Constable's phrase (2010). As the amount and variety of research into domestic worker organizing in Indonesia increased, activists and workers became adept at recounting experiences, not just of exploitation but of agency and transformation. If I began this chapter by sharing my recollections of hearing, from Bandung to Brighton, a seemingly unshakeable conviction that Indonesian domestic workers needed to be "spoken for", then the contribution of the knowledge producers profiled in this chapter has been to belie that belief. The preservation, publishing and circulation of domestic workers' own stories is creating a new archive, telling a different tale, a theme I take up in the conclusion.

Conclusion

Kami Tidak Akan Diam – "We Will Not Be Silent"

On 10 August 2017, 200 people attended a book launch in the glitzy Wisma Antara building in central Jakarta. The book was a collection of stories penned by PRT. Its title, *Kami Tidak Akan Diam: 31 Kisah Pekerja Rumah Tangga di Balik Tembok Ruang Domestik* (We Will Not Be Silent: 31 Stories of Domestic Workers behind the Domestic Wall), is apposite.[1] The word *tembok* refers to solid or retaining walls; used as an adjective or verb, it implies that something (or someone) has been walled in.

Walls, in this history, have been a matter of contention. While employers have seen the walls of their houses as offering shelter and opportunities to girls and women from poor communities, domestic workers have climbed those same walls in making their escape. The walls and gates of Indonesia's parliamentary complex have represented the gulf between PRT as an embodiment of Indonesia's "little people" and the politicians who failed to pass a domestic worker law over many years. As Sara Ahmed (2012: 175–6, 199) points out, much physical and emotional labour is expended by those who, like the supporters of the domestic worker movement in this story, bang their heads against institutional brick walls.

This book has brought to light some of that physical and emotional labour. It has revealed the importance of feminist theorizing, organizing, networking, advocacy, knowledge production, and modes of leadership in building a new social imaginary and politics of domestic work. By

1 The publication, funded by the US Department of Labor and published jointly by JALA PRT, the ILO, and AJI Jakarta, is available in Bahasa Indonesia on the ILO Jakarta website (Ujianto and Luviana 2017).

supporting domestic workers in *being together*, *being seen*, and *being heard* through what I have called the movement's feminist "politics of presence", the social actors featured in this account have added a localized legitimacy to global, rights-based claims and laid the foundations of a politically active Indonesian domestic worker class.

Books – like quilts – must eventually be completed. I long cherished the hope that this one might end with the news that, finally, Indonesia had passed a domestic worker law. As I write at the end of 2023, however, the fate of the Bill hangs in the balance.[2] Instead, this final chapter draws out some cross-cutting themes, seeing them as threads that have held the movement together; returns to "feminist triangles" to reflect on the book's broader contribution to the field of feminist activism and social movement organizing, and closes with an update of developments between 2016 and 2023 (drawn from internet sources) that give grounds for optimism, even amidst uncertainty.

Common Threads

Stitching sits symbolically at the centre of JALA PRT's argument for a domestic workers law. The giant *Serbet Cinta PRT* or "Love Napkin of Domestic Work" became a talisman. The word *serbet* came from the Dutch *servet*, itself derived from the French *serviette*, or napkin. A cheap item with direct connections to colonialism became an emblem of resistance to Dutch and Indonesian cultures of servitude. As one member of an OPERATA in South Jakarta told me: "we feel proud to wear the *serbet*, not embarrassed, it feels like a professional uniform".[3] Celebrating, not denigrating those who did domestic work and conveying the message that care work matters to everyone, the stitched together "Love Napkin" helped bind workers together and expressed the importance PRT attached to being valued as well as seen and heard.

Being Together

Gatherings, friendships, and longstanding loyalties have sustained Indonesia's domestic worker movement from the outset. JALA's network model had drawbacks: informants mentioned the lack of a secretariat,

2 On 12 September 2023, the DPR moved forward the date for the Bill's completion to 2024.

3 Fieldnote, Jakarta, 12 February 2016.

much time spent in meetings, heavy reliance on Lita Anggraini, and the difficulty of balancing their home organizations' priorities against JALA's needs. Hence, connections and commitment mattered enormously. For PRT, regular meetings fostered "communities of coping" (Jiang and Korczynski 2016). When workers attended protests or press conferences, their presence subverted stasis, upending notions that a domestic worker "belongs" to her employer's family and occupies only spaces apportioned to her. Instead, the movement nurtured "mobility, experimentation, risk-taking and aspiration" (Butcher and Maclean 2018) – graphically represented by the motorbikes and piles of shoes that collected outside the doors of houses or NGO offices being used as domestic workers schools.

The movement's meeting places were sites of resistance to hegemonic norms of women's destiny. They were rehearsal rooms where workers and activists could "think and practice space differently", incubators of new imaginaries of domestic work, and crucibles for the emergence of different "relational construction[s] of subjectivity" (Massey 2005: 58). Feminist emancipatory education helped workers seek redress and negotiate with employers. The PRT school prepared potential leaders to manage neighbourhood groups and represent their peers. Terms such as gender, patriarchy, harassment, solidarity, slavery, victim, protection, worker, rights, freedom, and experience became the movement's common parlance. Such feminist language countered familial constructs of servanthood while the home-like spaces of the JALA house and female-only OPERATA, where food, fellowship, celebrating, and recouping after disappointment went on year on year, nurtured feelings of solidarity.

Male supporters contributed, but leadership and decision-making rested with women. *Being together* under the JALA umbrella brought PRT into contact with Indonesia's activist "liberal left milieu" (Rinaldo 2013: 161). When PRT participated in conferences, they sat alongside representatives of secular feminist, Muslim feminist, women's rights, and human rights NGOs. They met journalists and trade unionists who shared the same pro-democracy and student activist pasts as the founders of RTND in Yogyakarta. Indeed, a photograph taken at the first JALA meeting I attended shows PRT gathered around a table with the silver-haired figure of "Pak Wiladi", aka Wiladi Budiharga, a noted democracy activist and intellectual whom Lita Anggraini describes as her mentor.

At the same time, JALA located itself in a transnational political arena. ILO resources, expertise, and influence with governments and unions were indispensable. A small number of activists and PRT attended regional or international meetings, building a sense of belonging to a global collective. One sceptical recruit to the Sapu Lidi domestic workers' union, for example, became an organizer only after meeting members of the International Domestic Workers Federation and hearing what workers elsewhere had achieved (Suryani 2017). In 2016, when PRT representatives from Jakarta, Yogyakarta, Semarang, Lampung (South Sumatra), and Makassar (Sulawesi) attended a weekend workshop facilitated by Elizabeth Tang, General Secretary of the IDWF, they spoke of "being proud" to see everyone assembled. Finding "together time" had not been straightforward; one attendee at the workshop confessed to not having told her husband where she was going, aware of his likely disapproval.[4] The weekend was geared towards planning a national domestic workers' confederation, akin to Brazil's National Federation of Domestic Workers, FENATRAD (Acciari 2019). As with other events chronicled in this book, that conference would become part of the movement's collective history and a waypoint on individual life journeys, documented in the selfies and group photographs participants took throughout the day I was there.

Being Seen

A second recurring theme has been visibility. *Being seen* had a material and a conceptual dimension. Materially, movement organizers paid attention to the presentation of PRT in public. Conceptually, organizers concentrated on changing the ways domestic workers visualized themselves. The activist T-shirt emblazed with the slogan "PRT=*Pekerja Rumah Tangga*" (PRT=Domestic Worker) brought the two elements together, making the movement's core message unmissable. Performing in "uniforms" in iconic protest spaces alongside union officials reminded PRT that being part of JALA linked them with a larger entity and longer protest tradition.

Images of the domestic worker's tools of the trade helped transform "helpers" into workers with rights. A small polythene bag sits among the papers I amassed in researching this book. It contains a kitchen sponge with a scratchy green surface on one side. Alongside it is a handwritten message from Titin, a domestic worker in East Java, urging the passage of the Domestic Workers Bill and ratification of C189. The sponge I salvaged as a keepsake was one of a (notional) 1,606 assembled from across the archipelago ready to be delivered

4 Field note, Tangerang, 3 December 2016.

to parliament on 16 June, International Domestic Workers' Day. Mops, brooms, napkins, washing lines, and pots and pans have all come under consideration in this story. While employers talked in the abstract of familial relationships and used gifts to reinforce patron–client relationships, PRT held up pictures of politicians' yellowed underpants awaiting the wash, told journalists about cleaning toilets without rubber gloves, and brandished brooms, buckets, saucepans, and irons during demonstrations. Such creative displays aligned Indonesia's domestic workers with a global movement – mops and aprons have universal currency – and with Indonesia's working class and urban poor, who have a history of bringing such items onto the forecourts of government offices or parliamentary buildings during protests (Juliawan 2011). Furthermore, as Steedman concluded in her study of domestic labour in late eighteenth-century England, it is in the tension between the hard physical labour associated with such objects – the repeated "back and forth movement of the human body with a rag" or the scraping of "baby's clouts"[5] – and the fact that these objects belong to the employer, not the servant, that the class identity of the domestic worker resides (2009: 348–50).

Being Heard

Throughout its history, the movement has challenged taboos against PRT speaking out. At the close of the New Order, as revealed in Chapter 1, domestic worker voices were expected to be deferential and self-deprecating. Progressive intellectuals and activists, meanwhile, aspired to speak for Indonesia's underclass. By contrast, much of JALA's legitimacy and resilience has derived from its investment in developing the capacity of workers to speak for themselves. As was the case amongst African American domestic workers in the US, the movement used storytelling to create an imaginary in which transformation, pride, self-worth, knowledge, and agency replaced victimization and acquiescence (Nadasen 2016: 156–7). PRT leaders learned to retell experiences of unfair practices, perform on stage, represent themselves or co-workers in court, conduct interviews with journalists or researchers, and contribute to discussions in the DPR. Press coverage amplified their voices and commanded political attention even though the number of organized PRT remained small.

Writing was a second strand of the *being heard* strategy. Part-way through my research, I came across Sara Ahmed's *Queer Phenomenology*.

5 Pieces of cloth used as nappies or diapers.

Her book has the image of Ciancarlo Neri's nine-metre-tall writer's table and chair installed on London's Hampstead Heath (a place dear to me as the site of many family walks) on its front cover. Reading Ahmed's text was revelatory. She argues that when women take up space at writing tables, they engage in re-gendering as they "turn the tables" on those who had hitherto shaped their lives (2006: 61–2). With such "re-gendering" in mind, the chairs, tables, pens, exercise books, flip chart paper, and photocopiers in use at domestic worker meetings I observed took on a new significance.

A New Domestic Worker Class

In the Introduction, I touched on the "making" of a working class in eighteenth-century England. Transposed to the contemporary moment, the trope of the "making of maids" frequently features in books and articles about migrant domestic work.[6] "Making" in such texts generally points to the disciplinary regimes imposed on overseas domestic workers to produce a commodity – "docile bodies with limited opportunities for formalised resistance" (Lyons 2005: 4). In this book, however, "making" signifies agency. The themes of *being together*, *being seen*, and *being heard*, conceptualized as a feminist "politics of presence", point to the proposition that the social actors studied in this book have enabled the emergence of a nascent Indonesian domestic worker class.

This proposition accords with Rina Agarwala and Shiny Saha's study of domestic worker organizations in India (2018). They found workers combining to confront employers who held down wages, refused to let workers join an association or withheld compensation in the case of accidents. As in Indonesia, workers made claims against the state. For Agarwala and Saha, such endeavours "indicate the 'making' of a new class of domestic workers" – a class well aware of its contribution to the economy and society (2018: 1221–2). Elsewhere, in a study of the construction and cigarette industries, Agarwala demonstrated that since informal labour is integral to modern capitalist economies, such workers can, if they choose, "organize, increase their visibility or improve their well-being as a class" (2013: 9). In Indonesia, organized PRT not only won concessions from employers but, as Rother (2017) argues is true of migrant domestic workers in Hong Kong, built a

6 Examples include Mary Romero's *Maid in the USA* (2002), Nicole Constable's *Maid to Order in Hong Kong* (2007), Lenore Lyons's "Embodying Transnationalism: The Making of the Indonesian Maid" (2005), Wanning Sun's *Maid in China* (2009), and Olivia Killias's *Follow the Maid* (2018).

store of class-based political capital. In their class roles, PRT have stood for election, written for journals, taught new recruits, appeared on television, and travelled overseas. When I left Jakarta at the end of 2016, one Sapu Lidi member was about to begin training as a lawyer, wanting to represent fellow workers in court.

It could be argued that the small number of PRT interviewed during this research raises questions about the top layer of this book's quilting, the notion of a "new class". Indeed, earlier studies drawing on much wider research bases have suggested that a "disconnect" between the task of creating collective worker identities at the local level and JALA PRT's national campaign has held up progress (Jordhus-Lier 2017: 50–51) and that the movement weakened its gender-based claims when it increased the emphasis on class (Eddyono et al. 2015). Both insights point to the balancing act required to conduct a campaign for national legislation and build broad support amongst domestic workers, employers, NGOs, trade unions, and politicians across a nation of some 273 million spread over the world's largest archipelago.

My own limited resources led me to concentrate on two cities in Java. Nevertheless, that focus has allowed me to extend earlier analyses and suggest that notions of Indonesia's domestic worker movement as an example of failed feminist or worker activism need reframing. In the global literature on domestic worker movements, Indonesia stands out. It is one of very few examples of a new organization – in this case JALA PRT – emerging and growing from "the very convergence" of women's rights issues and claims for domestic worker rights (Marchetti et al. 2021: 96–7). The stories retold here suggest that the movement's survival has depended on developing class identities as well as on feminist politics and praxis and an ability to shift spaces and emphases strategically as opportunities and agendas change.

Feminist Triangles Revisited

I began this book with feminist triangles. Starting with activists, journalists, and knowledge producers/academics provided an entry point. My findings, however, complicated such distinctions. Many of my informants were active across several fields. Furthermore, the question arose as to where, and how, PRT leaders featured in such a frame. Nevertheless, as I investigated biographies and intergroup relations, I unearthed material that gives this book resonance beyond the field of domestic work.

Indeed, if the stories retold are specific to Indonesia, their import contributes to broader analyses of feminist social movements and transnational activism. While one aspect of the 'politics of presence' explored in this book has been work done by, with, and for PRT, another has been flexible, cross-class coalition building. By paying close attention to the motivations and memories of supporters, this study adds depth to discussions of the role of emotion – and the more visceral 'affect' – in feminist social movements. Reliant on PRT, many of the middle-class professionals I met, for example, expressed feelings of discomfort about their privilege as well as shame at their nation's failure to protect domestic workers. At the same time, some of the most moving accounts shared with me were of the shock, anger, disgust, and disillusionment engendered by experiences of disregard by the state along with evidence of denial, self-interest, and intransigence from politicians. Both the everyday and extraordinary business of activists were shaped by listening to, acting on, publicizing, and processing reports of physical, sexual, and psychological abuse and harassment of domestic workers, refuelling the affect and emotion that helped recruit supporters and hold a loose intersectional alliance together.

This book is also a record of my own research and writing journey, a journey with its own discomforts and dilemmas. Organized domestic workers want research to advance their campaigns. Some criticize outsiders who arrive, take up their time, then disappear to publish academic papers (Grossman 2011; Azzarello et al. 2014). Such questions are demanding, especially for the lone PhD researcher. Three encounters towards the end of my fieldwork encapsulate the challenge of responding to such issues and to those raised by Nagar's "situated solidarities", discussed in Chapter 5. The first was when activist-turned-academic Muryanti, with whom I had just led a seminar at her university, suggested we co-author a paper for an English-language publication. It was a suggestion I should have been ready for. The second was at a conference marking the culmination of a collaboration between Dutch and Indonesian universities and institutes.[7] One of the speakers, Surya Tjandra, asked me about the "two trade unionists" mentioned in my presentation abstract. "Would one be Lita Anggraini? Have you invited Ririn Sulastri [from Tunas Mulia union] to join

7 "Citizenship as the politics of presence: Two trade unionists and the fight for an Indonesian Domestic Workers Law", paper presented at *From Clients to Citizens? Citizenship in Democratising Indonesia,* Universitas Gadjah Mada, Yogyakarta, Indonesia, 8–10 December 2016.

us today?" he inquired. At that moment, I was minded of Shireen Ally's description of the "fraught" tensions that arose when she and her colleagues experimented "in drawing domestic workers into the aegis of an academic conference" (2011a: 5). The third moment of discomfort was when I invited three PRT to my central Jakarta hotel for tea. We had all attended a workshop in a hotel almost next door to my own, and they had been keen to see where I was staying. Inevitably, one asked me how much it cost. Such situations pushed me to reflect on my positionality and, to build on Laura Pulido's response to Nagar's *Muddying the Waters*, consider "the path not taken" (Chowdhury et al. 2016: 1803). Just like Pulido, I was busy establishing my academic voice and competence. I too was coping with what she describes as the "corporeal politics of solidarity" – the heat, long hours sitting on floors, or navigating Jakarta's capricious and crowded public transport system (2016: 1803–4). And the further I ventured into writing, the more I realized that the seemingly unfashionable topic of domestic work offers rich insights into issues such as positionality, trust, accountability, and the use of names.

Update: New Voices, Alliances, and Arenas

While it remains for others to fill the missing pieces in this book's patchwork and continue the story, it seems fitting to end with an update since much has transpired since I finished my fieldwork. I had a foretaste of some of the political changes to come when, on 2 December 2016, staff at my Jakarta hotel urged me to stay indoors. They feared I might get caught up in what was expected to be a massive rally staged by a coalition of Islamist groups demanding that Jakarta's Christian Chinese Governor, Basuki Tjahaja Purnama – known as "Ahok" – be removed from office and tried for blasphemy. An estimated 500,000 to 750,000 Muslims turned out on the day. President Jokowi joined their prayers, made a short speech, and withdrew support from the man who had been his running mate for the governorship of Jakarta in 2012 (Fealy 2016). For some, this demonstration signified the rise of Islamic conservatism, a growing strength of hard-line Muslim organizations, increasing intolerance towards minorities and LGBTQI groups, and a threat to Indonesia as a pluralist state (Wieringa 2019). Like other women's and feminist movements in Indonesia, JALA PRT has witnessed a shift to a more conservative society, the passing of discriminatory by-laws by local and regional governments, and an online campaign for an "*Indonesia Tanpa Feminis*" (Indonesia without Feminists) (Mazrieva 2019).

In this context, exacerbated by a divisive 2019 presidential election in which populist deployment of motherhood identities played a role (Arifianto 2019; Dewi 2020), JALA has yet again forged new alliances. Between 2016 and 2023, the movement continued its politics of presence; won support from a new generation of feminists; found champions amongst influential women's rights activists; and used digital activism to extend its reach during and after COVID-19.

Presence

Building presence in neighbourhoods and the media has continued to be a priority. In 2022, Lita Anggraini was able to announce that some 8,000 PRT were enrolled in eight domestic workers' unions spread across ten provinces, compared with a membership of barely 1,000 at the close of 2016. New unions had opened in Bandar Lampung and Medan in Sumatra; Makassar in South Sulawesi; Malang and Surabaya in Central Java; and in Tangerang, part of what was by then known as Jabodetabek, adding to those already operating in Yogyakarta, Jakarta, and Semarang (Adityowati 2019; Tungku Menyala 2022) The domestic workers school continues, now renamed the "School of Insight". Lauded as a model of good practice by the ILO, it has a structured curriculum starting with a module for teaching new recruits to PRT unions their basic rights and leading up to training for paralegals and regional and national organizers. Sessions on decent work, sexual and reproductive health rights, complaint mechanisms, and elimination of harassment and violence in the workplace can be adapted to local needs. Public speaking and writing, developing campaign materials, and using social media for advocacy still feature (Nasution 2021; Kuswadi and Rahayu 2023). Vocational skills training can now lead to national certification; Leni Suryani from Sapu Lidi union, for example, completed a 200-hour, officially endorsed programme and used her certificate to negotiate a higher salary with an expatriate employer (Smith 2017). ILO monitoring and entries on the *Garuda* research portal reveal that PRT have gained more recognition in the media and the academy. In August 2017, *Jurnal Perempuan* published a follow-up to the 2005 edition on domestic work featured in Chapter 5. This time, one of the "expert" chapters had three co-authors: Jumiyem and Sargini, founder members of Tunas Mulia, who participated in the 2014 hunger strike, and Muryanti, a volunteer activist in 2005 but a university lecturer in 2017 (Sargini et al. 2017). Interviewed or written about in 2005, by 2017 PRT voices are being ascribed authorship.

Allies

Amongst the movement's new allies, a group calling itself "Jakarta Feminist" has introduced a new generation of young women to the movement. Established in 2014, Jakarta Feminist initiated the Women's March Jakarta in 2017. JALA PRT joined the organizing committee and the RUU PPRT became one of the rally's demands. A year later, when the March was repeated, PRT outfits caught the eyes of photographers. BBC Indonesia, for example, chose a photograph similar to Figure 6.1 when it reported the event.

Kate Walton's snapshot shows the striking red or black T-shirts, *serbet* headscarves, and woven bamboo hats worn by PRT on the Women's March. Some of the protestors carry kitchen utensils or traditional winnowing baskets painted with letters spelling out "PEKERJA" to highlight their cause. In the early days in Yogyakarta, I was told, PRT protestors hid their faces behind these same winnowing baskets; here, PRT bodies and faces radiate confidence. Headscarf and apron have evolved into a fun, fashionable, and feminist activist street style. The presence of PRT was further underlined when Leni Suryani, a leading member of the Sapu Lidi union, stood up on the platform as one of the day's main speakers.

Afterwards, four young, university-educated middle-class members of Jakarta Feminist reflected on the day. They were "impressed" by the PRT who participated. With PRT and women factory workers visibly

Fig. 6.1 JALA PRT at the Women's March Jakarta, 2018 (Photo: Kate Walton)

present, they had been able to leave their comfort zones "while feeling safe" and "show empathy" for women "from all layers of society" (Kwok 2018). Since 2017, Jakarta Feminist has continued to bring the issue of domestic worker rights to new audiences of younger women adept at influencing through social media.

If Jakarta Feminist influenced younger women on social media, two more established, older women's voices reached wider constituences. The first was that of Giwo Rubianto Wiyogo, chair of the Indonesian Women's Congress known as KOWANI. Early in 2016, Wiyogo attended a press conference with Lita Anggraini and the chair of the National Commission on Violence Against Women and pledged support for the RUU PPRT. Taking a prominent role, she has brought KOWANI's connections with ministers, politicians, the business world, and academia, as well as its international status to bear (Achmad 2016; RMOL.ID 2016; Indriani 2020). A federation of women's associations spread across the archipelago, KOWANI claimed a membership of 90 million in 2023 (Indriani 2023). Since many of its members employed PRT, KOWANI could circulate information about the Bill and reassure employers that work contracts would benefit them as well as their PRT.

Politicians recognized KOWANI's influence. In an increasingly populist political landscape, they wanted women's votes. In September 2018, for example, President Jokowi stood on stage next to Wiyogo at the opening of the 35th meeting of the International Council of Women in Yogyakarta, endorsing her use of the term "Mothers of the Nation" (*Ibu Bangsa*) to extol Indonesia's women. This was in preference to the term *emak-emak* or "ordinary working women" adopted by supporters of his political rival Prabowo Subianto (Dewi 2020: 237). Paying attention to PRT (an embodiment of Indonesia's "little people"), offered a counter to Prabowo's populist *emak-emak* and, in turn, heightened the political import of the Bill. PRT unions in Yogyakarta and Semarang seem to have taken up this "Bangsa" theme in their demonstrations. In December 2022 and February 2023, photographers from *Kompas.com* and *Liputan6.com* captured PRT in front of their regional parliaments wearing traditional batik *sarongs* paired with *serbet* headscarves, campaign T-shirts, or black umbrellas inscribed with the words "Pass the PRT Bill".

A second influential voice to join JALA's campaign was that of Eva Kusuma Sundari. Known as a staunch women's rights activist and academic, Sundari had entered the DPR in 2004 but lost her seat in 2019. Shen then became director of the Sarinah Institute (InSari), a think-tank started by members and former members of Indonesia's national student movement to advance a "Pancasila-based" feminism grounded in Indonesia's founding principles rather than western individualism – and began promoting the RUU PPRT. If, as informants have told me, politicians had dismissed demands for legislation as coming only from JALA, or even just from Lita Anggraini, enlisting Eva Sundari and Giwo Wiyogo to the cause put paid to such excuses.

By the middle of 2022, old and new allies had begun calling themselves the "Civil Coalition for the RUU PPRT". On 4 July, Aida Milasari (the founder member of Rumpun Tjoet Nyak Dien introduced in Chapter 2), headed a delegation to the DPR and informed leading politicians that the Coalition had 150 organizations, "including religious organizations and universities" on its side (mediakita 2022). Pressure on politicians was vital. Little or no progress had been made since July 2020 when the Legislative Council of the DPR had agreed that the Bill should proceed. This was even though the movement has given significant ground during negotiations – no longer calling for a standard minimum wage or legally specified hours of work, for example, but leaving these to be agreed with employers. The delay was not due to COVID-19; the government had pushed through a Job Creation Law and a new Criminal Code, both highly controversial, between 2020 and 2022.

Digital Activism

COVID-19 impacted disastrously on Indonesia's domestic workers. It also accelerated the use of digital activism. Initially, PRT used WhatsApp chat groups to support each other and circulate advice from JALA about unfair dismissals, wage cuts, increased workloads, pressure to become live-in staff, or failures to supply face masks and gloves. Some posted on the PRT's online news forum *Tungku Menyala*. Others published stories on *Konde.co*, the digital outlet established by journalist activist Luviana, featured in Chapter 4. *Magdalene.co*, an online magazine created to give space to "feminists, pluralists and progressives" (Winarnita et al. 2022: 8), and *JalaStoria*, a digital outlet created in 2018 to counter gender discrimination, both carried stories about PRT. Much advocacy and networking moved to the webinar. In Zoom meetings, often hosted by allies, Lita Anggraini and leading members of PRT unions appeared alongside lawyers, academics, activist students, religious leaders, trade unionists, sympathetic politicians, government ministers, and officials. Posted on Instagram, Facebook, NGO websites, uploaded to YouTube or picked up by journalists, such digital activism placed the domestic workers' cause in new arenas, reaching larger audiences. On 18 January 2023, for example, an episode of Metro TV's popular weekly show *HOTROOM* posted on YouTube showed fierce debate about the pros and cons of the RUU PPRT. Hosted by the controversial and flamboyant lawyer and businessman Hotman Paris Hutapea, the upload achieved 9834 views.

Once COVID-19 restrictions were lifted, PRT neighbourhood groups reopened their Sunday meeting spaces and schools. On Sunday 6 June 2022 at least 400 members of Sapu Lidi met for the first time in two years. An account of the event on *Tungku Menyala* describes the "broad smiles and joy" on the faces of the more than 400 PRT who attended. A photograph shows that almost all the attendees had dressed in red or black PRT T-shirts. With clenched fists raised, they resolved to grow their membership beyond the 5,000 already on their books and "be louder" in voicing their support for the RUU PPRT. Sapu Lidi membership was crucial: it accounted for more than half the national membership of domestic worker unions (Datu 2022; Tungku Menyala 2022). An air of renewal was boosted, in Jakarta at least, when, in October 2022, twenty or more "young feminist friends" attended a Sapu Lidi meeting. One PRT, Moy Soewartini, experienced their visit as "exciting" and "unusual" (Soewartini 2022). The visitors were very young, they came from "new organizations and alliances", they wanted to know what life as a PRT activist was like, they confessed to not understanding before how much PRT's live with anxiety and precarity. Drawing lessons from the meeting, Moy wanted more. With more "friends", she reasoned, PRT will not feel they struggle alone. The fight for the RUU PPRT might finally succeed.

*

On 21 December 2022, outside the Presidential Palace in Jakarta, JALA and the Civil Coalition staged the first of a series of regular Wednesday morning demonstrations. Featuring large umbrellas printed with "Pass the RUU PPRT", the protestors were creative with props and staging. Over the weeks they cooked breakfast for members of parliament; used chains, bags of sand, and bloodied bandages to symbolize enslavement and victimhood; and carried huge photographs of the Speaker of the House, Puan Maharani, demanding she accelerate the Bill. The Civil Coalition continued to lobby, garnering support from women's groups, academics, labour unions, students, and religious leaders. A newly revived Labour party, the Partai Buruh, looking to the 2024 elections, coveted the votes of informal workers, domestic and migrant workers, and the urban poor. In 2023, it repeatedly listed the RUU PPRT high on its demands and featured the Bill on protest banners. The party's leader, Said Iqbal, became a forceful advocate for the Bill (Ifhami 2023).

By the beginning of 2023, a circle had come round. Women's issues were high on politicians' agendas as they had been during *reformasi.* In January 2023, President Jokowi instructed two of his high-ranking ministers to accelerate the passage of the Bill. His Office established a Task Force. In February, spokespersons for, amongst others, Indonesia's second chamber (the People's Consultative Assembly), the Ministry for Women's Empowerment and Child Protection, the National Committee on Human Rights, Fatayat NU (the young women's branch of the mass Muslim organization NU), and several prominent politicians, expressed the need for urgency. On 21 March, nineteen years after a draft law first became a DPR priority, all nine party factions in parliament ceremonially handed over a written confirmation of their agreement to the RUU PPRT moving to its final stage. Since Indonesian law-making is based on the principle of consensus, this cross-party resolution was monumental. The Bill had never reached this point before in all its nineteen-year long journey.

No wonder that on the balcony of the hall, PRT who had asked employers for time off to attend clapped and cheered, hugged each other, and shed tears of joy and relief. This breakthrough, they said, was "a breath of fresh air", a "new chapter" and "a dream come true" (Tungku Menyala 2023).

Such moments of joy and achievement fuel hope for us all.

References

Acciari, L. 2019: Decolonising labour, reclaiming subaltern epistemologies: Brazilian domestic workers and the international struggle for labour rights. *Contexto Internacional* 41 (1), 39–63.

Achmad, A. 2016: PPRT Bill regulates employer–maid relations. *Hukumonline*, 12 January. https://www.hukumonline.com/berita/a/ruu-pprt-atur-hubungan-kerja-majikan-pembantu-lt5694493261a38 (Accessed 16 July 2022).

Adams, K. 2000: Negotiated Identities: Humour, kinship, rhetoric and mythologies of servitude in Southeast Asia. In K. Adams and S. Dickey (eds), *Homes and Hegemony: Domestic Service and Identity Politics in South and Southeast Asia*, Ann Arbor: University of Michigan Press, 157–78.

Adiprasetio, J. 2016: *Republika.co.id* and LGBT: Depiction of the failure of a watchdog. In *Conference Proceedings, Mass Media at Crossroads: A Survival between Technological Development and Cultural Change*, Faculty of Communication Science, Universitas Padjadjaran, 6–7 December 2016, 173–9.

Adityowati, P. 2019: Empowered domestic workers. *Tempo.co*, English Version, 2 February. https://en.tempo.co/read/1171614/empowered-domestic-workers (Accessed 8 August 2022).

Adriany, V., Pirmasari, D. A., and Umi, N. L. 2017: Being an Indonesian feminist in the north: An autoethnography. *Tijdschrift voor Genderstudies* 20 (3), 287–97.

Aftab, T., Poerwandari, K., and Porter, M. 2003: Triangular linkages between women's studies centers. *Gender, Technology and Development* 7 (2), 279–304.

Agarwala, R. 2013: *Informal Labor, Formal Politics, and Dignified Discontent in India*. Cambridge: Cambridge University Press.

Agarwala, R. and Saha, S. 2018: The employment relationship and movement strategies among domestic workers in India. *Critical Sociology* 44 (7–8), 1207–23.

Ahmed, S. 2006: *Queer Phenomenology: Orientations, Objects, Others*. Durham, NC/ London: Duke University Press.

Ahmed, S. 2008: Sociable happiness. *Emotion, Space and Society* 1 (1), 10–13.

Ahmed, S. 2010: Killing joy: Feminism and the history of happiness. *Signs: Journal of Women in Culture and Society* 35 (3), 571–94.

Ahmed, S. 2012: *On Being Included: Racism and Diversity in Institutional Life*. Durham, NC/London: Duke University Press.

Ahmed, S. 2017: *Living a Feminist Life*. Durham, NC/London: Duke University Press.

AJI Jakarta 2015: *Beasiswa Peliputan Urgensi Perlingdingan Hukum Bagi Pekerja Rumah Tangga*, 1 June. www.ajijakarta.org/2015/06/01/beasiswa-peliputan (Accessed 24 July 2017).

Alfin. 2015: *PRT adalah pekerja, penuhi hak-hak mereka*. [Blog] LBH Jakarta, 17 June. http://www.bantuanhukum.or.id/web/blog/prt-adalah-pekerja-penuhi-hak-hak-mereka/ (Accessed 28 October 2015).

Ally, S. 2008: Domestic worker unionisation in post-apartheid South Africa: Demobilisation and depoliticisation by the democratic state. *Politikon* 35 (1), 1–21.

Ally, S. 2011a: Domestics, "dirty work" and the affects of domination. *South African Review of Sociology* 42 (2), 1–7.

Ally, S. 2011b: On laws, rights and conventions: A provocation. *International Feminist Journal of Politics* 13 (3), 457–61.

Ally, S. 2013: "Ooh, eh…just one small cap is enough!" Servants, detergents, and their prosthetic significance. *African Studies* 72 (3), 321–52.

Amini, M. 2016: Anomali polah asuh: Keraton Yogyakarta, 1921–1939. *Paramita: Historical Studies Journal* 26 (2), 166–72.

Amiruddin, M. 2012: *Profil Jurnal Perempuan: 1995–sekarang*. http://www.jurnalperempuan.org/uploads/1/2/2/0/12201443/profil_jurnal_perempuan_1995-sekarang.pdf (Accessed 20 February 2020).

Amiruddin, M. 2013: *Jurnal Perempuan since 1995* [PowerPoint presentation]. http://www.jurnalperempuan.org/uploads/1/2/2/0/12201443/jurnal_perempuan_profile_english_version.ppt (Accessed 7 March 2020).

Amiruddin, M. 2014: *Mariana Amiruddin: Buku Harian untuk Jurnal Perempuan*. http://www.jurnalperempuan.org/2/post/2014/07/buku-harian-untuk-jurnal-perempuan.html (Accessed 16 February 2018).

Amnesty International 2007: *Indonesia: Exploitation and abuse: The plight of women domestic workers*, 14 February, ASA 21/001/2007. https://www.amnesty.org/en/documents/asa21/003/2007/en/ (Accessed 8 August 2022).

Anastasia, A., Anindhita, F., and Rahayuningtyas 2013: Organizational restructuring and network development. In A. Anastasia et al. (eds), *Indonesian Women's Movements: Making Democracy Gender Responsive*, Jakarta: Women's Research Institute, 153–72.

Anderson, B. 1970: In memoriam: Soe Hok-Gie. *Indonesia* 9, 225–7.

Anderson, B. 2006: *Imagined Communities: Reflections on the Origin and Spread of Nationalism*. Revised edn. London: Verso.

Andinda, P. 2022: Life is an impossible dream: The State has homework to do protect domestic workers, Lita Anggraini does it. *Project Multatuli*, 25 November. https://projectmultatuli.org/bagai-sebuah-mimpi-mustahil-negara-punya-pr-melindungi-prt-lita-anggraini-mengerjakannya/ (Accessed 8 August 2023).

Angarita, J. 2017: Indonesia: Workers not helpers – Organizing and empowering domestic workers. In *Decent Work for Domestic Workers: Eight Good Practices from Asia*, Geneva: International Labour Organization, 128–37. https://www.ilo.org/wcmsp5/groups/public/---asia/---ro-bangkok/---ilo-jakarta/documents/publication/wcms_571087.pdf (Accessed 8 August 2022).

Anggraini, L. 2012: *Meryakan Hari Pahlawan bagi Para Buruh Perempuan Indonesia. Ngalor-Nagidul* [Blog]. https://bangfir.wordpress.com/2012/11/06/merayakan-hari-pahlawan-bagi-para-buruh-perempuan-indonesia/ (Accessed 26 August 2022).

Anupamlata, R., Ansari, R., Bajpayee, V., Shashibala, S. V., Surbala, R. S., and Nagar, R. 2004: *Sangtin Yatra: Saat Zindgiyon Mein Lipta Nari Vimarsh*. Sitapur, India: Sangtin.

Anya, A. 2016a: Lawmaker to be questioned as suspect in abuse case. *Jakarta Post*, 24 February.

Anya, A. 2016b: Do people still need RT/ RW heads? *Jakarta Post*, 2 June.

Arifianto, A. R. 2019: What the 2019 election says about Indonesian democracy. *Asia Policy* 26 (4), 46–53.

Arivia, G. and Subono, N. 2017: *A Hundred Years of Feminism in Indonesia: An Analysis of Actors, Debates and Strategies*. Jakarta: Friedrich-Ebert-Stiftung Indonesia Office.

Ariyanti 2015: *Dalam Pelatihan Meliput Hak Pekerja Rumah Tangga–AJI*. [PowerPoint presentation], *Fellowship Training AJI*, Bogor, Indonesia, 6–7 June.

Ashoka 1999: *Maria Pakpahan*. https://www.ashoka.org/fellow/maria-pakpahan (Accessed 6 May 2016).

Aspinall, E. 2005: *Opposing Suharto: Compromise, Resistance, and Regime Change in Indonesia*. Stanford, CA: Stanford University Press.

Aspinall, E. 2012: Indonesia: Moral force politics and the struggle against authoritarianism. In M. Weiss and E. Aspinall (eds), *Student Activism in Asia: Between Protest and Powerlessness*, Minneapolis: University of Minnesota Press, 153–79.

Aspinall, E. and Weiss, M. 2014: The Limits of civil society: Social movements and political parties in Southeast Asia. In R. Robinson (ed.), *Routledge Handbook of Southeast Asian Politics*, London: Routledge, 213–28.

Astuti, R. 2012: *Pola Pendampingan Lemabarga Swadaya Masyarakat (LSM) Rumpun Tjoet Njak Dien, Yogyakarta, bagi Pekerja Rumah Tangga Berbasis Hak Asasi Manusia*, Undergraduate dissertation, Yogyakarta: Fakultas Ilmu Pemdidikan, Universitas Negeri. http://eprints.uny.ac.id/21629/ (Accessed 8 December 2015).

Augenbraum, H. and Schwalbe, W. 2000: Fear of the word: A conversation with Will Schwalbe on publishing Pramoedya Ananta Toer. *Mãnoa* 12 (1), 183–92.

Austin, M. 2014: Mopping up modernity: Domestic workers as modern citizens or fictive kin? [unpublished conference paper]. ASEAS Conference, University of Brighton, UK, 12–14 September.

Austin, M. 2017: Defending Indonesia's migrant domestic workers. In W. Berenschot, H. Schulte Nordholt, and L. Bakker (eds), *Citizenship and Democratization in Southeast Asia*, Leiden/Boston: Brill, 265–88.

Austin, M. 2022: Activist styling: Fashioning domestic worker identities in Indonesia. *International Quarterly for Asian Studies* 53 (1), 25–51.

Australia–Indonesia Partnership 2011: *ALAS 2011 Book of Profiles*. AusAID, Australia Indonesia Partnership. https://benaiahsoenarto.files.wordpress.com/2010/12/ebookofprofiles_v1.pdf (Accessed 25 April 2017).

Azzarello, S., Fish, J., Günther, S., Heimeshoff, L., Hobden, C., Kirchhoff, M., and Schwenken, H. 2014: *We Want to Be the Protagonists of Our Own Stories*. Research Network for Domestic Worker Rights, Kassel, Germany: Kassel University Press.

Bachtiar, I. 2010: Prof. Dr. Tapi Omas Ihromi: Ulang tahun ke-80 bersama anak, sahabat dan para murid. [Blog] *Kajian Gender.* https://kajiangender.wordpress.com/2010/04/06/prof-dr-tapi-omas-ihromi-ulang-tahun-ke-80-bersama-anak-sahabat-dan-para-murid/ (Accessed 23 January 2018).

Bailey, A. 2017: Tracking privilege-preserving epistemic pushback in feminist and critical race philosophy classes. *Hypatia* 32 (4), 876–92.

Bakker, L. and Timmer, J. 2014: Justice in Indonesia: The social life of a momentous concept. *The Asia Pacific Journal of Anthropology* 15 (4), 293–301.

Barbosa, G. and Varão, R. 2018: Error, doubt and gendered journalism: A look at the rape coverage in the feature "A rape on campus". *Brazilian Journalism Research* 14 (1), 12–29.

Barker, T. 2010: Historical Inheritance and film nasional in Post-Reformasi Indonesian cinema. *Asian Cinema* 21 (2), 7–24.

Beerkens, E. 2008: The student movement and the rise and fall of Suharto. *University World News.* http://www.universityworldnews.com/filemgmt_data/files/The%20rise%20and%20fall%20of%20Suharto.pdf (Accessed 8 August 2022).

Bennett, L. 2018: Infertility, Adoption, and Family Formation in Indonesia. *Medical Anthropology* 37 (2), 101–11.

Bergeijk, C. van 1986: *Movement and linkage in Yogyakarta: The case of domestic servants.* MA. University of Hawai'i at Manoa. https://www.proquest.com/openview/d7fd74843d7b05d9ac32191a62753408/1?pq-origsite=gscholar&cbl=18750&diss=y (Accessed 29 July 2022).

Bergstrom, P. 2004: *Women's/gender studies in Asia-Pacific.* Bangkok: UNESCO Office, Bangkok and Regional Bureau for Education in Asia and the Pacific. https://unesdoc.unesco.org/search/7420e470-2b65-4a34-a94c-1340c0c004e5 (Accessed 13 February 2020).

BeritaSatu 2015: Asa Anak Pantura. Jurnal Pagi. BeritaSatu TV. Live newscast on BeritaSatu TV, reporter Carlos Michael Kodoati [video]. 24 August. https://www.youtube.com/watch?v=CM_jKY_R_Xo (Accessed 14 May 2017).

Berninghausen, J. and Kerstan, B. 1992: *Forging New Paths: Feminist Social Methodology and Rural Women in Java.* London/New Jersey: Zed Books.

Blackburn, S. 2004: *Women and the State in Modern Indonesia.* Cambridge: Cambridge University Press.

Blackett, A. 2019: *Everyday Transgressions: Domestic Workers' Transnational Challenge to International Labour Law*. Ithaca, NY/ London: ILR Press.

Blackwood, E. 2010: *Falling into the Lesbi World: Desire and Difference in Indonesia*. Honolulu: University of Hawai'i Press.

Bodden, M. 2010: *Resistance on the National Stage: Theater and Politics in Late New Order Indonesia*. Athens, OH: Ohio University Press.

Boomgaard, P. 2003a: Bridewealth and birth control: Low fertility in the Indonesian archipelago, 1500–1900. *Population and Development Review* 29 (2), 197–214.

Boomgaard, P. 2003b: Human capital, slavery and low rates of economic and population growth in Indonesia, 1600–1910. *Slavery & Abolition* 24 (2), 83–96.

Boston Women's Health Book Collective 1973: *Our Bodies, Ourselves: A Book by and for Women*. New York: Simon and Schuster.

Bowen, R. 1986: On the political construction of tradition: *Gotong Royong* in Indonesia. *Journal of Asian Studies*, 45 (3), 545–61.

Brown, E. B. 1989: African American women's quilting. *Signs* 14 (4), 921–9.

Budianta, M. 2003: The blessed tragedy: The making of women's activism during the Reformasi years. In A. Heryanto and S. Mandal (eds), *Challenging Authoritarianism in Southeast Asia: Comparing Indonesia and Malaysia*, London: Routledge, 145–77.

Budianta, M. 2011: Negotiating boundaries and alterity: The making of a humanities scholar in Indonesia. In G. Beng-Lan (ed.), *Decentring and Diversifying Southeast Asian Studies: Perspectives from the Region*, Singapore: Institute of Southeast Asian Studies, 187–206.

Budiari, I. 2015: "Domestic workers" conditions at home no less worrying. *Jakarta Post*, 16 February.

Budiman, M. 2008: Treading the path of the Shari'a: Indonesian feminism at the crossroads of western modernity and Islam. *Journal of Indonesian Social Sciences and Humanities* 1, 73–93.

Butcher, M. and Maclean, K. 2018: Gendering the city: The lived experience of transforming cities, urban cultures and spaces of belonging. *Gender, Place and Culture: A Journal of Feminist Geography* 25 (5), 686–94.

Butler, J. 2016: *Frames of War: When is Life Grievable?* London: Verso.

Byerly, C. 2016: Stasis and shifts in feminist media scholarship. In C. Cerqueira, R. Cabecinhas, and S. Magalhães (eds), *Gender in Focus: (New) Trends in Media*, Braga: CECS, 15–27.

Chan, C. 2014: Gendered morality and development narratives: The case of female labour migration from Indonesia. *Sustainability* 6, 6949–72.

Chan, C. 2018: *In Sickness and in Wealth: Migration, Gendered Morality, and Central Java*. Bloomington, IN: Indiana University Press.

Chin, C. 1998: *In Service and Servitude: Foreign Female Domestic Workers and the Malaysian "Modernity" Project*. New York: Columbia University Press.

Chowdhury, E., Pulido, L., Heynen, N., Rini, L., Wainwright, J., Inayatullah, N., and Nagar, R. 2016: Muddying the waters: Coauthoring feminisms across scholarship and activism. *Gender, Place & Culture* 23 (12), 1800–1812.

Cislowski, H. and Purwadi, A. 2011: *Study of the Role of Indonesian Government Research Units (Baltibang) in Bridging Research and Development Policy*. Report commissioned by AusAID Tertiary Education and Knowledge Unit, 18 June. aid.dfat.gov.au/business/Documents/indo-ks3-balitbang.doc (Accessed 12 August 2014).

Clark, M. 2011: Indonesia's Jemek Suapardi: From pickpocket to mime artist. *Bijdragen tot de Taal-, Land- en Volkenkunde* 167 (2–3), 210–35.

Close, C. 2000: One thing leads to another: The making of Miyah: The life of a Javanese woman. *AEMS News and Reviews* 3 (1), 11–13.

Cole, R. 2012: A new tactical toolkit. *Inside Indonesia* 110 (Oct–Dec). https://www.insideindonesia.org/a-new-tactical-toolkit (Accessed 14 August 2022).

Committee on Women's Studies in Asia 1994: *Changing Lives: Life Stories of Asian Pioneers in Women's Studies*. New York: Feminist Press.

Connell, R. 2009: *Gender in World Perspective*, 2nd edn. Cambridge, UK: Polity Press.

Connell, R. 2018: Conclusion: Reckoning with gender. In J. W. Messerschmidt, P. Y. Martin, M. A. Messner, and R. Connell (eds), *Gender Reckonings: New Social Theory and Research*, New York: New York University Press, 331–46.

Constable, N. 2007: *Maid to Order in Hong Kong: Stories of Filipina Workers*, 2nd edn. Ithaca, NY: Cornell University Press.

Constable, N. 2010: Telling tales of migrant workers in Hong Kong: Transformations of faith, life scripts, and activism. *Asia Pacific Journal of Anthropology* 11 (4), 311–29.

Cornwall, A. 2002: *Making spaces, Changing Places: Situating Participation in Development. Institute of Development Studies Working Paper 170.* University of Sussex: Institute of Development Studies.

Crenshaw, K. 2011: Postscript. In H. Lutz, M. Vivar, and L. Supik (eds), *Framing Intersectionality: Debates on a Multi-faceted Concept in Gender Studies,* Farnham, Surrey: Ashgate: 221–33.

Da Costa, A. 2015a: Without contracts, domestic worker rights unprotected. ILO-CO Jakarta. Translation/version of article published by *Kontan.co.id*, 28 August. http://www.ilo.org/jakarta/info/public/fs/WCMS_464070/lang–en/index.htm (Accessed 15 October 2017).

Da Costa, A. 2015b: Tanpa kontrak, hak PRT tidak terlindungi. *Kontan.co.id*, 28 August. https://nasional.kontan.co.id/news/tanpa-kontrak-hak-prt-tidak-terlindungi (Accessed 7 February 2017).

Daly, M. 1973: *Beyond God the Father: A Philosophy of Women's Liberation.* Boston: Beacon Press.

Damanik, K. 1994: A decade in women's studies: 1979–1989. In Committee on Women's Studies in Asia (eds), *Changing Lives: Life Stories of Asian Pioneers in Women's Studies*, New York: Feminist Press, 92–106.

Datu, P. 2022: *Pandemi mereda, PRT gaspol perjuangkan pengesahan RUU perlindungan. PRT* [Blog]. https://www.tungkumenyala.com/pandemi-mereda-prt-gaspol-perjuangkan-pengesahan-ruu-perlindungan-prt/ (Accessed 5 July 2022).

Davidoff, L. and Hall, C. 2002: *Family Fortunes: Men and Women of the English Middle Class 1780–1850*, revised edn. London/New York: Routledge.

Davis, K. 2007: *The Making of Our Bodies, Ourselves: How Feminism Travels Across Borders*. Durham NC: Duke University Press.

detik.com 2011: Aksi Cuci dan Jemur Baju di Bundaran HI. *DetikNews*, 14 February. https://news.detik.com/foto-news/d-1570708/aksi-cuci-dan-jemur-baju-di-bundaran- hi (Accessed 10 May 2020).

Dewi, K. 2020: Motherhood identity in the 2019 Indonesian presidential elections: Populism and political division in the national women's movement. *Contemporary Southeast Asia: A Journal of International and Strategic Affairs* 42 (2), 224–50.

Diani, H. 2014: In the land where everyone's God: Interview with Musdah Mulia. *Magdalene*, 8 August. https://magdalene.co/story/in-the-land-where-everyones-god-interview-with-musdah-mulia (Accessed 29 August 2022).

Dibley, T. 1966: Maria Pakpahan: "Feminism is a choice of life". *Inside Indonesia* 47, 12.

Downs, L. 2019: Gender history. In L. Downs, M. Tomm, and P. Burke (eds), *Debating New Approaches to History*, London: Bloomsbury Academic Press, 101–25.

Dragojlovic, A. and McGregor, K. 2022: "They call me babu": The politics of visibility and gendered memories of Dutch colonialism in Indonesia. *Women's History Review* 31 (6), 933–52.

D'Souza, A. 2010: *Moving Towards Decent Work for Domestic Workers: An Overview of the ILO's Work*. Working Paper 2/2010. Geneva: International Labour Organization.

Dukut, E. M. 2018: Semiotics for interpreting quilt's cultural values from the U.S. and Indonesia. *K@ta: A Biennial Publication in the Study of Language and Literature* 20 (1) 18–26.

Eddyono, S.W., Fanani, E. R., and Maurice, Y. 2015: Mobilizing voices for domestic worker protection in Indonesia [Conference Paper]. ILO 4th Conference on Regulating for Decent Work: Developing and Implementing Policies for a Better Future at Work (RDW), 8–10 July, Geneva, Switzerland. https://studylib.net/doc/7238748/full-paper--conference-of-the-regulating-for-decent-work (Accessed 24 August 2022).

Eddyono, S. W., Fanani, E. R., Sababiah, D., Maurice, Y., Ghaza li, H., Warlif, J., Velayati, S., and Ciciek, F. 2016: *When and Why the State Responds to Women's Demands*. Geneva: United Nations Research Institute for Social Development.

Eldridge, P. 1996: Development, democracy and non-government organizations in Indonesia. *Asian Journal of Political Science* 4 (1), 17–35.

Elmhirst, R. 2003: "Learning the ways of the Priyayi": Domestic servants and the mediation of modernity in Jakarta, Indonesia. In J. H. Momsen (ed.), *Gender, Migration and Domestic Service*, London/New York: Routledge, 237–58.

Elmhirst, R. 2012: Methodological dilemmas in migration research in Asia: Research design, omissions and strategic erasures. *Area* 44 (3), 274–81.

Ernawati, E. 2016: *Keistemewaan Serikat Pekerja Rumah Tangga (SPRT) Yogyakarta*, TURC Trade Union Rights Centre. https://www.turc.or.id/informasi-perburuhan-istimewanya-jogja-tercermin-dalam-keistimewaan-sprtnya-berdasarkan-hasil-assessment-ilo-project-tentang-pekerja-rumah-tangga-prt/ (Accessed 10 January 2017).

Errington, J. 1984: Self and self-conduct among the Javanese "priyayi" elite. *American Ethnologist* 11 (2), 275–90.

Faizal, E. 2011: Activists file lawsuit against SBY, aides on negligence. *Jakarta Post*, 7 April.

Falanta, E. 2015: Mogok makan demi nasib PRT. *KBR.id*, 18 March. http://kbr.id/berita/03-2015/mogok_makan_demi_nasib_prt/68868.html (Accessed 25 July 2018).

Fealy, G. 2016: Bigger than Ahok: Explaining the 2 December mass rally [Blog]. *Indonesia at Melbourne*, 7 December. https://indonesiaatmelbourne.unimelb.edu.au/bigger-than-ahok-explaining-jakartas-2-december-mass-rally/ (Accessed 20 December 2023).

Fechter, A.-M. 2007: *Transnational Lives: Expatriates in Indonesia*. Aldershot: Ashgate Publishing.

Firman, T. and Fahmi, F. Z. 2017: The privatization of metropolitan Jakarta's (Jabodetabek) urban fringes: The early stages of "post-urbanization" in Indonesia. *Journal of the American Planning Association* 83 (1), 68–79.

Fish, J. 2017: *Domestic Workers of the World Unite! A Global Movement for Dignity and Human Rights*. New York: New York University Press.

Flannery, M. 2001: Quilting: A feminist metaphor for scientific inquiry. *Qualitative Inquiry* 7 (5), 628–44.

Florey, M. and Healey, C. 2002: Work well and guard your honour: Temporary labour migration and the role of adolescent women in eastern Indonesia. *Asian Studies Review* 26 (3), 355–81.

Ford, M. 2003: *NGO as outside intellectual: A history of non-governmental organisations' role in the Indonesian labour movement*. PhD. University of Wollongong. http://ro.uow.edu.au/theses/150 (Accessed 8 August 2022).

Ford, M. 2004: Organizing the unorganizable: Unions, NGOs, and Indonesian migrant labour. *International Migration* 42 (5), 99–119.

Ford, M. 2006: Migrant working in Indonesia. *Asian and Pacific Migration Journal* 15 (3), 313–33.

Ford, M. 2008: Women's labor activism in Indonesia. *Signs* 33 (3), 510–15.

Ford, M. 2014: A challenge for business? Developments in Indonesian trade unionism after Soeharto. In M. Basri and P. van der Eng (eds), *Business in Indonesia: New Challenges, Old Problems*, 221–33.

Forum-Pembaca-KOMPAS 2010: *Mohon Dukungan: Aksi "Serbet Cinta Untuk PRT"* [Google group posting], posted by Joanna Kebo and Uma Farida, 25 January. https://groups.google.com/forum/#!topic/komunitas-fpk/fq5gWXmS7LY (Accessed 5 March 2020).

Fox, M. 2010: Mary Daly, a leader in feminist theology, dies at 81. *The New York Times*, 7 January.

Fraser, N. 1998: *Social justice in the age of identity politics: Redistribution, recognition, participation*. Working Paper, Wissenschaftszentrum Berlin für Sozialforschung, Forschungsschwerpunkt Arbeitsmarkt und Beschäftigung, Abteilung Organisation und Beschäftigung, 98–108. Berlin: Wissenschaftszentrum Berlin für Sozialforschung. https://nbn-resolving.org/urn:nbn:de:0168-ssoar-126247 (Accessed 8 August 2022).

Fraser, N. 2013: *Fortunes of Feminism: From State-Managed Capitalism to Neoliberal Crisis*. Brooklyn, NY: Verso Books.

Freire, P. 1996: *Pedagogy of the Oppressed*. London: Penguin Books.

Friend, T. 1998: Indonesia in flames. *Orbis* 43 (3), 387–407.

Font Perjuangan Rakyat 2009: *Pernyataan bersama Jakerla PRT (Jaringan Kerja Layak Pekerja Rumah Tangga)* [Blog]. August 1. *Front Perjuangan Rakyat*. https://fprsatumei.wordpress.com/2009/08/01/pernyataan-bersama-jakerla-prt-jaringan-kerja-layak-pekerja-rumah-tangga/ (Accessed 18 August 2022).

Ganie-Rochman, M. and Achwan, R. 2005: Inclusion and exclusion: NGOs and critical social knowledge. In V. Hadiz and D. Dhakidae (eds), *Social Science and Power in Indonesia*, Jakarta/Singapore: Equinox Publishing and Institute of Southeast Asian Studies, 197–220.

Gastaldi, M. 2017: Indonesia: RAP – a method for organizing domestic workers. In *Decent Work for Domestic Workers: Eight Good Practices from Asia*, Geneva: International Labour Organization, 98–123.

Gastaldi, M., Jordhus-Lier, D., and Prabawati, D. 2017: Domestic workers and their struggle for citizenship and collective identity in Indonesia. In E. Hiariej and K. Stokke (eds), *Politics of Citizenship in Indonesia*, Jakarta: Yayasan Pustaka Obor Indonesia, 153–76.

Gibbings, S. 2017: Sosialisasi, street vendors and citizenship in Yogyakarta. In W. Berenschot, H. Schulte Nordholt, and L. Bakker (eds), *Citizenship and Democratization in Southeast Asia*, Leiden: Brill, 96–117.

Gouda, F. 1999: Gender and hyper-masculinity as post-colonial modernity during Indonesia's struggle for independence, 1945–1949. In A. Burton (ed.), *Gender, Sexuality and Colonial Modernities*, London/New York: Routledge, 161–74.

Gouda, F., Raben, R., Schulte Nordholt, H., and Stoler, A. 2009: Ann Laura Stoler, Along the Archival Grain: Epistemic Anxieties and Colonial Common Sense [round table]. *Bijdragen tot de Taal-, Land- en Volkenkunde/Journal of the Humanities and Social Sciences of Southeast Asia* 165 (4), 551–67.

Grossman, J. 2011: The researched on research and researchers: Conversations with SADSAWU. *South African Review of Sociology* 42 (2), 122–7.

Gunawan, A. 2008: Ahmad Sofian: Protecting child victims of violence. *Jakarta Post*, 13 November.

Gutiérrez-Rodríguez, E. 2009: *Migration, Domestic Work and Affect: A Decolonial Approach on Value and the Feminization of Labor.* London/New York: Routledge.

Hadiwinata, B. S. 2003: *The Politics of NGOs in Indonesia: Developing Democracy and Managing a Movement.* London and New York: Routledge Curzon.

Hadiz, V. and Dhakidae, D. (eds) 2005: *Social Science and Power in Indonesia.* Jakarta/Singapore: Equinox Publishing and Institute of Southeast Asian Studies.

Hanitzsch, T. 2005: Journalists in Indonesia: Educated but timid watchdogs. *Journalism Studies* 6 (4), 493–508.

Hanitzsch, T., Hanusch, F., and Lauerer, C. 2016: Setting the agenda, influencing public opinion, and advocating for social change: Determinants of journalistic interventionism in 21 countries. *Journalism Studies* 17 (1), 1–20.

Harding, S. (ed.) 2004: *The Feminist Standpoint Theory Reader: Intellectual and Political Controversies.* New York/London: Routledge.

Harsaputra, I. 2007: New program empowers domestic helpers. *Jakarta Post*, 17 February.

Harsono, A. 1994: *Sirnagalih Declaration*, *Andreas Harsono* [Blog]. 8 August. http://www.andreasharsono.net/1994/08/sirnagalih-declaration.html (Accessed 10 March 2020).

Haryanti, N. 2011: *Ruang Kata-kata: Pembantu Rumah Tangga dalam Sastra: Konstruksi Budaya Kelas Menengah* [Blog]. Ruang Kata-kata, 29 June. http://ruangkata-katavie.blogspot.com/2011/06/pembantu-rumah-tangga-dalam-sastra.html (Accessed 1 July 2019).

Haryanto, I. 2011: Media ownership and its implications for journalists and journalism in Indonesia. In K. Sen and D. Hill (eds), *Politics and the Media in Twenty-First Century Indonesia: Decade of Democracy*, London: Routledge, 104–18.

Heath, J. 1994: Kissing and telling: Turning round in *A Room with a View*. *Twentieth Century Literature* 40 (4), 393–433.

Hemmings, C. 2005: Telling feminist stories. *Feminist Theory* 6 (2), 115–39.

Hemmings, C. 2012: Affective solidarity: Feminist reflexivity and political transformation. *Feminist Theory* 13 (2), 147–61.

Heider, K. 2000: Miyah: The Life of a Javanese Woman: A film by Laurie Rothstein in collaboration with Sandeep Ray. *AEMS News and Reviews* 3 (1): 6.

Herjanjam, I. 2015: National Child Protection Commission: Urgent, the abolition of child domestic workers. ILO-CO Jakarta, translation/version of article published by *Suara Pembaruan*, 20 August. https://www.ilo.org/jakarta/info/public/fs/WCMS_464076/lang–en/index.htm. (Accessed 3 February 2020).

Hivos 2009: *Yayasan Jurnal Perempuan Jakarta*. http://www.hivos.nl (Accessed 2 December 2014).

Hiz, O. 2014: Puluhan PRT Letakkan Replika Toilet dan Sapu Raksasa di Depan Gedung DPR. *BeritaSatu*, 1 October 2014.

Hoadley, M. 1983: Slavery, bondage and dependency in precolonial Java: The Cirebon-Priangan region, 1700. In A. Reid and J. Brewster (eds), *Slavery, Bondage and Dependency in Southeast Asia*, London/New York: University of Queensland Press, 90–117.

Holli, A. M. 2008: Feminist triangles: A conceptual analysis. *Representation* 44 (2), 169–85.

Holliday, J. 2023: *Skilled to Care, Forced to Work: Recognizing the Skills of Migrant Domestic Workers in ASEAN amid Forced Labour and Exploitation*. Bangkok: International Labour Organization.

hooks, bell, 1994: *Teaching to Transgress: Education as the Practice of Freedom*. New York: Routledge.

Hoskins, J. 2004: Slaves, brides and other "gifts": Resistance, marriage and rank in eastern Indonesia. *Slavery & Abolition* 25 (2), 90–107.

HRW 2005: *Always on Call: Abuse and Exploitation of Child Domestic Workers in Indonesia*. Human Rights Watch Report 17 (C). New York: Human Rights Watch.

HRW 2006: *Swept Under the Rug: Abuses against Domestic Workers around the World*. Human Rights Watch Report 18 (C). New York: Human Rights Watch.

HRW 2009: *Workers in the Shadows: Abuse and Exploitation of Child Domestic Workers in Indonesia*. New York: Human Rights Watch. https://www.hrw.org/report/2009/02/11/workers-shadows/abuse-and-exploitation-child-domestic-workers-indonesia (Accessed 29 August 2022).

Hudalah, D. and Firman, F. 2012: Beyond property: Industrial estates and post-suburban transformation in Jakarta Metropolitan Region. *Cities* 29, 40–48.

Hudalah, D., Zulfahmi, F., and Firman, T. 2013: Regional governance in decentralizing Indonesia: Learning from the success of urban-rural cooperation in Metropolitan Yogyakarta. In T. Bunnell, D. Parthasarathy, and E. Thompson (eds), *Cleavage, Connection and Conflict in Rural, Urban and Contemporary Asia*, Dordrecht/Heidelberg: Springer, 65–82.

Hudaya, I. 2011*: A book of wisdom and self-being, Our Bodies, Ourselves* [Blog]. 28 May. https://www.ourbodiesourselves.org/2011/05/a-book-of-wisdom-and-self-being/ (Accessed 15 February 2020).

Husni, H., Abdullah, I. and Cahyowati, R. 2017: The review of Act Number 39, year 2004 concerning the review and placement and protection for Indonesian workers abroad. *Umran Law Review* 1 (2), 1–17.

Idrus, N. 2008: "Makkunrai passimokolo": Bugis migrant women workers in Malaysia. In M. Ford and L. Parker (eds), *Women and Work in Indonesia*, London: Routledge, 155–72.

IDWFED 2013: *Towards sustainable and strong domestic worker union with paid up membership building – A report on reviving Tunas Mulia Domestic Workers' Union in Yogyakarta, Indonesia*. http://idwfed.org/en/resources/towards-sustainable-and-strong-domestic-worker-union-with-paid-up-membership-building-2013-a-report-on-reviving-tunas-mulia-domestic-workers-union-in-yogjakarta-indonesia (Accessed 5 July 2022).

IDWFED 2014: *Indonesia: Domestic workers hunger strike action*, 26 November. https://idwfed.org/en/updates/indonesia-domestic-workers-hunger-strike-action (Accessed 30 December 2014).

IDWFED 2020: Indonesia: Lobbying for the C190 [Blog]. 18 March International Domestic Workers Federation. https://idwfed.org/en/updates/indonesia-lobbying-for-the-c190-i-had-to-explain-to-them-why-domestic-violence-is-an-issue-for-workers (Accessed 18 August 2022).

Ifhami, I. 2023: Perjuangkan RUU PPRT, Said Iqbal Sayap Partai Buruh. *Tribunnews.com* 14 March. https://www.tribunnews.com/nasional/2023/03/14/perjuangkan-ruu-pprt-said-iqbal-dukung-sayap-partai-buruh-lakukan-aksi-mogok-makan-besok (Accessed 28 December 2023).

Ikhbal, A. M. 2015a: Workers who are still considered as "housemaids". ILO-CO Jakarta. Translation/version of article published in *Republika,* 19 August. https://ww.ilo.org/jakarta/info/public/fs/WCMS_470249/lang–en/index. (Accessed 5 March 2020).

Ikhbal, A. M. 2015a/ind: Para Pekerja yang Masih Dianggap "Membantu" (Bagian I). *Republika*, 19 August. https://republika.co.id/berita/koran/halaman-1/15/08/19/ntbi4l1-para-pekerja-yang-masih-dianggap-membantu-bagian-1 (Accessed 7 February 2020).

Ikhbal, A. M. 2015b: House "ping-pongs" the draft law on domestic workers. ILO-CO Jakarta. Translation of article published in *Republika*, 21 August. https://www.ilo.org/jakarta/info/public/fs/WCMS_470250/lang–en/index.htm (Accessed 3 February 2020).

Ikhbal, A. M. (2015b/ind): DPR 'Pingpong' RUU PRT (Bagian 2). *Republika*, 20 August. https://republika.co.id/berita/koran/halaman-1/15/08/20/ntdlux1-dpr-pingpong-ruu-prt-bagian-2 (Accessed 10 November 2019).

Ikhbal, A. M. 2015c: No maximum efforts yet to protect domestic workers. ILO-CO Jakarta. Translation of article published in *Republika*, 21 August. http://www.ilo.org/jakarta/info/public/fs/WCMS_470251/lang–en/index.htm (Accessed 5 March 2020).

Ikhbal, A. M. 2015c/ind: Belum Ada Usaha Maksimal Lindungi PRT (Bagian 3 Habis). *Republika*, 21 August. https://republika.co.id/berita/ntf1w623/belum-ada-usaha-maksimal-lindungi-prt-bagian-3-habis (Accessed 7 February 2020).

ILO 2004: *The Real Story of Cinderella: Children in Domestic Labour* [video], 11 June. http://www.ilo.org/global/about-the-ilo/multimedia/video/video-news-releases/WCMS_074388/lang–en/index.htm (Accessed 2 October 2017).

ILO 2006: *The Regulation of Domestic Workers in Indonesia: Current Laws, International Standards, and Best Practices*, Working Paper, 1 June. Jakarta: International Labour Office.

ILO 2013: *Domestic Workers across the World: Global and Regional Statistics and the Extent of Legal Protection*. Geneva: International Labour Organization.

ILO 2017: *Mempromosikan kerja layak bagi pekerja rumah tangga di Indonesia: Sari Nila*, [video]. https://www.ilo.org/jakarta/info/public/pr/WCMS_585487/lang–en/index.htm (Accessed 3 March 2020).

ILO 2018: *Promoting Decent Work for Domestic Workers and Elimination of Child Labor in Domestic Work: Ten Emerging Good Practices from Indonesia*. Geneva: International Labour Organization.

ILO 2021: *Making Decent Work a Reality for Domestic Workers: Progress and Prospects Ten years after the Adoption of the Domestic Workers Convention, 2011 (No.189)*. Geneva: International Labour Organization.

ILO Jakarta 2010a: *National Domestic Workers' Day: Recognizing domestic work as work*. 12 February. http://www.ilo.org/jakarta/info/public/pr/WCMS_122352/lang–en/index.htm (Accessed 12 June 2018).

ILO Jakarta 2010b: *Special edition on domestic work: Recognizing domestic work as work*. April. http://www.ilo.org/wcmsp5/groups/public/@asia/@ro-bangkok/@ilo-jakarta/documents/publication/wcms_125946.pdf (Accessed 20 July 2022).

ILO-IPEC 2004: *Flowers on the Rock: The Phenomenon of Child Domestic Workers in Indonesia (in Bahasa Indonesia)* [Report]. http://www.ilo.org/jakarta/whatwedo/publications/WCMS_121307/lang–en/index.htm (Accessed 7 April 2015).

Indriani, K. 2020: Kowani desak RUU Perlindungan PRT segera disahkan. *Antara*, 16 June. https://www.antaranews.com/berita/1557520/kowani-desak-ruu-perlindungan-prt-segera-disahkan (Accessed 29 August 2022).

Indriani, K. 2023: Indonesia presents good practices of gender equality at UN. *Antara*, 13 March. https://en.antaranews.com/news/275337/indonesia-presents-good-practices-of-gender-equality-at-un (Accessed 30 August 2023).

IOM 2010: *Labour Migration from Indonesia: An Overview*. Jakarta: International Organization for Migration.

Irawati, H. 2006: Profil: Saparinah Sadli: Women's studies di Indonesia. *Jurnal Perempuan* 48, 119–24.

Irawaty, D. 2005: Yang Khas dari Masalah Perempuan dan Pendampingannya. *Jurnal Perempuan* 39: 19–39.

Irawaty, D. 2011: *Redefining Cultural Practices and Reconstructing a Colonial Legacy*. Saarbrucken, Germany: VDM Verlag.

IRENE and IUF 2008: *Respect and Rights: Protection for Domestic/Household Workers!* Tilburg, Netherlands: IRENE and IUF.

Irham, M. and Andapita, V. 2015a: When domestic workers united in trade union. ILO-CO Jakarta, translation of article published by *Varia News*, 15th August. https://www.ilo.org/jakarta/info/public/fs/WCMS_470252/lang–en/index.htm (Accessed 3 June 2022).

Irham, M. and Andapita, V. 2015b: When domestic workers united in trade union (Part 2). ILO-CO Jakarta, translation of article published by *Varia News*, 15th August. http://www.ilo.org/jakarta/info/public/fs/WCMS_470253/lang–en/index.htm (Accessed 25 August 2022).

Irham, M. and Andapita, V. 2015c: Steep road of draft law on protection of domestic workers. ILO-CO Jakarta, translation of article published by *Varia.id*, 15 August. http://ilo.org/jakarta/info/public/fs/WCMS_470254/lang–en/index.htm (Accessed 25 August 2022).

Isin, E. F. 2009: Citizenship in flux: The figure of the activist citizen. *Subjectivity* 29 (1), 367–88.

Ismail, G. and Ogando, A. 2023. *Domestic Workers during the COVID-19 Crisis: Pathways of Impact, Recovery, and Resilience.* Resource Document No. 3. Manchester: WIEGO.

Ito, T. 2017: Everyday citizenship in Java. In W. Berenschot, H. Schulte Nordholt, and L. Bakker (eds), *Citizenship and Democratization in Southeast Asia*, Leiden, Brill, 51–67.

IWMF 2013: *Prodita Sabarini 2013/14. International Women's Media Foundation* [Blog], 17 August. https://www.iwmf.org/blog/2013/08/17/prodita-sabarini-201314/ (Accessed 3 March 2020).

Jakarta Post 2015: NGOs praise regulation on domestic worker protection. *Jakarta Post*, 19 January.

Jakarta Post 2016: Ideal wage for Jakarta journalists $572, says association. *Jakarta Post*, 3 May.

Jasanoff, S. 2015: Future imperfect: Science, technology, and the imaginations of modernity. In S. Jasanoff and S.-H Kim (eds), *Dreamscapes of Modernity: Sociotechnical Imaginaries and the Fabrication of Power*. Chicago: University of Chicago Press, 1–33.

Jenkins, L. 2019: Annie Kenney and the politics of class in the women's social and political union. *Twentieth Century British History* 30 (4), 477–503.

Jiang, Z and Korczynski, M. 2016: When the "unorganizable" organize: The collective mobilization of migrant domestic workers in London. *Human Relations* 69 (3), 813–38.

Johns, Y. and Stokes, R. 1977: *Bahasa Indonesia Book One: Introduction to Indonesian Language and Culture*. Singapore: Periplus Editions.

Jones, C. 2004: Whose stress? Emotion work in middle-class Javanese homes. *Ethnos* 69 (4), 509–28.

Jordhus-Lier, D. 2017: Claiming industrial citizenship: The struggle for domestic worker rights in Indonesia. *Norsk Geografisk Tidsskrift – Norwegian Journal of Geography* 71 (4), 243–52.

Jordhus-Lier, D. and Prabawati, D. 2018: Mobilities and moralities of domestic work in Indonesia. In K. Ward, A. E. Jonas, B. Miller, and D. Wilson (eds), *The Routledge Handbook on Spaces in Urban Politics*, London: Routledge, 270–80.

Juliawan, B. H. 2011: Street-level politics: Labour protests in post-authoritarian Indonesia. *Journal of Contemporary Asia* 41 (3), 349–70.

Jumiyem, L. 2017: Mogok Makan dan Nadi Perjuangan Kami. In E. Ujianto and Luviana (eds) *Kami Tidak Akan Diam: 31 Kisah Pekerja Rumah Tangga di Balik Tembok Ruang Domestik*, Jakarta: AJI Jakarta, JALA PRT and ILO Jakarta, 147–51.

Jurnal Perempuan 2005a: Tips-PRT—Majikan Berbagi Hak dan Kewajiban. *Jurnal Perempuan* 39, 82–84.

Jurnal Perempuan 2005b: *JP 39 Pekerja Rumah Tangga*. Jakarta: Yayasan Jurnal Perempuan.

Kajian Gender 2012: *Abstrak Tesis Program Studi Kajian Gender.* http://kajiangender.pps.ui.ac.id/abstrak-tesis/ (Accessed 20 April 2014).

Karlekar, M. and Lazarus, B. 1994: Introduction. In Committee on Women's Studies in Asia (ed), *Changing Lives: Life Stories of Asian Pioneers in Women's Studies*, New York: Feminist Press, 5–22.

Kartika, S. 2016: Yanti Muchtar: Pendidikan Alternatif untuk Perempuan. Interview posted 1 August (originally published in *Jurnal Perempuan* 44, 2005). http://www.jurnalperempuan.org/9/post/2016/08/yanti-muchtar-pendidikan-alternatif-untuk-perempuan.html (Accessed 25 May 2022).

Katjasungkana, N. and Wieringa, S. (eds) 2012: *The Future of Asian Feminisms: Confronting Fundamentalisms, Conflicts and Neo-Liberalism*. Newcastle-upon-Tyne: Cambridge Scholars Publishing.

Kennedy, K. 2013: The daw and the honeybee: Situating metaphors for originality and authorial labor in the 1728 *Chambers' Cyclopædia*. *College English* 76 (1), 35–8.

Killias, O. 2009: The politics of bondage in the recruitment, training and placement of Indonesian migrant domestic workers. *Sociologus* 59 (2), 145–72.

Killias, O. 2018: *Follow the Maid: Domestic Worker Migration in and from Indonesia*. Copenhagen: NIAS Press.

Koelsch, L. 2012: The virtual patchwork quilt. *Qualitative Inquiry* 18, 823–9.

Koentjaraningrat, R. 1985: *Javanese Culture*. Singapore: Oxford University Press.

Kompas 2004a: Ingin Masalah Maryati Cepat Selesai. *Kompas*, 12 January.

Kompas 2004b: Pramuwisma Minta Diperhatikan Nasibnya. *Kompas*, 8 June.

Kompas 2008a: Cagub Lampung Harus Dihukum. *Kompas.com*, 10 July.

Kompas 2008b: Warga Bali di Lampung desak polisis tuntaskan kasus pelecehan. *Kompas*, 10 July.

Kompas 2008c: Jelang Lebaran, Permintaan PRT Pengganti Mulai Meningkat. *Kompas.com*, 5 September.

Kompas 2010a: "Serbet Cinta Raksasa" untuk PRT. *Kompas.com*, 14 February.

Kompas 2010b: Serbet Cinta Raksasa Dibentangkan di Bundaran HI. *Kompas.com*, 14 February.

Kongres Operata Yogyakarta 2009: *Festival and teater PRT digelar di TBY*. *Kongres Operata* [Blog]. http://kongresoperatayogya.blogspot.com/2009/12/festival-dan-teater-prt-digelar-di-tby.html (Accessed 25 August 2016).

Kramer, E. A. 2015: *What's in a symbol? Emerging parties and anti-corruption symbols in Indonesia's 2014 National Legislative Election campaigns*. PhD. University of Sydney. https://ses.library.usyd.edu.au/bitstream/2123/15992/1/KRAMER_EA_Thesis.pdf (Accessed 25 August 2022).

Kraube, D. 2018: Polite vocabulary in the Javanese language of Surabaya. *Wacana* 19 (1), 58–99.

Kumar, A. 1980: Javanese court society and politics in the late eighteenth century: The record of a lady soldier. *Indonesia* 29, 1–46.

Kurnianingsih, Y. and Brata, N. 2015: Tradisi Ngenger dalam Konteks Bride Service di Desa Botoreco Kecamatan Kunduran Kabupaten Blora. *Solidarity* 4 (1). https://journal.unnes.ac.id/sju/index.php/solidarity/article/view/6039 (Accessed 18 August 2022).

Kusno, A. 2006: "Back to the city": A note on urban architecture in the new Indonesia. In M. Leaf (ed.), *Arts, Popular Culture and Social Change in the New Indonesia*, Vancouver: University of British Columbia, Institute of Asian Research, 59–94.

Kusno, A. 2010: *The Appearances of Memory: Mnemonic Practices of Architecture and Urban Form in Indonesia*. Durham, NC: Duke University Press.

Kusumawati, U. 2015a: Kisah para pemburu "receh" dari tenaga domestik anak. *CNN Indonesia*, 19 September. https://www.cnnindonesia.com/nasional/20150919170224-20-79755/kisah-para-pemburu-receh-dari-tenaga-domestik-anak (Accessed 24 August 2022).

Kusumawati, U. 2015b: Menjadi PRT, jalan keluar gadis desa hindari pernikahan. *CNN Indonesia*, 19 September. https://www.cnnindonesia.com/nasional/20150919115712-20-79733/menjadi-prt-jalan-keluar-gadis-desa-hindari-pernikahan (Accessed 24 August 2022).

Kuswadi, W. and Rahayu, Y. 2023: Education and unionizing are keys to effect change. In A. Gordo and B. Pattaanik (eds), *Our Work, Our Lives (10)*, Bangkok: Global Alliance Against Trafficking in Women, 96–103.

Kuswandini, D. 2010: The rise and fall of Indonesia's women's movement. *Jakarta Post*, 21 April.

Kutanegara, P. M. 2017: *Poverty, Crises and Social Solidarity in Sriharjo, Rural Java*. Jakarta: PT Kanisius.

Kwok, Y. 2018: Jakarta feminist discussion group talks About Women's March Jakarta. *April Magazine*, 8 March. https://www.aprilmag.com/2018/03/08/jakarta-feminist-discussion-group-talks-about-womens-march-jakarta/ (Accessed 22 July 2022).

Lan, P.-C. 2006: *Global Cinderellas: Migrant Domestics and Newly Rich Employers in Taiwan*. Durham, NC: Duke University Press.

Lane, M. 2008: *Unfinished Nation: Indonesia Before and After Suharto*. London: Verso Books.

LBH Jakarta. 2014: *Baleg DPR RI: RUU Perlindungan PRT Penting untuk Menjadi Prioritas. LBH Jakarta*. https://www.bantuanhukum.or.id/web/baleg-dpr-ri-ruu-perlindungan-prt-penting-untuk-menjadi-prioritas/ (Accessed 26 July 2018).

Lee, D. 2009: Aktivis, activist. In J. Barker and J. Lindquist (eds), Figures of Indonesian modernity, *Indonesia* 29 (April), 48–50.

Lee, D. 2011a: Images of youth: On the iconography of history and protest in Indonesia. *History & Anthropology* 22 (3), 307–36.

Lee, D. 2011b: Styling the revolution: Masculinities, youth, and street politics in Jakarta, Indonesia. *Journal of Urban History* 37 (6), 933–51.

Lee, D. 2016: *Activist Archives: Youth Culture and the Political Past in Indonesia*. Durham, NC/London: Duke University Press.

Leeuwen, L. van 2008: *Lost in Mall: An Ethnography of Middle-class Jakarta in the 1990s*. Leiden: KITLV Press.

Leitner, H. and Sheppard, E. 2018: From kampungs to condos? Contested accumulations through displacement in Jakarta. *Environment and Planning A: Economy and Space* 50 (2), 437–56.

Levitt, P. and Merry, S. 2009: Vernacularization on the ground: Local uses of global women's rights in Peru, China, India and the United States. *Global Networks* 9 (4), 441–61.

Lindquist, J. 2010: Labour recruitment, circuits of capital and gendered mobility: reconceptualizing the Indonesian migration industry. *Pacific Affairs* 83 (1), 115–32.

Lindsey, T. 2017: Is Indonesia sliding towards a 'Neo-New Order'? *Indonesia at Melbourne*, 10 October. https://indonesiaatmelbourne.unimelb.edu.au/is-indonesia-sliding-towards-a-neo-new-order/ (Accessed 22 August 2023).

Lister, R. 1997: Citizenship: Towards a feminist synthesis. *Feminist Review* 57, 28–48.

Listyowati and Herdiyani, R. n.d.: Lessons from Indonesia's Nationality Law Campaign. https://equalnationalityrights.org/news/80-lessons-indonesia-nationality-law-reform-campaign?highlight=WyJpbmRvbmVzaWEiLCJpbmRvbmVzaWEncyJd (Accessed 28 January 2023).

Locher-Scholten, E. 2000: "So close and yet so far": European ambivalence towards Javanese servants. In *Women and the Colonial State: Essays on Gender and Modernity in the Netherlands Indies 1900–1942*, Amsterdam: Amsterdam University Press, 131–53.

Lucas, A. 1992: Land disputes in Indonesia: Some current perspectives. *Indonesia* 53, 79–92.

Luttikhuis, B. and van der Meer, A. 2020: 1913 in Indonesian History: Demanding equality, changing mentality. *TRaNS: Trans-Regional and -National Studies of Southeast Asia* 8 (2), 115–33.

Luviana 2012: *Jejak Jurnalis Perempuan: Pemetaan kondisi kerja jurnalis perempuan di Indonesia*. Jakarta: Aliansi Jurnalis Independen (AJI). https://www.aji.or.id/read/buku/6/jejak-jurnalis-perempuan.html (Accessed 25 August 2022).

Luviana 2013: *Luviana: Di Negeri Tanpa Selebrasi. Catatan Luviana* [Blog]. 16 June. https://catatanluviana.wordpress.com/2013/06/16/luviana-di-negeri-tanpa-selebrasi/ (Accessed 5 January 2017).

Luviana and Utami, E. 2022: Not recognized as a worker: 18 years of domestic workers neglected by the state. *Konde.co*, 20 March. https://www.konde.co/2022/03/not-recognized-as-a-worker-18-years-of-domestic-workers-neglected-by-the-state.html/ (Accessed 17 July 2022).

Lyons, L. 2005: Embodying transnationalism: The making of the Indonesian maid. In E. Lorek-Jezinski and K. Wieckowska (eds), *Corporeal Inscriptions: Representations of the Body in Cultural and Literary Texts and Practices*, Torun, Poland: Nicolas Copernicus Press, 171–85.

Madewanti, L. 2015: *Leadership Interview: Lita Anggraini (JALA PRT)*. Institute for Women's Empowerment, 10 December. https://iwe-asia.org/2015/12/10/leadership-interview-lita-anggraini-jala-prt/ (Accessed 4 March 2020).

Madhok, S. 2017: On vernacular rights cultures and the political imaginaries of *Haq*. *Humanity: An International Journal of Human Rights, Humanitarianism and Development* 8 (3), 485–509.

Mahy, P., Mitchell, R., Cooney, S. and Howe, J. 2017: *The Plural Regulation of Work: A Pilot Study of Restaurant Workers in Yogyakarta, Indonesia*. Melbourne: Melbourne Law School.

Manan, N. 2015a: Lack of OSH protection for domestic workers. ILO-CO Jakarta, translation/version of text of radio broadcast aired on *KBR Saga*, 25 August. https://www.ilo.org/jakarta/info/public/fs/WCMS_464066/lang–en/index.htm (Accessed 3 February 2020).

Manan, N. 2015a/ind.: 'PRT Sunarti: Tangan Saya Melepuh Saat Mencuci Pakaian', *KBR Saga* [Podcast], 25 August. https://kbr.id/saga/08-2015/prt_sunarti__tangan_saya_melepuh_saat_mencuci_pakaian/75221.html (Accessed 10 February 2020).

Manan, N. 2015b: Lack of OSH protection for domestic workers (2). ILO-CO Jakarta, translation/version of text of radio broadcast aired on *KBR Saga*, 25 August. https://www.ilo.org/jakarta/info/public/fs/WCMS_464068/lang–en/index.htm. (Accessed 2 February 2020).

Manan, N. 2015b/ind.: *Lita Anggraini: Hidup Mati Kami di UU Perlindungan PRT* [Podcast]. KBR Saga, 25 August. https://kbr.id/saga/082015/lita_anggraeni__hidup_mati_kami_di_uu_perlindungan_prt/75222.html (Accessed 7 February 2020).

Marchetti, S., Cherubini, D., and Garofalo Geymonat, G. 2021: *Global Domestic Workers: Intersectional Inequalities and Struggles for Rights*. Bristol: Bristol University Press.

Marchetti, S. and Schwenken, H. 2018: The research network for domestic workers' rights. *Global Dialogue: Magazine of the International Sociological Association* 10 (1). http://globaldialogue.isa-sociology.org/the-research-network-for-domestic-workers-rights/ (Accessed 4 March 2020).

Marsinah FM 2012: *Tentang Radio Komunitas Marsinah FM*. https://marsinahfm.wordpress.com/about/ (Accessed 9 May 2017).

Massey, D. 1994: *Space, Place and Gender*. Minneapolis: University of Minnesota Press.

Massey, D. 2005: *For Space*. London: Sage.

Massey, D., Human Geography Research Group, Bond, S., and Featherstone, D. 2009: The possibilities of a politics of place beyond place? A conversation with Doreen Massey. *Scottish Geographical Journal* 125 (3–4), 401–20.

Mather, C. 2008: *Respect and Rights: Protection for Domestic/Household Workers!* Tilburg, Netherlands: IRENE. http://www.idwfed.org/en/resources/report-of-the-international-conference-respect-and-rights-protection-for-domestic-workers/@@display-file/attachment_1 (Accessed 17 July 2016).

Mather, C. 2010: *Platform of Demands*. Geneva: IDWF and IUF. https://idwfed.org/platform-of-demands/ (Accessed 17 July 2016).

May-Ron, R. 2016: Rejecting the glass slipper: The subversion of Cinderella in Margaret Atwood's *The Edible Woman*. In M. Rochère, G. Lathey, and M. Woźniak (eds), *Cinderella Across Cultures: New Directions and Interdisciplinary Perspectives*. Detroit: Wayne State University Press, 141–61.

Mazrieva, E. 2019: *"Indonesia Tanpa Feminis"; Krtitikatan atau Bunga Tidur?* 4 February. https://www.voaindonesia.com/a/indonesia-tanpa-feminis-kritik-atau-bunga-tidur-/4858116.html (Accessed 8 August 2022).

Meer, A. van der 2017: Performing colonial modernity: Fairs, consumerism, and the emergence of the Indonesian middle classes. *Bijdragen tot de Taal-, Land- en Volkenkunde* 173, 503–38.

Meer, A. van der 2020: *Performing Power: Cultural Hegemony, Identity, and Resistance in Colonial Indonesia*. Ithaca, NY and London: Cornell University Press.

Meerkerk, E. van Nederveen 2016: Grammar of difference? The Dutch colonial state, labour policies, and social norms on work and gender, c.1800–1940. *International Review of Social History* 61 (S24), 137–64.

Meitzner, M. 2007: Party financing in post-Soeharto Indonesia: Between state subsidies and political corruption. *Contemporary Southeast Asia* 29 (2), 238–63.

Meitzner, M. 2013: Fighting the hellhounds: Pro-democracy activists and party politics in post-Suharto Indonesia. *Journal of Contemporary Asia* 43 (1), 28–50.

Messerschmidt, J. W., Martin, P. Y., Messner, M. A. and Connell, R. 2018: *Gender Reckonings: New Social Theory and Research*. New York: New York University Press.

Milasari, A. 2005: Penting Namun Terabaikan: Potret Pekerja Rumah Tangga (PRT) di Indonesia. *Jurnal Perempuan* 39, 31–9.

Milasari, A. 2009: *Curriculum Vitae: Name: Aida Milasari, S. Si.* http://xa.yimg.com/kq/groups/16067427/1467385598/name/CV+Aida.doc (Accessed 3 May 2018).

Mills, M. B. 2017: Gendered Morality Tales: Discourses of gender, labour, and value in globalising Asia. *Journal of Development Studies* 53 (3), 316–30.

Mitra Imadei 2011: Mitra Imadei: Profile. Presentation at Workshop on Public-Private-Local Community Partnership against Child Labour in Indonesia, 12 June, Jakarta. https://www.ilo.org/jakarta/WCMS_158832/lang–en/index.htm (Accessed 14 June 2022).

Miyah: The Life of a Javanese Woman 1999: directed by L. Rothstein and S. Ray [Film]. Watertown, MA: Documentary Educational Resources (DER). 30 minutes.

Moeliona, L., Milasari, A., Wibawa, D. S. and Marinta, D. 2010: *Modul Sosialisasi dan Pelatihan Untuk Pencegahan dan Penarikan Pekerja Rumah Tangga Anak (PRTA)*, Jakarta: Kementarian Pemberdayaan Perempuan dan Perlindungan Anak (KPP-PA); ILO-IPEC Jakarta & Rumpun Gema Perempuan (RGP).

Mrazek, R. 2010: *A Certain Age: Colonial Jakarta through the Memories of its Intellectuals*. Durham, NC: Duke University Press.

Mulia, M. M. 2015: Family law reform in Indonesia: A progressive interpretation of The Qur'an. *Al-Mawarid Journal of Islamic Law* 15 (1), 1–18. https://www.neliti.com/publications/42613/muslim-family-law-reform-in-indonesia-a-progressive-interpretation-of-the-quran (Accessed 29 August 2022).

Mullally, S. and Murphy, C. 2014: Migrant domestic workers in the UK: Enacting exemptions, exclusions, and rights. *Human Rights Quarterly* 36 (2), 397–427.

Munt, S. 2016: "Argumentum ad misericordam": The cultural politics of victim media. *Feminist Media Studies* 17 (5), 866–83.

Murniati, A. 2004: *Getar Gender: Perempuan Indonesia dalam Perspektif Sosial, Politik, Ekonomi, Hukum, dan Ham*. Magelang, Indonesia: Yayasan Indonesia Tera.

Muryanti, M. 2005: Upaya Perlindungan PRT. *Jurnal Perempuan* 39, 7–17.

Muryanti, M. 2012: *Perempuan Pedesaan (Kajian Sosiologi Pekerja Rumah Tangga)*. Yogyakarta: Bima Sakti Publishing.

Muryanti, M. 2015: Dilemma of the kinship and formality relationship between employer and domestic worker in Yogyakarta, Indonesia. *KOMUNITAS: International Journal of Indonesian Society and Culture* 7, 191–214.

Nababan, H. 2008: Weleh...Cagub Dilaporkan Memerkosa PRT. *kompas.com*, 18 June. https://regional.kompas.com/read/2008/06/18/11511449/Weleh...Cagub.Dilaporkan.Memerkosa.PRT (Accessed 8 August 2022).

Nadasen, P. 2016: Domestic worker organizing: Storytelling, history, and contemporary resonances. *Souls* 18 (1), 155–60.

Nagar, R. 2014: *Muddying the Waters: Coauthoring Feminisms across Scholarship and Activism*. Urbana: University of Illinois Press.

Newberry, J. 2010: The global child and non-governmental governance of the family in post-Suharto Indonesia. *Economy and Society* 39 (3), 403–26.

Newberry, J. 2014: Class MOBIL: Circulation of children in the making of Middle Indonesia. In G. van Klinken and W. Berenschot (eds), *In Search of Middle Indonesia*, Leiden/ Boston: Brill, 69–86.

Newberry, J. 2017: "Anything can be used to stimulate child development": Early childhood education and development in Indonesia as a durable assemblage. *The Journal of Asian Studies* 76 (1), 25–45.

Nilan, P., Demartoto, A., Broom, A., and Germov, J. 2014: Indonesian men's perceptions of violence against women. *Violence Against Women* 20 (7), 869–88.

Niner, S., Cuthbert, D., and Ahmad, Y. 2014: Good mothers, bad mothers: Motherhood, modernity and politics in representations of child abuse in Malaysia's English-language newspapers. *Feminist Media Studies* 14 (6), 993–1011.

Nooteboom, G. and Kutanegara, P. 2002: "Will the storm soon be over?" Winners and losers in the 1997 crisis in rural Java. *Moussons: Recherche en Sciences Humaines sur L'Asie-Est* 6, 3–36.

Nurbaiti, A. 2000: Labor migration and media coverage in Indonesia. [online conference paper]. Regional Consultation on Media and Labor Migration, Manila, 21–23 August 2000. https://dr.ntu.edu.sg//handle/10356/87390 (Accessed 15 February 2020).

Nurbaiti, A. 2008: "No sense of urgency" to help Indonesia's heroes. *Jakarta Post*, 20 July.

Nurbaiti, A. 2009: Annual reflection of the value of cheap help. *Jakarta Post*, 6 October.

Nurgiyantoro, B. 2019: Students' character learning through internalization of character values from wayang figures. In E. Retnowati, A. Ghufron. K. Marzuki, Kasiyan, A. Pierawan, and Ashadi (eds), *Character Education for 21st Century Global Cities*, London/New York: Routledge, 425–30.

OECD/Asian Development Bank 2015: *Education in Indonesia: Rising to the Challenge*, Reviews of National Policies for Education. Paris: OECD Publishing.

Ogilvy 2012: *Jala PRT: Mop*. Ads of the World, 21 April. http://adsoftheworld.com/media/print/jala_prt_mop (Accessed 21 April 2014).

Olcott, J. 2017: *International Women's Year: The Greatest Consciousness-Raising Event in History*. Oxford: Oxford University Press.

Padawangi, R. 2013: The cosmopolitan grassroots city as megaphone: Reconstructing public spaces through urban activism in Jakarta. *International Journal of Urban and Regional Research* 37 (3), 849–63.

Padawangi, R. 2014: Reform, resistance, and empowerment: Constructing the public city from the grassroots in Jakarta, Indonesia. *International Development Planning Review* 36 (1), 33–50.

Pakpahan M. 1996: "Feminism is a choice of life". *Inside Indonesia* 47. https://www.insideindonesia.org/feminism-is-a-choice-of-life (Accessed 18 August 2022).

Pakpahan, M. 2010: Letters: Gus Dur's legacies. *Jakarta Post*, 9 January.

Papachan, S. 2009: *Manual for Domestic Workers: Organizing for a Better Future*. Bangkok: Committee for Asian Women.

Pasaribu, Q. 2015a: Sunarti: My hands blister when washing clothes'. ILO-CO Jakarta, translation of radio reporting posted on KBR 68H News Portal, 24 August. https://www.ilo.org/jakarta/info/public/fs/WCMS_461057/lang–en/index.htm (Accessed 3 February 2020).

Pasaribu, Q. 2015b: Lita Anggraini: Our life and death is for the Law on Protection of Domestic Workers. Translation of radio reporting by KBR 68H News Portal, 25 August. https://www.ilo.org/jakarta/info/public/fs/WCMS_464074/lang–en/index.htm (Accessed 17 July 2017).

Pemberton, J. 1994: *On the Subject of "Java"*. Ithaca, NY/London: Cornell University Press.

Perempuan Mahardhika 2014: *Ingin Tahu Siapa Kami? Perempuan Mahardhika*. https://perempuanmahardhika.wordpress.com/2014/01/20/ingin-tahu-siapa-kami/ (Accessed 8 May 2017).

Pintak, L. and Setiyono, B. 2011: The mission of Indonesian journalism: Balancing democracy, development, and Islamic values. *International Journal of Press/Politics* 16 (2), 185–209.

Poerwandari, K., Eveline, R., Bachtiar, I., Tilawati, K., and Lestari, N. 2011: *Study of Knowledge Needs and Supply Constraints for Gender Research in Indonesia's Knowledge Sector*. Canberra: AusAID.

Poerwandari, E., Munti, R., and Vienilawati, J. 2018: Pro-women's policy advocacy movements in Indonesia: Struggles and reflections. *Asian Journal of Women's Studies* 24 (4), 489–509.

Polindo 2012: Okky Asokawati: UU Perlindungan PRT Akan Terus Diperjuangkan. *PolitikIndonesia*, 15 February. https://www.polindo.id/okky-asokawati-uu-perlindungan-prt-akan-terus-diperjuangkan (Accessed 8 August 2022).

Poo, A.-J. 2009: Domestic worker Bill of Rights: A feminist approach for a new economy. *The Scholar and Feminist Online* 8 (1).

Poo, A.-J. 2011: *Organizing with love: Lessons from the New York Domestic Workers Bill of Rights Campaign*. Centre for the Education of Women, University of Michigan. https://www.yumpu.com/en/document/read/42959388/organizing-with-love-center-for-the-education-of-women (Accessed 20 March 2020).

Prasad, A. and Zulfiqar, G. 2021: Resistance and praxis in the making of feminist solidarity: A conversation with Cynthia Enloe. *Gender, Work & Organization* 28, 722–34.

Pratiwi, A. 2017: Lita Anggraini: Bias Kelas Masih Menjadi Hambatan Besar dalam Advokasi RUU Perlindungan Pekerja Rumah Tangga. *Jurnal Perempuan* 94, 203–14.

Prichard, S. 2010: Negotiating space: Fabric and the feminine 1945–2010. In S. Prichard (ed.), *Quilts 1700–2010: Hidden Histories, Untold Stories*, London: V&A Publishing, 131–50.

Protschky, S. 2012: Teacups, cameras and family life: Picturing domesticity in elite European and Javanese family photographs from the Netherlands Indies, ca. 1900–42. *History of Photography* 36 (1), 44–65.

Putranto, P., Utami, A., and Usman, H. 2004: *Flowers on the Rock: The Phenomenon of Child Domestic Workers in Indonesia (in Bahasa Indonesia)*, [Report] 30 April. Jakarta: ILO-IPEC. https://www.ilo.org/jakarta/whatwedo/publications/WCMS_121307/lang–en/index.htm (Accessed 26 August 2022).

Putranto, P, Utami, A., and Usman, H. 2004/Ind.: *Bunga-bunga diatas padas: fenomena pekerja rumah tangga anak di Indonesia*. Geneva: International Labour Organization.

Qayum, S. and Ray, R. 2003: Grappling with modernity: India's respectable classes and the culture of domestic servitude. *Ethnography* 4 (4), 520–55.

Qibtiyah, A. 2010: Self-identified feminists among gender activists and scholars at Indonesian universities. *ASEAS-Austrian Journal of Southeast Asian Studies* 3 (2), 151–74.

Qibtiyah, A. 2012: Women's studies and gender studies centres: How they contribute to feminism. *Pakistan Journal of Women's Studies Aalam-e-Niswan* 19 (2), 167–92.

Ramirez, H. 2005: A living archive of desire: Teresita La Campesina and the embodiment of queer Latino community histories. In A. Burton (ed.), *Archive Stories: Facts, Fictions, and The Writing of History*, Durham, NC/London: Duke University Press, 111–35.

Ratnawati, A. 2013: *Project brief, PROMOTE: Decent work for domestic workers to end child domestic work*. ILO Jakarta Office. http://www.ilo.org/wcmsp5/groups/public/--asia/--ro-bangkok/---ilo-jakarta/documents/projectdocumentation/wcms_211363.pdf (Accessed 27 July 2022).

Ray, R. and Qayum, S. 2009: *Cultures of Servitude: Modernity, Domesticity, and Class in India*. Stanford, CA: Stanford University Press.

Reuters, T. 2015: Political parties and the power of money in Indonesia and beyond. *TRaNS: Trans-Regional and -National Studies of Southeast Asia* 3 (2), 267–88.

Ricklefs, M. 2008: *A History of Modern Indonesia since c. 1200*, 4th edn. Basingstoke: Palgrave Macmillan.

Rinaldo, R. 2013: Mobilizing piety: Women, Islam, and the public sphere in Indonesia. *Indonesia* 66, 45–73.

RMOL.ID 2016: *Aktivis Perempuan Desak RUU PRT Segera Disahkan*. 12 January. https://rmol.id/read/2016/01/12/231576/aktivis-perempuan-desak-ruu-prt-segera-disahkan (Accessed 30 July 2022).

Robertson, K. 2014: Quilts for the twenty-first century: Activism in the expanded field of quilting. In J. Jeffries, H Clark, and D. Conroy (eds), *The Handbook of Textiles*, London: Bloomsbury Academic, 197–210.

Robinson, K. 1991: Housemaids: The effect of gender and culture on the internal and international migration of Indonesian women. In G. Bottomley, M. de Lepervanche, and J. Martin (eds), *Intersexions: Gender/Class/Culture/Ethnicity*, Sydney: Allen & Unwin, 33–51.

Robinson, K. 2009: *Gender, Islam and Democracy in Indonesia*. ASAA Women in Asia Series. Abingdon: Routledge.

Roces, M. 2010: Asian feminisms: Women's movements from the Asian perspective. In M. Roces, and L. P. Edwards (eds), *Women's Movements in Asia: Feminisms and Transnational Activism*, Abingdon: Routledge, 1–20.

Roces, M. 2012: *Women's Movements and the Filipina, 1986–2008*. Honolulu: University of Hawai'i Press.

Romano, A. 2003: *Politics and the Press in Indonesia: Understanding an Evolving Political Culture*, Abingdon/Oxford: RoutledgeCurzon.

Romero, M. 2002: *Maid in the USA*. New York/London: Routledge.

Rother, S. 2017: Indonesian migrant domestic workers in transnational political spaces: Agency, gender roles and social class formation. *Journal of Ethnic and Migration Studies* 43 (6), 956–73.

RTND n.d.: *Tentang Sekolah Pekerja Rumah Tangga* [Blog]. Rumpun Tjoet Nyak Dien. http://rumpuntjoetnjakdien.blogspot.com/search?updated-min=2008-12-31T09:00:00-08:00&updated-max=2009-08-12T04:35:00-07:00&max-results=50&start=20&by-date=false (Accessed 2 March 2020).

RTND 2009: *"SEMILOKA": Mau Kemana (Quo Vadis) Gerakan PRT?* [Blog]. Rumpun Tjoet Nyak Dien, 2 May. http://rumpuntjoetnjakdien.blogspot.com/2009/05/semiloka-mau-kemana-quo-vadis-gerakan.html (Accessed 19 September 2016).

RTND 2010: *Rumpun Tjoet Njak Dien: Aksi Hari PRT: Serbet Cinta untuk PRT* [Blog]. Rumpun Tjoet Njak Dien, 15 February. http://rumpuntjoetnjakdien.blogspot.com/2010/02/aksi-hari-prt-serbet-cinta-untuk-prt.html (Accessed 26 June 2018).

Rudnyckyj, D. 2004: Technologies of servitude: Governmentality and Indonesian transnational labor migration. *Anthropological Quarterly* 77 (3), 407–34.

Ruoho, I. and Torkkola, S. 2018: Journalism and gender: Toward a multidimensional approach. *Nordicom Review* 39, 67–79.

Ruwaida, I. 2017: Kondisi Kerja Layak bagi PRT dan Majikan: Hasil Studi di Makassar, Surabaya, dan Bandung. *Jurnal Perempuan 94* (Pekerja Rumah Tangga Domestik dan Migran). Jakarta: Yayasan Jurnal Perempuan.

Ruzuar, A. H. (ed.) 2016: *Kami, Jurnal Perempuan (setelah 20 Tahun).* Jakarta: Yayasan Jurnal Perempuan.

Ryter, L. 1998: Pemuda Pancasila: The last loyalist free men of Suharto's order? *Indonesia* 66, 45–73.

Sabarini, P. 2009: Domestic Workers ask for national day, more days off. *Jakarta Post*, 16 February.

Sadli, S. 2002: Feminism in Indonesia in an international context. In K. Robinson and S. Bessell (eds), *Women in Indonesia: Gender, Equity and Development*, Singapore: ISEAS: Institute of Southeast Asian Studies, 80–91.

Sadli, S. and Porter, M. 1999: Importing/applying western feminism: A women's studies university linkage project. *Women's Studies International Forum* 22 (4), 441–9.

Saherman, H. 2010: *Serbet Cinta untuk PRT* [Blog]. 19 February. http://sahermankoe.wordpress.com/2010/02/19/serbet-cinta-untuk-prt/ (Accessed 25 August 2022).

Samodro, D. 2014: Rieke: RUU PPRT Diupayakan Masuk Prolegnas. *Antara News*, 14 December. https://www.antaranews.com/berita/469176/rieke-ruu-pprt-diupayakan-masuk-prolegnas (Accessed 17 July 2022).

Sangtin Writers [with Richa Nagar] 2006: *Playing with Fire: Feminist Thought and Activism through Seven Lives in India*. New Dehli: Zubaan Books and Minneapolis University Press.

Santos, A., Cerqueira, C., and Cabecinhas, R. 2018: "Challenging it softly": A feminist inquiry into gender in the news media context. *Feminist Media Studies* 22, 66–82.

Saragih, B. 2010: Protection asked for domestic workers. *Jakarta Post*, 26 February.

Saraswati, L. A. 2013: *Seeing Beauty, Sensing Race in Transnational Indonesia*. Honolulu, University of Hawai'i Press.

Sargini, Jumiyem, L. and Muryanti, M. 2017: Pengesahan Peraturan Daerah Pekerja Rumah Tangga di Daerah Istimewa Yogyakarta dan Tantangannya. *Jurnal Perempuan 94*, 22 (3), 123–40.

Sarumpaet, R. and McGlynn, J. 2000: Marsinah Accuses. *Manoa* 12 (1), 155–66.

Sassen, S. 2006: *Territory, Authority, Rights: from Medieval to Global Assemblages*. Princeton, NJ: Princeton University Press.

Schlehe, J. 2017: Contesting Javanese traditions. *Indonesia and the Malay World* 45 (131), 3–23.

Schrauwers, A. 1999: Negotiating parentage: The political economy of "kinship" in Central Sulawesi, Indonesia. *American Ethnologist* 26 (2), 310–23.

Schulte Nordholt, H. 2011: Modernity and cultural citizenship in the Netherlands Indies. *Journal of Southeast Asian Studies* 42 (3), 435–57.

Schulte Nordholt, H. 2014: Decentralization and democracy in Indonesia: Strengthening citizenship or regional elites? In R. Robinson (ed.), *Routledge Handbook of Southeast Asian Politics*, London/New York, Routledge, 229–41.

Schwenken, H., Prügl, E., Pabon, R., Hobden, C., and Ally, S. 2011: Conversations. *International Feminist Journal of Politics* 13 (3), 437–61.

Scott, J. W. 1986: Gender: A useful category of historical analysis. *The American Historical Review* 91 (5), 1053–75.

Scott, J. W. 2011: *The Fantasy of Feminist History*. Durham, NC/London: Duke University Press.

Seiffarth, M., Bonnet F., and Hobden, C. 2023. *The Road to Decent Work for Domestic Workers*. Geneva: International Labour Office.

*Sekolah PRT RTND (part 1) c.*2011a: [video]. Edited by Hayu Primaningtyas. Yogyakarta: rtnvideo. (Script: members of domestic workers school. Music: Sarwanto). https://www.youtube.com/watch?v=E9m3hrL7eTg (Accessed 4 February 2020).

*Sekolah PRT RTND (part 2) c.*2011b: [video]. Edited by Hayu Primaningtyas, Yogyakarta, RTND. Script: members of domestic workers school. Music: Sarwanto. https://www.youtube.com/watch?v=WPe6vNXy2nQ (Accessed 14 February 2020).

Sen, K. and Hill, D. 2007: *Media, Culture and Politics in Indonesia*, first Equinox Edn. Jakarta: Equinox Publishing.

Sendjaja, H. 2009: *Teologi Kristiani: Potret Tiga Teolog Feminis Mengeakkan Komunitas Demokratis* [Blog]. Teologi Kristiani, 30 January. http://teologikristiani.blogspot.co.uk/2009/01/potret-tiga-teolog-feminis-menegakkan.html (Accessed 17 April 2016).

Sentilles, R. 2005: Toiling in the archives of cyberspace. In A. Burton (ed.), *Archive Stories: Facts, Fictions and the Writing of History*, Durham, NC/London: Duke University Press, 136–56.

Septi, D. and Ariane, Z. 2013: Indonesia: From statistics to fighters against sexual violence. *Politik Rakyat Online*, 15 November. https://politikrakyatdotcom.wordpress.com/2013/11/15/indonesia-from-statistics-to-fighters-against-sexual-violence/ (Accessed 20 July 2022).

Setiawan, Y. B., Fanani, F., and Julianto, E. 2013: Bias Gender Dalam Cerita Rakyat. *The Messenger* 5 (2), 1–13.

Setiawati, I. 2008: Mentally ill woman "beat maids to death". *Jakarta Post*, 24 July.

Setiogi, S. 2003: Bill prepared on woman and child trafficking. *Jakarta Post*, 21 June.

Sheppard, B. 2009: *Workers in the Shadows: Abuse and Exploitation of Child Domestic Workers in Indonesia*. New York: Human Rights Watch.

Sherlock, S. 2003: *Struggling to Change: The Indonesian Parliament in an Era of Reformasi*. Canberra: Centre for Democratic Institutions, ANU.

Sherlock, S. 2012: Made by committee and consensus: Parties and policy in the Indonesian parliament. *South East Asia Research* 20 (4), 551–68.

Sherlock, S. 2020: Alliances of instrumental advantage: Supporting women's agency in civil society organisations of Indonesia. *Politics and Governance* 8 (4), 147–56.

Shiraishi, S. 1986: Silakan Masuk. Silakan Duduk: Reflections in a sitting room in Java. *Indonesia* 41, 89–130.

Siapno, J. 2002: *Gender, Islam, Nationalism, and the State in Aceh: The Paradox of Power, Co-optation and Resistance.* London: RoutledgeCurzon.

Siegel, J. 1986: *Solo in the New Order: Language and Hierarchy in an Indonesian City.* Princeton: Princeton University Press.

Silvey, R. 2018: From Java to Saudi Arabia and Dubai: Precarious itinerary of Indonesian domestic workers. In R. Hoefte and P. Meel (eds), *Departing from Java: Javanese Labour, Migration and Diaspora*, Copenhagen: NIAS Press, 188–208.

Sim, A. 2009: Women versus the State: Organizing resistance and contesting exploitation in Indonesian labor migration to Hong Kong. *Asian and Pacific Migration Journal* 18 (1), 47–75.

Simanjuntak, T. 2015: Toeti Heraty: For love of writing and Indonesian people. *Jakarta Post*, 14 December.

Sisters for Change/JALA PRT 2018: *Unsafe to work in the home: Workplace exploitation and violence against women domestic workers in Indonesia* [report]. https://www.sistersforchange.org.uk/2018/10/20/unsafe-to-work-in-the-home/ (Accessed 4 November 2019).

Smith, N. 2017: In Indonesia, education is the key for domestic workers' empowerment [Blog]. *Women in and beyond the Global*, 21 October. http://www.womeninandbeyond.org/?p=21711 (Accessed 28 December 2023).

Soewartini, M. 2022: Kedatangan Teman Feminis Muda, Kami Berbagi Suka Duka Jadi PRT [Blog]. https://www.tungkumenyala.com/kedatangan-teman-feminis-muda-kami-berbagi-cerita/ (Accessed 28 December 2023).

Sofiani, T, Rahmawati, R., and Rismawati, S. 2012: *Membangun Kosep Ideal Hubungan Kerja Antara Pekerja Rumah Tangga dan Majikan Berbasis Hak-Hak Buruh Dalam Islam.* Conference Proceedings Annual International Conference on Islamic Studies (ALCIS VII), 5–8 November 2012, Surabaya, Indonesia. http://digilib.uinsby.ac.id/7575/ (Accessed 17 February 2020).

Solidaritas Luviana 2016: *Solidaritas Luviana* [Facebook] 25 May. http://facebook.com/permalink.php?id=281723571901066& (Accessed 2 July 2017).

Solidaritas Perempuan n.d.: *Sejarah SP*. http://www.solidaritasperempuan.org/tentang-sp/struktur-kepengurusan/ (Accessed 3 February 2020).

Solidarity Center 2011: *By organizing, we are not alone* [Blog]. 19 July. https://organizesolidarity.blogspot.com/2011/07/by-organizing-we-are-not-alone.html (Accessed 8 August 2022).

Soparianti, P. and Narulita, S. 2022: Musdah Mulia, the Reformist Muslima. *Swararahima*, 10 March. https://swararahima.com/en/2022/03/10/musdah-mulia-the-reformist-muslima/ (Accessed 29 August 2022).

Steedman, C. 2009: *Labours Lost: Domestic Service and the Making of Modern England*. Cambridge: Cambridge University Press.

Steele, J. 2011: Indonesian journalism post-Suharto: Changing ideals and professional practices. In K. Sen and D. Hill (eds), *Politics and the Media in Twenty-first Century Indonesia: Decade of Democracy*, London and New York: Routledge, 85–104.

Steele, J. 2013: From fashion to the hereafter: Indonesia's *Republika*, a modern Islamic newspaper. *Media Asia* 40 (1), 27–33.

Stoler, A. 2009: *Along the Archival Grain: Epistemic Anxieties and Colonial Common Sense*. Princeton, NJ: Princeton University Press.

Stoler, A. with Strassler, K. 2002: Memory-work in Java: A cautionary tale. In *Carnal Knowledge and Imperial Power: Race and the Intimate in Colonial Rule*, Berkeley, CA: University of California Press, 183–99.

Stone-Mediatore, S. 2016: Storytelling/narrative. In L. Disch and M. Hawkesworth (eds), *The Oxford Handbook of Feminist Theory*, Oxford: Oxford University Press, 934–54.

Strassler, K. 2004: Gendered visibilities and the dream of transparency: The Chinese-Indonesian rape debate in post-Suharto Indonesia. *Gender and History* 16 (3), 689–725.

Strassler, K. 2006: Reformasi through our eyes: Children as witnesses of history in post-Suharto Indonesia. *Visual Anthropology Review* 22 (2), 53–70.

Strassler, K. 2010: *Refracted Visions: Popular Photography and National Modernity in Java*. Durham, NC: Duke University Press.

Stroud, M. 2015: *Ripples, echoes, and reverberations: 1965 and now in Indonesia*. PhD. University of California, Berkeley.

Subiyantoro, E. B. 2005: Yuli Maiheni: Matahari Pekerja Rumah Tangga. *Jurnal Perempuan* 39, 101–9.

Subiyantoro, E. B. 2007: Buruh Anak Perempuan: Bekerja tanpa jaminan hukum. *Jurnal Perempuan* 56, 41–52.

Suchocki, M. 1994: The idea of God in feminist philosophy. *Hypatia* 9 (4), 57–68.

Sudibyo, A. and Patria, N. 2013: The television industry in post-authoritarian Indonesia. *Journal of Contemporary Asia* 43 (2), 257–75.

Sufa, T. 2014: Police general's wife accused of abusing maids. *Jakarta Post*, 21 February.

Suhaimi, U. and Farid, M. 2017: *Toward a Better Estimation of Total Population of Domestic Workers in Indonesia*. Report, 31 January. Jakarta: ILO Jakarta.

Sukarno, S. 2010: The reflection of the Javanese cultural concepts in the politeness of Javanese. *K@ta* 12 (1), 59–71.

Sukendar, A. 1999: *Profil sosial dan problematika pekerja rumah tangga di Daerah Istimewa Yogyakarta*. Yogyakarta: Yayasan Rumpun Tjoet Njak Dien with INPI-Pact (Indonesian NGOs Partnership Initiative).

Sukesi, K. 2009: Bias Gender Dalam Pekerjaan Rumah Tangga Domestik dan Buruh Migran. *Jurnal Analisi Sosial* 14 (1), 105–24.

Sun, W. 2009: *Maid in China: Media, Morality, and the Cultural Politics of Boundaries*. London: Routledge.

Sunindyo, S. 1998: When the earth is female and the nation is mother: Gender, the armed forces and nationalism in Indonesia. *Feminist Review* 58, 1–21.

Supardo, S. 2007: Address term in a family of Javanese priyayi. *Leksika* 1 (2), 1–13.

Suryadinata, L. (ed.) 2012: *Southeast Asian Personalities of Chinese Descent: A Biographical Dictionary, Volume 1*. Singapore: Institute of Southeast Asian Studies.

Suryakusuma, J. 2012: Is state ibuism still relevant? *Inside Indonesia* 109 (July–September). https://www.insideindonesia.org/editions/edition-109-jul-sep-2012/is-state-ibuism-still-relevant (Accessed 28 December 2023).

Suryakusuma, J. 2013: *Julia's Jihad: Tales of the Politically, Sexually, and Religiously Incorrect Living in the Chaos of the Biggest Muslim Democracy*. Jakarta: Komunitas Bambu.

Suryakusuma, J. 2016: VAW and the Janus Face of social media. *Jakarta Post*, 14 December.

Suriyani, L. 2008: Most employers overlook domestic workers' rights. *Jakarta Post*, 15 September.

Suryani, L. 2017: Dari organisasi, saya menjadi tahu bagaimana berjuang. In A. Ujianto and Luviana (eds), *Kami Tidak Akan Diam: 31 Kisah Pekerja Rumah Tangga di Balik Tembok Ruang Domestik*, Jakarta: AJI Jakarta, JALA PRT and ILO Jakarta, 85–95.

Susanto, S. 2004: School no chore as domestic workers helpers learn their rights. *Jakarta Post*, 17 July.

Sushartami, W. 2012: *Representation and beyond: Female victims in post-Suharto media*. PhD. Leiden University.

Sutradani 2012a: 1000 serbet ala demo buruh. *Beritagar.id*, 22 November. https://beritagar.id/artikel/waini/1000-serbet-ala-demo-buruh (Accessed 20 August 2022).

Sutradani 2012b: Buruh PRT menolak disebut pembantu. *Beritagar.id*, 22 November. https://beritagar.id/artikel-amp/berita/buruh-prt-menolak-disebut-pembantu (Accessed 20 August 2022).

Suwignyo, A. 2019: *Gotong royong* as social citizenship in Indonesia, 1940s to 1990s. *Journal of Southeast Asian Studies* 50 (3), 387–408.

Swara Rahima 2009: Islam dan pekerja rumah tangga. *Swara Rahima* 28 (August). https://swararahima.com/wp-content/uploads/2021/03/SR-28-Combine.pdf (Accessed 30 June 2022).

Syafina, D. 2012: PRT tuntut pengesahan Undang-Undang PRT. *kontan.co.id*, 22 November. http://nasional.kontan.co.id/news/prt-tuntut-pengesahan-undang-undang-prt (Accessed 26 August 2022).

Tapsell, R. 2012: Old tricks in a new era: Self-censorship in Indonesian journalism. *Asian Studies Review* 36 (2), 227–45.

Tarida, S. 2013a: *Luviana!* [Blog]. *Kompasiana,* 13 June. http://www.kompasiana.com/sahida/luviana_552a43666ea8342c53552d35 (Accessed 27 April 2017).

Tarida, S. 2013b. *Award untuk Luviana* [Blog]. *Kompasiana*, 8 July. https://www.kompasiana.com/sahida/552e0bde6ea834f9288b4619/award-untuk-luviana (Accessed 9 February 2020).

Tarigan, M. 2015a: Never escaping from modern slavery. ILO-CO Jakarta, translation of an article published in *Koran Tempo*, 1 September. https://www.ilo.org/jakarta/info/public/fs/WCMS_470263/lang–en/index.htm (Accessed 3 February 2020).

Tarigan, M. 2015b: Tak Kunjung Keluar Dari Perbudakan Modern. *Koran Tempo*, 31 August. https://koran.tempo.co/read/nasional/381359/tak-kunjung-keluar-dari-perbudakan-modern (Accessed 15 March 2017).

Tarrant, B. 2008: *Reporting Indonesia: The Jakarta Post Story*. Jakarta: Equinox Publishing.

Taylor, C. 2004: *Modern Social Imaginaries*. Durham, NC/London: Duke University Press.

Thompson, E. P. 1963: *The Making of the English Working Class*. Harmondsworth: Penguin Books.

Tjandra, S. 2014: The Indonesian trade union movement: A clash of paradigms. In J. Suryomenggolo (ed.), *Worker Activism After Reformasi 1998: A New Phase for Indonesian Unions?* Hong Kong: Asia Monitor Resources Centre, 45–66.

Tungku Menyala 2018: *Tentang Kami* [Blog]. https://www.tungku-menyala.com/tentang-kami/ (Accessed 25 July 2022).

Tungku Menyala 2022: *Hari PRT Nasional: Perjalanan panjing RUU Perlindungan PRT* [Blog]. 15 February. https://www.tungkumenyala.com/hari-prt-nasional-perjalanan-panjang-ruu-perlindungan-prt/ (Accessed 3 August 2022).

Tungku Menyala 2023: *DPR Sahkan RUU PPRT Menjadi Inisiatif DPR, PRT: Selangkah Lagi Mimpi Kami Terwujud* [Blog]. https://www.tungkumenyala.com/dpr-sahkan-ruu-pprt-menjadi-inisiatif-dpr-prt-selangkah-lagi-mimpi-kami-terwujud/ (Accessed 29 December 2023).

Ujianto, A. and Luviana (eds) 2017: *Kami Tidak Akan Diam: 31 Kisah Pekerja Rumah Tangga di Balik Tembok Ruang Domestik*. Jakarta: AJI Jakarta, JALA PRT and ILO Jakarta.

Ulung, A. K. 2017: Saparinah Sadli continues to fight for justice. *Jakarta Post*, 25 July.

US Department of Labor 2012: *Technical cooperation project summary, PROMOTE: Decent work for domestic workers to end child domestic work*. US Department of Labor, International Labor Affairs Bureau. https://www.dol.gov/ilab/projects/summaries/Indonesia_PROMOTE.pdf (Accessed 23 February 2017).

Utama, A. 2015a: Menjadi PRT anak, pilihan gegabah Yantri. *CNN Indonesia*, 19 September. https://www.cnnindonesia.com/nasional/20150919105134-20-79724/menjadi-prt-anak-pilihan-gegabah-yantri/ (Accessed 24 August 2015).

Utama, A. 2015b: PRT anak dalam lingkaran kekerasan. *CNN Indonesia,* 19 September. https://www.cnnindonesia.com/nasional/20150919113509-20-79729/prt-anak-dalam-lingkaran-kekerasan/ (Accessed 24 August 2022).

Utama, A. and Kusumawati, U. 2015a: Stories of child domestic workers hunting for "small change". ILO-CO Jakarta [Feature Story], 19 September. Translation/version of article published by *CNN Indonesia*. https://www.ilo.org/jakarta/info/public/fs/WCMS_461055/lang–en/index.htm (Accessed 24 August 2022).

Utama, A. and Kusumawati, U. 2015b: Child domestic workers in cycle of abuse. ILO-CO Jakarta [Feature Story], 19 September. Translation/version of article published by *CNN Indonesia*. https://www.ilo.org/jakarta/info/public/fs/WCMS_461056/lang–en/index.htm (Accessed 24 August 2022).

Utama, A. and Kusumawati, U. 2015c: Being domestic workers, way out for countryside girls to avoid marriage. ILO-CO Jakarta [Feature Story], 19 September. Translation/version of article published by *CNN Indonesia*, https://www.ilo.org/jakarta/info/public/fs/WCMS_461057/lang–en/index.htm (Accessed 24 August 2022).

Utama, A. and Kusumawati, U. 2015d: Being child domestic worker, Yantri's careless choice. ILO-CO Jakarta [Feature Story], 19 September. Translation/version of an article published by *CNN Indonesia*. http://www.ilo.org/jakarta/info/public/fs/WCMS_461058/langen/index.htm (Accessed 24 August 2022).

Utami, A. 2005: PRTA (Pekerja Rumah Tangga Anak): "Fenomena pekerja anak yang terselubung dan termarginalkan". *Jurnal Perempuan* 39, 45–57.

Utari, P. and Nilan, P. 2004: The lucky few: Female graduands of communication studies in the Indonesian media industry. *Asia Pacific Media Educator* 15, 63–80.

Vargas, V. and Wieringa, S. 1998: The triangle of empowerment: Processes and actors in the making of public policy for women. In G. Lycklama, G. Nijeholt, and S. Wieringa (eds), *Women's Movements and Public Policy in Europe, Latin America and the Caribbean*, New York: Garland Publishing, 3–20.

Venny, A. 2005: Prolog: Pekerja domestik dari masa ke masa. *Jurnal Perempuan* 39, 4–5.

Vickery, A. 2009: *Behind Closed Doors: At Home in Georgian England*. New Haven, CT/ London: Yale University Press.

Volkman, T. A. 1984: Great performances: Toraja cultural identity in the 1970s. *American Ethnologist* 11 (1), 152–69.

VOI 2023: NasDem Legislator Sad, Ratification of the PPRT Bill is postponed by the leadership of the DPR. *VOI* 23 March. https://voi.id/en/news/261903 (Accessed 7 July 2023).

Wahyuni, S. 2004: Women's Forum struggles to improve the lot of domestic helpers. *Jakarta Post,* 11 December.

Waisbord, S. 2009: Advocacy journalism in a global context. In K. Wahl-Jorgensen and T. Hanitzsch (eds), *The Handbook of Journalism Studies*, New York/London: Routledge, 371–85.

Wanandi, J. 2004: The Indonesian general elections 2004. *Asia-Pacific Review* 11 (2), 115–31.

Warburton, E. 2022. Indonesia in 2021: A year of crisis, development, and democratic decline. *Asian Survey* 62 (1), 93–104.

Wardoyo, H. 2008: *Siti Noor Laila (1967–...). Tokoh Lampung* [Blog]. 29 October. http://paratokohlampung.blogspot.com/2011/10/siti-noor-laila-1967-kebangkitan-bangsa.html (Accessed 18 April 2016).

Warouw, N. 2004: *Assuming modernity: Migrant industrial workers in Tangerang, Indonesia*. PhD. Australian National University.

Weix, G. G. 1990: *Following the family/firm: Patronage and piecework in a Kudus cigarette factory*. PhD. Cornell University.

Weix, G. G. 2000a: Inside the home and outside the family. In S. Dickey and K. Adams, (eds), *Home and Hegemony: Domestic Service and Identity Politics in South and Southeast Asia*, Michigan: University of Michigan Press, 137–55.

Weix, G. G. 2000b: Hidden managers at home: Elite Javanese women running New Order family firms. In J. Koning et al. (eds), *Women and Households in Indonesia: Cultural Notions and Social Practices*, Richmond, Surrey: Curzon Press, 299–314.

Weix, G. G. 2002: Resisting history: Indonesian labour activism in the 1990s and the "Marsinah" case. In B. Yeoh, P. Teo, and S. Huang (eds), *Gender Politics in the Asia-Pacific Region*, London/New York: Routledge, 120–36.

Welch, A. 2007: "Blurred vision?" Public and private higher education in Indonesia. *Higher Education: The International Journal of Higher Education and Educational Planning* 54 (5), 655–87.

Wichelen, S. van 2010: *Religion, Politics and Gender in Indonesia: Disputing the Muslim Body*. London: Routledge.

Wieringa, S. 1993: Two Indonesian women's organizations: Gerwani and the PKK. *Bulletin of Concerned Asian Scholars* 25 (2), 17–30.

Wieringa, S. 2011: Sexual slander and the 1965/66 mass killings in Indonesia: Political and methodological considerations. *Journal of Contemporary Asia* 41 (4), 544–65.

Wieringa, S. 2015: Gender harmony and the happy family: Islam, gender and sexuality in post-Reformasi Indonesia. *South East Asia Research* 23 (1), 27–44.

Wieringa, S. 2019: Criminalisation of homosexuality in Indonesia: The role of the constitution and civil society. *Australian Journal of Asian Law* 20 (1), 227–45.

Wieringa, S., Melvin, J., and Pohlam, A. (eds) 2019: *The International People's Tribunal for 1965 and the Indonesian Genocide*. London/New York: Routledge.

Wijaksana, W. B. 2005a: Perlindungan hukum pekerja rumah tangga beda antara Indonesia dan Filipina. *Jurnal Perempuan* 39, 67–81.

Wijaksana, W. B. 2005b: Wawancara: Tati Krisnawati. *Jurnal Perempuan* 39, 86–91.

Williams, C. P. 2005: "Knowing one's place": Gender, mobility and shifting subjectivity in eastern Indonesia. *Global Networks* 5 (4), 401–17.

Wilson, C. A. 2001: Reciprocal work: Bees and the meaning of neighbourhood. *Canadian Historical Review* 82 (3), 431–64.

Wilson, I. 2019: Urban poor activism and political agency in post–New Order Jakarta. In T. Dibley and M. Ford (eds), *Activists in Transition: Progressive Politics in Democratic Indonesia*, Ithaca, NY/London: Cornell University Press, 99–116.

Winarnita, M., Bahfen, N., Mintarsih, R., Height, G., and Byrne, J. 2022: Gendered digital citizenship: How Indonesian female journalists participate in gender activism. *Journalism Practice* 16 (4), 621–36.

Women Research Institute 2005: *Perspektif feminis, mengungkap yang tak terungkap*. 8 October. http://www.wri.or.id/media-wri/liputan-media/2005/187-perspektif-feminis-mengungkap-yang-tak-terungkap (Accessed 23 August 2022).

Wulandari, I. 2014: Kado Toilet Raksasa Buat Anggota DPR Baru. *Republika Online*, 1 October. https://republika.co.id/berita/nasional/umum/14/10/01/ncre7g-kado-toilet-raksasa-buat-anggota-dpr-baru (Accessed 23 July 2018).

Wulandari, I. and Thaniago, R. 2012: Luviana: Jurnalis harus sadar bahwa mereka adalah kelas buruh [Interview]. *Remotivi*, 2 December. http://www.remotivi.or.id/wawancara/112/Luviana:-Jurnalis-Harus-Sadar-Bahwa-Mereka-Adalah-Kelas-Buruh (Accessed 23 August 2022).

Yanco, J. 1996: "Our bodies, ourselves" in Beijing: Breaking the silence. *Feminist Studies* 22 (3), 511–17.

Yazid, M. 2008: Protecting workers' rights abroad should begin at home. *Jakarta Post*, 18 July.

Yoedtadi, M. and Pribadi, M. 2020: *Alternative media as counter-hegemony: A case study of Konde.co and Magdalene.co.* Proceedings of the 2nd Tarumanagara International Conference on the Applications of Social Sciences and Humanities (TICASH 2020). https://dx.doi.org/10.2991/assehr.k.201209.013 (Accessed 27 July 2022).

Yuni, S. R. 2019: *Menulis, Menjadi Api Gerakan Bagi Kami* [Blog]. *indonesiana,* 27 April. https://www.indonesiana.id/read/103891/menulis-menjadi-api-gerakan-bagi-kami (Accessed 20 July 2022).

Yuniasari 2015: *Notulasi Lokakarya Kerja Layak Bagi PRT.* Notes circulated after workshop organized by Komnas Perempuan held at Hotel Oria, Jakarta, 30 July.

Zoonen, L. van 1998: A professional, unreliable, heroic marionette (m/f): Structure, agency and subjectivity in contemporary journalisms. *European Journal of Cultural Studies* 1 (1), 123–43.

Appendices

Appendix 1

Timeline: Towards an Indonesian Domestic Workers Law, National & International Context

Period	INDONESIA	INTERNATIONAL /ILO	DRAFT DOMESTIC WORKERS BILL
1965–1966	Alleged coup and mass killings end President Sukarno's "Old Order". General Suharto takes power.		
1966–1997	President Suharto establishes a repressive military dictatorship known as New Order Indonesia.	1971: Household Technicians of America trade union founded. 1975–1985: UN Decade for Women 1979: Convention on Elimination of all Forms of Discrimination against Women (CEDAW). 1989: UN Convention on the Rights of the Child. 1995: Fourth World Conference on Women. Beijing Declaration and Platform for Action.	Human Rights activists research and advocate for better provincial regulation of domestic work in Jakarta. 1995: Rumpun Tjoet Nyak Dien begins work with PRT.
1997–1998	Asian Financial Crisis. Collapse of Indonesian economy. President Suharto resigns. End of New Order regime. Beginning of *reformasi*.		1997: Rumpun Tjoet Nyak Dien submits draft regulation on domestic work to regional parliament in Yogyakarta.

Period	INDONESIA	INTERNATIONAL /ILO	DRAFT DOMESTIC WORKERS BILL
1998–2004	*Reformasi* Transition to democracy. Decentralization to the regions. Three presidents in succession: B. J. Habibie (1998–1999); Abdurrahman Wahid (1999–2001); Megawati Sukarnoputri (2001–2004).	1986: South African Domestic Workers Union founded. 1997: South Africa includes domestic workers in labour laws. 1998: Latin American & Caribbean Confederation of Domestic Workers founded in Bogotá, Colombia.	Tunas Mulia Domestic Workers Union established in Yogyakarta. 2004: JALA PRT established. 2004: JALA submits Draft Domestic Workers Bill (RUU PPRT) to parliament.
2004–2014	President Susilo Bambang Yudhoyono (SBY). Law No. 23 of 2004 on Elimination of Household Violence. Pace of reform slows. Yudhoyono supports ILO Convention in Geneva.	2006: First International Conference of domestic worker activists, Amsterdam. Standard-setting on decent work for domestic workers on agenda for ILO Labour Conference (ILC) in 2010. 2008: International Domestic Workers Network (IDWN) sends *Platform of Demands* to the ILO. 2009: ILO consults member states on proposed Convention. 2010: ILC debates global standards for domestic work 16 June 2011: ILC adopts **ILO Convention 189** on Decent Work for Domestic Workers. 2012: Philippines amongst the first nations to ratify C189. United Domestic Workers of the Philippines established. 2012: UN includes decent work in Sustainable Development Goals. 2013: IDWN renamed the International Domestic Workers Federation (IDWFED).	2004: RUU PPRT listed as priority legislation for 2004 to 2009 parliament. 2010: RUU PPRT re-enters list of DPR priority bills in 2010 2011–2013: DPR Commission 1X undertakes research, public consultation, and sends fact-finding delegation to South Africa and Argentina. 2013: RUU PPRT moves to next stage in the DPR but then stalls.

Period	INDONESIA	INTERNATIONAL /ILO	DRAFT DOMESTIC WORKERS BILL
2014–2023	President Joko Widodo (Jokowi). 2014: Jokowi promises support for RUU PPRT during his election campaign. 2019: Jokowi wins second term. 2023: Jokowi urges ministers to progress the RUU PPRT.	2014–2018: ILO PROMOTE project continues. 2021: ILO reports on severe impact of COVID-19 on domestic workers and urges nations in the Asia and Pacific region to include domestic workers in labour laws. 2023: ILO launches new strategy for achieving decent work for domestic workers. 2023: thirty-six nations have ratified C189.The Philippines only ASEAN nation to have done so.	Hunger strikes November 2014 and February to March 2015. RUU PPRT not on priority list for legislation for 2014–2019 parliament. 2019: RUU PPRT back on priority list. 1 July 2020: DPR Legislative Body agrees RUU should proceed. 21 March 2023: All factions in DPR agree RUU PPRT should move to final stage.

Appendix 2

List of Interviewees/Informants

This list includes the date and place of meetings. The few informants who preferred not to be named, and the details of the interviews conducted on my behalf by my research assistants are listed separately.

Ade Indriani Zuchri, Jakarta, 8 July 2015
Agustine (Nunuk) Prasetyo Murniati, Yogyakarta, 1 March 2016
Ahmad Nurhasim, Jakarta, 15 July 2015
Aida Milasari, Jakarta, 2 July 2015 and 6 July 2015
Alimatul Qibtiyah, Yogyakarta, 5 August 2014
Ani Widyani Soetjipto, Jakarta, 28 July 2015
Arum Ratnawati, Jakarta, 1 August 2014 and 9 July 2015
Asih Nur Candra, Yogyakarta, 25 February 2016
Ati Nurbaiti, Jakarta, 27 June 2012 and 29 August 2014
Caecilia Mediana, Jakarta, 13 August 2015
Debbie Prabawati, Yogyakarta, 5 December 2016
Dedi H., Jakarta, 18 February 2016
Dewi Astuti, Jakarta, 18 February 2016
Dewi Tjakrawinata, Jakarta, 29 July 2015
Diah Rofika, Jakarta, 16 November 2016
Dian Septi Trisnanti, Jakarta, 3 July 2015
Edriana Noerdin, Jakarta, 22 November 2016
Elizabeth Kristi Poerwandari, Jakarta, 5 August 2015
Endy Bayuni, Jakarta, 23 November 2016
Gadis Arivia, Jakarta, 21 November 2016
Gita Nasution, Jakarta, 11 July 2015
Ida Ruwaida Noor, Jakarta, 3 August 2015
Irma Suryani, Jakarta, 3 August 2015
Julia Suryakusuma, London, 24 October 2015
Lek Jumiyem, Yogyakarta, 24 February 2016
Lita Anggraini, Jakarta, 27 August 2014, 2 July 2015, and 30 July 2015
Luviana Ariyanti, Jakarta, 30 June 2015
Magdalena Sitorus, Jakarta, 14 February 2016
Manna Nababan, Jakarta, 3 August 2015
Maria Pakpahan, Edinburgh, 9 August 2017

Melani Budianta, Jakarta, 24 June 2015
Mitra Tarigan, Jakarta, 14 July 2015
Muhamad Nour, Jakarta, 9 July 2015 and 23 November 2016
Muryanti Muryanti, Yogyakarta, 7 December 2016
Nisaa Yura, Jakarta, 29 July 2015
Nurika Manan, Jakarta, 24 November 2016
Nursyahbani Katjasungkana and Wiladi Budiharga, Jakarta, 4 August 2015
Nurul Hamami, Jakarta, 21 August 2015
Nusya Kuswantin, Yogyakarta, 2 March 2016
Pratiwi Febry, Jakarta, 28 July 2015
Ratna Batara Munti, Jakarta, 31 July 2015
Razian Agus Toniman, Jakarta, 17 February 2016
Rena Herdiyani, Jakarta, 23 June 2015
Rina Satdewi, Jakarta, 27 July 2015
Ririn Sulastri, Yogyakarta, 24 February 2016
Santi Sunarti, Jakarta, 28 June 2015
Sargini, Yogyakarta, 24 February 2016
Shelly Adelina, Jakarta, 5 August 2015
Siti Aripurnami, Jakarta, 22 November 2016
Sofia Opie, Jakarta, 22 June 2015
Solita Sarwono, Jakarta, 22 August 2015
Sri Djoharwinarlien, Yogyakarta, 2 July 2012
Sri Wahyuni, Yogyakarta, 1 March 2016
Sri Wiyanti Eddyono, Yogyakarta, 9 December 2016
Sulistri Sulistri, Jakarta, 15 February 2016
Surya Tjandra, Jakarta, 16 February 2016
Tarech Rasyid, Palembang, 7 August 2015
Tiasri Wiandani, Jakarta, 20 August 2015
Valentina Utari, Jakarta, 30 June 2016
Vebri Al Lintani, Palembang, 7 August 2015
W. B. Wijaksana, Jakarta, 15 November 2016
Wiwin Winarsih Farisca, Jakarta, 3 July 2015
Yuli Maiheni, Yogyakarta, 24 February 2016
Yuni Satia Rahayu, Yogyakarta, 23 February 2016
Yuni Sri Rahayu, Jakarta, 3 July 2015
Yuniyanti Chuzaifah, Jakarta, 12 August 2015

Interviewees Not Named

AJI Jakarta journalist, Jakarta, 15 July 2015
Kompas journalists, Jakarta, 27 June 2012
University of Indonesia academic, Jakarta, 1 December 2016

Additional Interviews Conducted by Research Assistants on My Behalf

Intan Bedisa (RTV), Jakarta, 2 December 2016 (interviewer Zahra Sakinaruzzahara)
Michael Kodoati, BeritaSatu TV, Jakarta, 27 November 2016 (interviewer Tyas Pusposari)
Monique Rijkers, Jakarta, 27 February 2016 (interviewer Tyas Pusposari)
Mawa Kresna, Jakarta, 23 November 2016 (interviewer Zahra Sakinaruzzahara)
Gusti (Reuters), Jakarta, 4 March 2016 (interviewer Tyas Pusposari)
Shelly Adelina, UI Kajian Gender, Jakarta, 25 January 2017 (interviewer Zahra Sakinaruzzahara)

Appendix 3

Original Text of Extracts from Account Written by Lek Jumiyem, Member of Tunas Mulia Domestic Workers' Union, Yogyakarta, Published in Indonesian in *Kami Tidak Akan Diam: 31 Kisah Pekerja Rumah Tangga di Balik Tembok Ruang Domestik* (Jumiyem 2017: 147–51).

Lek Jumiyem: Mogok Makan dan Nadi Perjuangan Kami

> Mungkin orang lain yang melawati jalan di sekitar tempat itu tidak akan pernah melirik apa yang kami lakukan saat itu. Namun bagiku pengalaman waktu itu merupakan hal yang tidak pernah terbayangkan. Dan kami senang menjalaninya.
>
> Demikian pertempuran kecil telah terselesaikan tapi perang maish panjang dan tidak akan pernah selesai selama masih ada penindasan dan belum ada perlindungan pekerja rumah tangga.
>
> Aksi keprihatinan telah rampung. Satu babak drama kehidupan telah terwarnai oleh nadi-nadi perjuangan, semangat dan cinta. Jalan terbentang sangat meruncing untuk mewujudkan harapan cita-cita menjadi bagian warga negara yang mendapatkan pekerjaan layak sebagaimana pekerja lain [...]'.
>
> *Kami Tidak Akan Diam* can be viewed at this link:
>
> http://www.ilo.org/wcmsp5/groups/public/---asia/---ro-bangkok/---ilo-jakarta/documents/publication/wcms_569568.pdf (Accessed 12 August 2022).

Appendix 4

Sample of Articles Published in *Kompas* in 2004 and 2008 Used in the Discussion of Stock Stories in Chapter 4

Kompas now has a paywall. Articles published in 2004 do not have a URL. Links to the 2008 articles are listed below.

http://megapolitan.kompas.com/read/2008/03/25/08284536/Pelaku.Hipnotis.Cegat

http://megapolitan.kompas.com/read/2008/02/15/08121564/Hati-hati.Pilih.PRT

http://regional.kompas.com/read/2008/06/18/11511449/Weleh...Cagub.Dilaporkan

http://regional.kompas.com/read/2008/06/19/17464779/Polisi.Terus.Selidiki.Kasus

http://regional.kompas.com/read/2008/06/19/17262126/Kapolda.Lampung.Ingatkan

http://megapolitan.kompas.com/read/2008/07/07/21043480/PRT.Tewas.di.Kolam

http://regional.kompas.com/read/2008/08/26/00193562/Polisi.Kembali.Periksa..Lampung

http://megapolitan.kompas.com/read/2008/09/05/03063921/Jelang.Lebaran..Permintaan

http://megapolitan.kompas.com/read/2008/09/25/08411843/PRT.Korban.Perampokan.Tewas

http://regional.kompas.com/read/2008/10/05/21004656/Majikan.Cemas.PRT.Tak.Kembali

http://megapolitan.kompas.com/read/2008/09/08/01354293/Pemprov.DKI.Belum.Atur

The table that follows shows the date, headlines, and key themes for each article in the sample. Zahra Sakinaruzzahara, one of my research assistants, located the items, translated the headlines, and did the preliminary analysis.

YEAR	NO.	DATE	HEADLINES	THEMES
2004	1	Saturday, 10 January	**Buried in Backyard**	murder/abuse
2004	2	Monday, 12 January	**Hoping Maryati Case Completed Soon** (*Ingin Masalah Maryati Cepat Selesai*)	abuse/murder/ neighbours
2004	3	Tuesday, 13 January	**Domestic Worker Blinded after Employer Put Balsam on Her Eyes** (*Mata PRT Buta Karena Dibalsem Majikan*)	abuse
2004	4	Wednesday, 14 January	**Underage Domestic Workers Need Education to Improve Their Skills** (*PRT Anak Perlu Pendidikan Keterampilan*)	empowerment
2004	5	Wednesday, 14 January	**Domestic Worker Kidnapped Two Children of Her Employer Only to Ask Rp.200,000** (*PRT Menculik 2 Anak Majikan Untuk Dapat Komisi Rp 200.000*)	crime
2004	6	Saturday, 2 February	**Taking Her Employer's Saving Book and ID, a Domestic Worker Steals Employer's Money** (*Curi Buku Tabungan dan KTP, PRT Ambil Uang Majikan*)	crime
2004	7	Monday, 3 March	**A Domestic Worker Abused by Her Employer** (*PRT Dianiaya Majikan*)	abuse
2004	8	Saturday, 27 March	**Efforts to Empower Underage Domestic Workers** (*Upaya Memberdayakan PRTA*)	empowerment
2004	9	Tuesday, 8 June	**Domestic Workers Asking for More Attention to Their Misfortune** (*Pramuwisma Minta Diperhatikan Nasibnya*)	protest
2004	10	Friday, 18 June	**A Domestic Workers Service Center Is Proposed** (*Digagas, Pendirian Pusat Pelayanan Terpadu PRT*)	ministry, government, protection

YEAR	NO.	DATE	HEADLINES	THEMES
2004	11	Monday, 28 June	**Fallen from 25th Floor, a Domestic Worker is Found Dead** (*PRT Tewas, Jatuh Dari Lantai* 25)	suicide
2004	12	Thursday, 29 July	**Susanti's Murderer Arrested** (*Pembunuh Susanti Ditangkap*)	murder, victims
2004	13	Saturday, 31 July	**Tangerang Women (Underage) Prison Full of Domestic Workers** (*LP Anak Wanita Tangerang "Penuh" Pembantu*)	underage domestic workers, crime
2004	14	Sunday, 1 August	**Domestic Worker Found Hanging on the Second Floor of Employer's House** (*Seorang Pembantu Gantung Diri di Lantai 2 Rumah Majikan*)	suicide
2004	15	Monday, 9 August	**Police Investigating Domestic Worker Kidnap Case** (*Polisi Selidiki Kasus Penculikan PRT*)	kidnap
2004	16	Friday, 13 August	**Working for a Day, Domestic Workers Stole Diamonds** (*Baru Sehari Bekerja, Pembantu Curi Berlian*)	crime, stealing
2004	17	Tuesday, 31 August	**Victim of Abuse, Domestic Worker Will Be Examined** (*PRT Korban Aniaya Akan Diperiksa*)	abuse
2004	18	Thursday, 30 September	**Denying Accusation of Stealing, Domestic Worker Abused by Employer** (*Menolak Dituduh Mencuri, PRT Dianiaya Majikan*)	abuse
2004	19	Monday, 4 October	**Domestic Worker's Abuser Arrested** (*Pengaiaya PRT Ditangkap*)	abuse
2004	20	Tuesday, 12 October	**Catching Thieves, Domestic Worker Raped** (*Pergoki Pencuri, PRT Ditangkap*)	rape, victim
2004	21	Tuesday, 19 October	**Persuaded by Friend, Domestic Worker Robs Her Employer** (*Dibujuk Teman, PRT Nekat Kuras Harta Majikan*)	crime, stealing

YEAR	NO.	DATE	HEADLINES	THEMES
2004	22	Sunday, 24 October	**Disguising as Domestic Workers Recruitment Agency** (*Berkedok Yayasan PRT*)	crime
2004	23	Sunday, 24 October	**Stealing After Being Hypnotized** (*Mencuri Karena Dibipnotis*)	crime, stealing
2004	24	Thursday, 28 October	**Domestic Worker Found Dead after Doing Laundry** (*PRT Tewas Saat Mencuci*)	accident
2004	25	Sunday, 7 November	**Poked and Kidnapped** (*Dicolak-Colek Culik*)	abuse
2004	26	Monday, 8 November	**Domestic Workers Go Home on IED** (*PRT Bubaran Lebaran*)	IED, Culture
2004	27	Friday, 12 November	**Difficulties when Domestic Workers Take Leave** (*Repotna Ditinggal PRT*)	IED, Culture, Need
2004	28	Friday, 26 November	**Domestic Worker Raped by Four Men** (*PRT Dicabuli 4 Pemuda*)	rape, victim
2004	29	Sunday, 12 December	**Families Depend on Domestic Workers** (*Ketergantungan Keluarga Kepada "Simbok"*)	dependency, need
2004	30	Wednesday, 29 December	**Aiming at Women's Abuse** (*Membidik Kekerasan Terhadap Perempuan*)	abuse

YEAR	NO.	DATE	HEADLINES	THEMES
2008	31	Wednesday, 9 January	**Ex-Domestic Worker Suspect in Police Officer's Whole Family Murder Case** (*Mantan PRT Jadi Tersangka Pembunuhan Keluarga Polisi*)	crime, murder
2008	32	Wednesday, 16 January	**Torturer of Domestic Helper Sentenced to Ten Years** (*Penyiksa Pembantu Divonis 10 Tahun*)	victim, torture, justice system
2008	33	Friday, 15 February	**Be Careful in Choosing Domestic Workers from Agency** (*Hati-hati Pilih PRT di Yayasan*)	crime
2008	34	Tuesday, 25 March	**Hypnotic Criminal Stops Domestic Worker in the Street** (*Pelaku Hipnotis Cegat PRT di Jalan*)	victim, crime, hypnotism
2008	35	Wednesday, 4 April	**Domestic Worker Steals Jewellery** (*Pembantu Curi Perhiasan*)	crime, stealing
2008	36	Saturday, 19 April	**Experiences of Using Recruitment Agency** (*Pengalaman Dengan Penyalur PRT*)	recruitment agency
2008	37	Monday, 21 April	**Domestic Worker Hammered by Employer's Brother** (*PRT Dimartil Adik Majikan*)	abuse
2008	38	Saturday, 3 May	**Domestic Worker Rights Left Unfulfilled** (*Hak-Hak PRT Belum Terpenuhi*)	domestic worker rights
2008	39	Sunday, 5 May	**Changing Bill Is Not a Piece of Cake** (*Perubahan UU Bukan Perkara Mudah*)	Bill
2008	40	Wednesday, 18 June	**Governor Candidate Rapes Domestic Worker** (*Weleh...Cagub Dilaporkan Memerkosa PRT*)	rape, victim
2008	41	Thursday, 19 June	**Police Keep Investigating Domestic Helper Sexual Abuse Case** (*Polisi Terus Selidiki Kasus Pencabulan PRT*)	sexual abuse

YEAR	NO.	DATE	HEADLINES	THEMES
2008	42	Thursday, 19 June	**Lampung Chief of Police Warns Media to Be Careful** (*Kapolda Lampung Ingatkan Media Untuk Hati-hati*)	sexual abuse, bupati, media
2008	43	Monday, 7 July	**Domestic Worker Died Learning How to Swim** (*PRT Tewas di Kolam Renang*)	accident
2008	44	Tuesday, 8 July	**Learning To Swim, Domestic Worker Ended Up Dead** (*Belajar Renang, PRT Tewas*)	accident
2008	45	Wednesday, 9 July	**Robbery in Wealthy Family, and Domestic Worker Rape Case** (*Perampokan di Rumah Elit dan PRT Diperkosa*)	rape, victim
2008	46	Thursday, 10 July	**After Murder, Babysitter Examined by Police** (*Pasca Pembunuhan.Babysitter Diperiksa Polisi*)	suspect, murder
2008	47	Monday, 14 July	**Stop Sexual Assault** (*Menolak Tindak Pelecehan Seksual*)	sexual abuse
2008	48	Thursday, 7 August	**After One Day's Work, Domestic Helper Kidnaps Employer's Child** (*Baru Sehari Kerja, PRT Culik Anak Majikan*)	kidnap, theft, deceit
2008	49	Monday, 18 August	**Again! Domestic Helper Tortured and Killed by Employer** (*Lagi! PRT Tewas Dianiaya Majikan*)	murder, torture
2008	50	Tuesday, 26 August	**Police Examine the Victim of Governor Candidate Sexual Abuse Case** (*Polisi Kembali Periksa Korban Pencabulan Cagub Lampung*)	sexual abuse
2008	51	Monday, 1 September	**Hurt by Her Employer, Domestic Worker Mutilates the Employer** (*PRT Mutilasi Majikannya Karena Sakit Hati*)	crime, murder
2008	52	Wednesday, 3 September	**Domestic Worker Raped by Five Men** (*PRT Digilir 5 Pria*)	rape, victim, abuse

YEAR	NO.	DATE	HEADLINES	THEMES
2008	53	Friday, 5 September	**Getting Close to *Lebaran*, Demand for Substitute Domestic Helpers Increases** (*Jelang Lebaran: Permintaan PRT Pengganti Mulai Meningkat*)	mudik, needs
2008	54	Monday, 8 September	**DKI Government Has Not Regulated Domestic Worker Wages** (*Pemprov DKI Belum Atur Gaji Pembantu*)	DPRD, government, wages
2008	55	Thursday, 11 September	**Recruitment Agency Reduced Demand for Domestic Workers** (*Penyalur PRT Sepi Order*)	recruitment agency
2008	56	Monday, 22 September	**Huge Difference between Filipina and Indonesian Domestic Workers** (*Perbedaan Mencolok PRT Filipina dan Indonesia*)	wages, comparison
2008	57	Monday, 22 September	**Jakarta Left with No Domestic Workers When They Need Them the Most** (*Jakarta Ditinggalkan Saat Membutuhkan*)	mudik, culture, dependency
2008	58	Thursday, 25 September	**Domestic Worker, Victim of Robbery Found Dead** (*PRT Korban Perampokan Tewas*)	victim, robbery
2008	59	Monday, 5 October	**Employers Worried That Their Domestic Workers Will Not Return** (*Majikan Cemas PRT Tak Kembali*)	mudik, urbanization
2008	60	Monday, 3 November	**There Won't Be Any Migrant Workers in Five Years** (*5 Tahun Lagi Tak Ada Pengiriman PRT ke Luar Negeri*)	BNPPTKI, migrant workers
2008	61	Tuesday, 2 December	**Accused of Stealing a Laptop, Domestic Worker Abused by Police** (*Diduga Mencuri Laptop, PRT Dianiaya Polisi*)	abuse, theft
2008	62	Thursday, 11 December	**Beaten Up by Employers, Domestic Worker Reports to the Police** (*Dikeroyok Majikan,PRT Lapor Polisi*)	abuse

Index

Bold page numbers refer to figures

Printed and bound by CPI Group (UK) Ltd, Croydon, CR0 4YY

13/09/2026

14961102-0005